PROFILING AND CRIMINAL JUSTICE IN AMERICA

A Reference Handbook

Other Titles in ABC-CLIO's
**CONTEMPORARY
WORLD ISSUES**
Series

Books in the Contemporary World Issues series address vital issues in today's society such as genetic engineering, pollution, and biodiversity. Written by professional writers, scholars, and nonacademic experts, these books are authoritative, clearly written, up-to-date, and objective. They provide a good starting point for research by high school and college students, scholars, and general readers as well as by legislators, businesspeople, activists, and others.

Each book, carefully organized and easy to use, contains an overview of the subject, a detailed chronology, biographical sketches, facts and data and/or documents and other primary-source material, a directory of organizations and agencies, annotated lists of print and nonprint resources, and an index.

Readers of books in the Contemporary World Issues series will find the information they need in order to have a better understanding of the social, political, environmental, and economic issues facing the world today.

PROFILING AND CRIMINAL JUSTICE IN AMERICA

A Reference Handbook

WITHDRAWN

Jeffrey B. Bumgarner

CONTEMPORARY WORLD ISSUES

A B C 🞄 C L I O

Santa Barbara, California
Denver, Colorado
Oxford, England

To Kathy, Jack, Alex, and Carl. Your patience
with me has been above and beyond the call.
I love each of you very much.

Library of Congress Cataloging-in-Publication Data
Bumgarner, Jeffrey B.
   Profiling and criminal justice in America : a reference handbook /
Jeffrey B. Bumgarner.
      p.   cm. — (Contemporary world issues)
   Includes index.
   ISBN 1-85109-469-5 (hardcover : alk. paper); 1-85109-474-1 (eBook)
   1. Criminal justice, Administration of—United States.   2. Racial
profiling in law enforcement—United States.   I. Title.   II. Series.

HV9950.B86 2004
363.2'3'08900973—dc22

2004014005

08 07 06   10 9 8 7 6 5 4 3

This book is also available on the World Wide Web as an eBook. Visit
abc-clio.com for details.

ABC-CLIO, Inc.
130 Cremona Drive, P.O. Box 1911
Santa Barbara, California 93116-1911

This book is printed on acid-free paper ∞.
Manufactured in the United States of America

CONTENTS

PREFACE

*P*rofiling and Criminal Justice in America: A Reference Handbook serves as an introduction to the issue of profiling within the criminal justice system in the United States. The term *profiling* means different things to different people. When the term is mentioned, many people who are consumers of popular cinema and television crime drama productions think immediately of the process of drawing up psychological composite sketches of unknown offenders who have invariably left "calling cards" at crime scenes. Although this type of profiling does exist as an investigative tool and is addressed in some portions of this book, this is not the bulk of what this publication is about. Rather, this book is primarily concerned with the use of race and other dubious identifiers by criminal justice officials in making decisions about enforcement, prosecution, guilt, and punishment.

In the wake of the terrorist attacks of September 11, 2001, it is not sufficient simply to say that profiling along racial or ethnic lines is always immoral or ill advised. Such a position may be a legitimate one to hold; in these dangerous times, however, positions must be informed ones. The traveling public, for example, has little patience for the random screening of elderly white women at airports while Middle Eastern men board unmolested. The public, by and large, would prefer to be more safe than fair.

Likewise, it is not a foregone conclusion even after 9–11 that profiling along racial, ethnic, or religious lines is appropriate. There is no question that considerable opportunity for error and abuse exists when criminal justice officials rely on such criteria, and history seems to bear this out. What's more, the public, when queried, does not think for the most part that a person's race or religion should doom that individual to a lifetime of chronic suspicion and inconvenience.

Profiling is a tough issue in this day and age and requires a comprehensive understanding of all sides to it. Although this book may not convey all information that can be conveyed, it is my hope that readers will find *Profiling and Criminal Justice in America: A Reference Handbook* to be a useful and balanced introduction to the topic and a springboard for further research about profiling within the context of our criminal justice system.

Jeffrey B. Bumgarner
Minnesota State University
Mankato, Minnesota

1

Introduction

On July 27, 1996, in the early morning hours and amid well-attended all-night festivities in Atlanta's Centennial Olympic Park, a security guard named Richard Jewell came across a green, military-style backpack placed under a bench. This bench was located next to a row of additional benches; it was also next to the NBC Sound Tower that had been erected to manage the sound from a stage nearby where one band after another performed for the crowds in attendance. Even though it was 1:20 A.M., the park was crowded with bystanders in town to enjoy the Olympic events and associated celebrations.

To Jewell's horror, the backpack contained an apparent bomb. Immediately, Jewell radioed law enforcement officers of his situation and started clearing the area of people. Another security officer arrived on scene, and Jewell informed him of the bomb. Jewell said "Let's get out of here." A few seconds later, the bomb exploded. The explosion killed one woman instantly, caused a fatal attack in another individual, and seriously injured more than 100 others. Immediately after the bomb, Jewell, who aspired to a career in law enforcement, began administering aid to the wounded. By all accounts, Jewell had acted heroically before and after the explosion . . . by all accounts except that of the Federal Bureau of Investigation (FBI).

Almost immediately after the FBI investigation began, federal authorities began to focus their suspicion on Richard Jewell. According to their profile of the likely offender, Jewell measured up. FBI profilers suspected that the bomber was white, male, in the thirty-something age group, politically conservative, a relative loner, and a southerner. Additional information received by the FBI further solidified their suspicions. For example, former coworkers of Jewell described him as wanting to be in the middle of the action if anything happened at the Olympics. He was characterized as an "adrenaline junkie." His passion for a career in law enforcement was read by FBI investigators as Jewell's possessing a "hero complex"—in other words, they thought Jewell relished the idea of coming in and saving the day during some crisis. The FBI believed this about Jewell despite the fact that Jewell himself never claimed to be a hero or to be doing anything other than his job—even in the immediate hours after the incident when everyone else believed that he was, indeed, a hero.

On July 30, 1996, the *Atlanta Journal-Constitution*, which is Atlanta's major daily newspaper, ran a front-page story identifying Jewell as a suspect of the FBI in the bombing. The paper cited several unidentified law enforcement sources. This was a huge national and international story. From that point on, every major media organization referred to Richard Jewell as the Olympic Park bombing suspect.

For over eighty days, Richard Jewell was officially a suspect of the FBI in the Olympic Park bombing. Although no physical evidence was ever found tying him to the bombing, the FBI clung to Jewell and his remarkable resemblance to the suspected profile of the bomber. The facts (as opposed to the profile), however, simply could not sustain long-term suspicion against Jewell.

After search warrants were executed on his car and at the residence of Jewell and his mother, and after countless interviews, the FBI could not tie Jewell in any way to the bombing or even produce evidence of a motive. In late October 1996, the U.S. Department of Justice sent Jewell a letter stating that he was no longer a suspect in the bombing.

Indeed, in November 2000, Eric Robert Rudolph was indicted on twenty-one counts related to the Olympic Park bombing by a federal grand jury. He was also indicted for a bombing at a Birmingham, Alabama, abortion clinic in which an off-duty police officer was killed. In some ways, the FBI profile held up with Rudolph. He was white, male, thirty-something, ultraconservative politically, a southerner. But given the misdirected attention by the FBI toward Jewell and the apparent unwillingness early on to look elsewhere given Jewell's fit with the profile, can it be said that the profile worked?

Definitions

There is no disagreement in the United States today that criminal justice profiling is a controversial and sensitive issue. The presence of controversy implies that there is more than one side to the issue. Indeed there is. In this handbook, we will examine the issue of criminal justice profiling from what I hope is an objective, nonjudgmental perspective. The goal is to simply provide you, the reader, with information about the issue and expose you to all sides of it.

As criminal justice profiling is controversial, it should not be surprising that there is more than one definition that governs the topic. What is criminal justice profiling? In its plainest sense, criminal justice profiling occurs when criminal justice officials strategically consider characteristics such as race, gender, religion, or sexual orientation as they make discretionary decisions in the course of their duties. In considering such characteristics, criminal justice officials may select some action or actions over others, in part because of the profile of the suspect, convicted offender, victim, witness, or other relevant party under consideration. Although many writers on the subject use the expression *criminal profiling,* this handbook will regularly refer to *criminal justice profiling* because it is not necessarily suspects alone who are profiled by the criminal justice system.

It is easier to imagine legitimate uses of profiles by law enforcement than it is to imagine legitimate prosecutorial or judicial uses. This does not mean, however, that profiling does not take place at some level or another in the prosecutorial and judicial realms. This handbook will present in a later chapter some scholarly evidence that decisions are made by prosecutors and judges at least in part on the basis of race, gender, and other offender characteristics. For example, a prosecutor may attempt to strike an individual from consideration for jury duty during jury selection (voir dire) because of the gender of that potential juror. Prosecutors may believe, for example, that women will be less likely to invoke the death penalty, and so the more men on the jury, the better (from the prosecutor's standpoint).

Although this book concerns itself with profiling throughout the criminal justice system, it is incontrovertible that the most pressing profiling debates today revolve around the use of profiles by law enforcement. This fact was true prior to the suicide hijackings on September 11, 2001; it is even more true afterward. Although this book by design will avoid spending too much time on profiling in the war against terrorism, the impact that 9–11 has had on breathing new life into the pro-profiling movement cannot be overstated.

Just when it seemed politicians were in agreement that race or ethnicity had been receiving too much weight by law enforcement in decision making and that it must stop, the terrorist attacks took place. Now policymakers are asking why airport security personnel are randomly selecting passengers for searches, including elderly ladies from North Dakota, when clearly the most likely threat is going to come from a male, young adult of Middle Eastern descent.

Profiled characteristics can certainly include race, ethnicity, gender, sexual orientation, and religious affiliation. These are not the only characteristics considered in profiling, however. Things such as travel patterns, socioeconomic status, geographic location, age, clothing, and many other factors can weigh into a profile that is used by criminal justice professionals. What is so controversial, however, about race, sex, and religion's being utilized in profiling is the fact that these characteristics all are explicitly protected statuses, or classes, in our laws. Further, these are not behaviors; these are characteristics that simply "are."

Although a neutral definition of profiling may be simply the consideration of certain characteristics in criminal justice decision making, less neutral definitions also exist. For example, some may define criminal justice profiling as the targeting of racial, sexual, and religious minorities for criminal justice action on the basis of their class or group affiliation. Such a definition is by and large a negative portrayal of profiling. Indeed, profiling that results in criminal justice action solely on the basis of these characteristics is generally illegal, as we shall see.

Others (especially within the criminal justice system) may choose, however, to define profiling as the consideration of racial, sexual, or religious characteristics, when relevant, along with other characteristics in a law enforcement officer's decision to stop, question, arrest, or search someone, in a prosecutor's decision to prosecute someone, or in a judge's decision of how to adjudicate someone. This definition, although a little unwieldy, allows criminal justice professionals some flexibility and freedom to account for any number of obvious observations of or association with criminal tendencies.

Daniel Carlson, author of the book *When Cultures Clash* (2002), distinguished between rational and irrational profiling. He noted that rational profiling is a legitimate investigative tool in the fight against crime, and police officers, relying on a commonsense analysis of the observed environment and the activities of suspicious people in context, use the tool frequently.

Irrational profiling, by contrast, is when a police officer decides to stop and question someone when the sole rationale for the stop is the person's race or some other protected classification (Carlson 2002).

Although there are numerous instances of irrational profiling in the criminal justice system past and present, most profiling advocates argue that legitimate and proper criminal justice profiling actually guards against random harassment and discrimination by law enforcement. This is because profiling offers criminal justice officials the opportunity to pool together collective criminal justice experience into comprehensive and accurate information, as opposed to selectively remembered war stories of individual officials (Harris 2002).

Importance of Studying Criminal Justice Profiling

The importance behind the issue of criminal justice profiling is as plain as the commonsense arguments for and against the use of profiling. First and foremost, it is important because fighting crime and ensuring the safety of all people in a community is among the chief purposes of government. Any tool that can be enlisted in that fight has got to be thoroughly considered prior to any decision to disregard such tool.

Likewise, another purpose of our government—perhaps a greater purpose than fighting crime—is to ensure the equality of all people before the law. The image of Lady Justice blindfolded while holding her scale is rooted in a very important American (and generally Western) concept: that all people, regardless of class, race, sex, religion, disability, and so on, are of fundamentally equal worth and should therefore be treated as equals. Class should not have its privileges before the bar of justice.

American history teaches that this concept of equal justice, although lauded from our beginnings, has been in fact a work in progress. But progress has been made. More than ever before, it has become the goal of the criminal justice system, and government generally, to treat men and women, blacks and whites, Jews and Christians, heterosexuals and homosexuals, as equals.

The extent to which criminal justice profiling negatively impacts the steady movement in the United States toward equality of all before the law necessitates that the issue be carefully thought out and studied—certainly before any final verdicts about its legitimacy as a criminal justice tool are made at the public policy level.

There are arguably no two greater aims of government than to protect its citizens from other citizens who would do people harm and to protect its citizens from government itself, by abiding by constitutional and statutory restrictions and through self-restraint. In the case of criminal justice profiling, these two aims appear somewhat at odds with each other. As with any issue having two or more compelling sides to it, only the possession of an informed understanding of the issue by policymakers and the public will result in the proper balance being struck.

The issue of criminal justice profiling and its potential discriminatory effects was hotly debated in a number of statehouses in the 2001 and 2002 legislative sessions. In the state of Virginia, the legislature passed a measure to require and expand cultural diversity training for law enforcement officers in part because of perceived racial profiling. West Virginia's legislature passed a measure outlawing any stop or search of a person solely on the basis of his or her race or ethnicity. Such a stop was already unconstitutional, but legal redundancy rarely gets in the way of good politics. The measure also established procedures for investigating claims of biased policing and for disciplining officers found to engage in it.

In South Carolina, the state senate passed a bill that would require police officers to collect data on traffic stops to determine if law enforcement is engaging in racial profiling. Similar requirements already exist in several other states. The state of Utah passed legislation requiring driver's licenses and state identification cards to record the holder's race so that the race of individuals being checked in the system by law enforcement can be tracked. Additionally, officers are required to record why a person is being checked every time the officer runs someone in the system. The information of race is then matched up with the reasons people are being stopped and which officers are stopping them.

The aggregate information is passed on to the departments and to the state legislature. Utah law enforcement agencies are also required under the law to adopt policies against bias-based policing (International Association of Chiefs of Police 2003).

In 1994, the National Commission on Crime Control and Prevention was established by the Violent Crime Control and Law Enforcement Act. This commission, like national crime commissions in the past, was tasked with the responsibility to make broad and realistic recommendations to improve the U.S. criminal justice system. Among the mandates given to it by Congress, the commission was to:

1. develop a comprehensive proposal for preventing and controlling crime and violence in the United States
2. bring attention to the successful models and programs in crime prevention and crime control
3. reach out beyond the traditional criminal justice community for ideas for controlling and preventing crime
4. recommend improvements in the coordination of local, state, federal, and international crime control and prevention efforts, including efforts relating to crime near international borders
5. make a comprehensive study of the economic and social factors leading to or contributing to crime and violence, including the causes of illicit drug use and other substance abuse, and to develop specific proposals for legislative and administrative actions to reduce crime and violence and the factors that contribute to it
6. recommend means of utilizing criminal justice resources as effectively as possible, including targeting finite correctional facility space to the most serious and violent offenders, and considering increased use of intermediate sanctions for offenders who can be dealt with adequately by such means
7. examine distinctive crime problems and the impact of crime on members of minority groups, Native Americans living on reservations, and other groups defined by race, ethnicity, religion, age, disability, or other characteristics and to recommend specific responses to the distinctive crime problems of such groups
8. examine the problem of sexual assaults, domestic violence, and other criminal and unlawful acts that partic-

ularly affect women and to recommend federal, state,
and local strategies for more effectively preventing and
punishing such crimes and acts

9. examine the treatment of victims in federal, state, and
local criminal justice systems and to develop recommendations to enhance and protect the rights of victims

10. examine the ability of federal, state, and local criminal
justice systems to administer criminal law and criminal
sanctions impartially without discrimination on the
basis of race, ethnicity, religion, gender, or other legally
proscribed grounds and to make recommendations for
correcting any deficiencies in the impartial administration of justice on these grounds

11. examine the nature, scope, causes, and complexities of
violence in schools and to recommend a comprehensive
response to that problem

Interestingly, two of the mandates concern the issue of race,
ethnicity, religion, and other protected classifications. Mandate
number seven implores the criminal justice system to concern
itself with the specific and unique problems associated with particular classes of people; the tenth mandate, however, essentially
demands that the criminal justice system ignore the variety of
classifications in pursuit of justice, lest it be unequal in its application. In other words, the former mandate proposes consciousness regarding groups and classes whereas the latter proposes
neutrality.

This seeming, and certainly unintentional, contradiction
exemplifies in a broad way some of the dilemmas felt in the more
narrowly framed issue of criminal justice profiling. In the following sections, criminal justice profiling will be examined for what
it is and is not and for the contradictory aims and achievements
it yields.

The Criminal Justice System

In understanding criminal justice profiling, it is important to
know something about the criminal justice system in the United
States. In particular, what are its goals? Criminal justice scholars
are not in agreement on the degree to which American criminal
justice operates as a system to begin with. Generally, when we

speak of the criminal justice system, we think of the police, the prisons, and the courts as the triad comprising the system.

It could be argued, however, that American criminal justice is distinctly a "nonsystem," as the police, prisons, and courts have different, and sometimes competing, goals. In a true system, the component parts of the system are all designed to work toward the bigger objective. Instead, the component criminal justice parts are working frequently at odds with each other, and in any case rarely act in concert with each other.

Add to the differing goals of these three criminal justice components the fact that the United States has one federal and fifty state criminal justice systems existing at the same time, and you will have the epitome of decentralization that marks our federalist approach to government. Calling it a "system" that can be universally characterized as "racist" or "nonracist" or "sexist" or "just" may be giving it too much credit.

This point notwithstanding, most criminal justice professionals and scholars believe there are some overall objectives of all who work in the U.S. justice system. These broad objectives can be said to be the goals of the American criminal justice "system." And it is within the context of these goals that profiling takes place. The overarching goal of the U.S. criminal justice system is to "do justice" (Cole and Smith 2001, 14). There are two values associated with doing justice. Although these values are somewhat in competition, they are not mutually exclusive. The first is that of crime control. This value requires our free society to make every effort to allow law-abiding citizens to live in freedom and safety by repressing crime that would otherwise be perpetrated against them. This means there is an emphasis placed on efficiency, speed, and finality in the prevention, apprehension, and punishment of criminals.

The other value characterizing U.S. criminal justice is that of due process. This value requires us to make every effort to ensure that our criminal justice decisions and actions are based on fair and reliable information. There is an emphasis on the adversarial process, the rights of defendants, and formal decision-making procedures over ad hoc, impulsive, or emotion-driven decisions.

Those who stress crime control tend to support the expansion of police numbers and police powers; they tend to want to limit the ability of judges to be lenient on defendants; and they tend to oppose probation and parole, preferring instead to build more prisons and jails. Those who stress due process, on the other hand, make every effort to ensure that individual rights are protected; they tend to prefer treatment and rehabilitation efforts over punishment for punishment's sake; and they insist that the system err on the side of offenders rather than risk unjustly depriving innocent people of their rights or their liberty.

The relative value one places on crime control and due process will likely shape one's view on the worthwhileness of criminal justice profiling. Those who value crime control over due process will find profiling to be an invaluable crime-fighting tool that is not used enough or to great enough lengths to preserve law-abiding citizens' safety and security from criminal elements. Those who value due process above crime control will find profiling to be an oppressive and illegitimate tool of government to single out some of its citizens for action. Even if it works, the cost to individual dignity and rights is too high to warrant its use.

Profiling and Political Philosophy

The issue of criminal profiling has broader implications than those just for the law enforcement community, or the criminal justice system for that matter. Profiling raises questions that are the heart of the political philosophies of the United States. Indeed, exactly what America's philosophies and core values are continues to be debated to this day. At the root of the debate are the models of "consensus" and "conflict."

The debate of consensus versus conflict amounts to two competing models of explanation as to where our laws (and the enforcement mechanisms that follow) come from. The consensus model holds that criminal law, as an expression of the social consciousness of the whole society, reflects widely shared values and beliefs (Cole and Smith 2001). In other words, the laws of American society reflect a consensus that has been arrived at by society's members.

The main principles commonly associated with the consensus model are that (1) the law reflects the need for order; (2) the law results from a consensus on the values that are widely shared in society; (3) the law is an impartial system that protects the public interest; and (4) the law provides a neutral means for resolving disputes.

Crimes that tend to be emphasized by those adhering to this model are known as *mala in se* offenses. These offenses are thought to be wrong by their very nature, with or without a criminal code telling us so. Offenses such as murder, assault, rape, and so on are considered *mala in se* crimes. The fact that there are criminal codes against these offenses reflects the fact that society's members widely agree that committing these acts is wrong.

The conflict model rejects the notion that most of the criminal laws are written as a result of widespread consensus. Instead, subscribers of this model hold that the criminal laws and enforcement mechanisms have been crafted by powerful political groups. The model assumes that people act in their own self-interests; therefore, people who have power are the ones whose preferred wishes will be codified into law (Cole and Smith 2001).

The conflict model emphasizes crimes known as *mala prohibita* offenses to prove its point. *Mala prohibita* crimes are prohibited by law but are not necessarily evil or wrong in and of themselves. These offenses include gambling, vagrancy, prostitution, and drug use. Many critics of the notion of consensus in our criminal laws point out that the statutes articulating *mala prohibita* offenses tend to be largely enforced against the lower classes in society—especially against racial and sexual minorities.

Pluralism: The American Ideal

Often associated with the criminal justice notion of consensus is the broader political philosophy of pluralism. Pluralism postulates that self-rule by all the people of a society can be achieved through competition among multiple organized groups and that individual members of society can genuinely participate in societal and political decisions through group memberships and elections (Dye 2001). Things get done, including the crafting of the criminal justice system, by debating, bargaining, and compromising among various interest groups in competition.

Public policy that emerges from a pluralistic system is generally thought to be rationally derived. Through open and free debate, all policy options are aired and considered according to their relative costs and benefits. In the end, policy is crafted according to the maximum social gain, which is consistent with the consensus model.

That the government has the right to do this is based on the long-standing adherence of the United States to social contract theory. The notion of social contract in America can be traced back to seventeenth-century political philosopher John Locke, among others. Social contract is the idea that government originates as an implied contract among individuals who agree to obey the law in exchange for the protection of their rights.

Locke argued that government is based on consensus. It exists because the people have allowed it to . . . and for good reason. As Thomas Hobbes said in his classic work *Leviathan*, life without any government would be "solitary, poor, nasty, brutish, and short" (Hobbes 1651, 65). Indeed, we the people have consented to the existence of our government. In doing so, we have agreed to give up some of our liberties and responsibilities, such as to avenge ourselves (and to a lesser degree protect ourselves), and have delegated them to the government instead. As the Preamble of the U.S. Constitution says, we have agreed to delegate to the government our national defense, the preservation of our welfare, the establishment of justice and tranquility, and the securing of our liberties. If the government lives up to its portion of the contract and provides these things, then the people will continue to let the government exist and rule. Locke suggested, however, that when government—any government—fails to deliver in these—its essential responsibilities—then the government can and should be dissolved by the people and replaced with a new one.

Clearly, John Locke's social contract served as the justification for the American Revolution. American colonists had decided that the British Crown no longer deserved power over them as it no longer (if it had ever) met its contractual obligations. Hence, Locke's language appears practically verbatim in the American Declaration of Independence.

Elitism: The American Reality?

The political philosophy of elitism is generally aligned with the conflict model of criminal justice. Elitism posits that public policy of all types boils down to the preferences and values of the governing elite. Those who argue that the United States is an elitist society note that most policymakers are drawn from the upper socioeconomic strata of society. What's more, so are those who have access to the policymakers. It is estimated that half of the nation's total assets are concentrated in the 100 largest corporations and fifty largest banks in the United States (Dye 2001). Leaders of these businesses have regular access to politicians and high-ranking bureaucrats. C. Wright Mills coined the term *power elite* to describe those leaders in government, the military, and private corporations who comprise the decision makers in U.S. society. He noted that they tend to be white, male, wealthy, educated, and Protestant and together form the pinnacle of a pyramid of power, with the masses positioned below (Mills 1956).

Elitism manifests itself in the criminal justice system with two types of discriminatory laws. Historically, many laws in this country were designed to treat people differently based upon their minority racial, ethnic, gender, sexual orientation, or religious status. A well-known example would be the Jim Crow laws of the South, which well into the twentieth century enforced racial segregation.

In recent years, however, the Supreme Court has been scrutinizing laws that were directed against particular classes of people. Most laws specifically directed against a particular class of people—favorably or unfavorably—have been found to be violations of the Equal Protection clause of the Fourteenth Amendment and therefore unconstitutional. But many people point out that elitism also manifests itself in laws that are classification neutral but are enforced in a way that causes an adverse impact on a class or group of people (Schott 2001).

In these instances, the law applies to everyone equally, but the impact tends to be greater among a particular group because of that group's tendencies or because of selective enforcement. For example, possession or sale of crack cocaine carries a harsher penalty in many jurisdictions than does powder cocaine. African American cocaine users tend to prefer crack cocaine, whereas white users favor powder.

Supporters of such laws note that crack cocaine is more dangerous and more addictive. Critics point out, however, that blacks and other ethnic minorities tend to use crack cocaine because it is cheaper, whereas middle- and upper-class whites can afford the more expensive powder cocaine. Although a white person using crack cocaine may be subject to the same penalties as minorities who use it, the net effect is that harsher penalties tend to be doled out to black cocaine users more than white cocaine users because of the preference and affordability of crack cocaine over powder among the black population.

Another example is the existence of antisodomy laws that remain on the books in most states. Although heterosexuals and homosexuals alike live under such laws, homosexuals are much more likely to engage in sodomy and therefore be prosecuted for it because sodomy is the preferred sexual activity among homosexuals. Therefore antisodomy laws, which in appearance are neutral when it comes to sexual orientation, generally impact one particular group more than others. The Supreme Court struck down these laws in 2003. Many see such laws as prima facie evidence of an elitist society and an elitist criminal justice system.

As is the case in so many social contexts, the polar extremes may not reflect the reality that is our criminal justice system. Instead, we may think of the degree of fairness or unfairness in criminal justice as a continuum. Samuel Walker, Cassia Spohn, and Miriam DeLone conceptualized discrimination in the American criminal justice system as existing along a continuum ranging from "systematic discrimination" to "pure justice" (Walker, Spohn, and DeLone 2002).

The view that the criminal justice system is discriminatory at all stages, at all times, and in all places throughout the United States is one that holds to "systematic discrimination." It is the view that the criminal justice system, as presently constituted, is hopelessly flawed with bias against all types of people.

Next along the continuum is the notion that the criminal justice system is characterized by "institutional discrimination." This position asserts that disparities in outcomes along racial, ethnic, gender, or other lines are due to the application of otherwise neutral factors, such as criminal record or family status, but these factors nevertheless adversely impact some groups more than others. The previously mentioned crack cocaine and antisodomy laws are also examples.

"Contextual discrimination" is next on Walker, Spohn, and DeLone's continuum. People believing that this level of discrimination exists in the system hold that discrimination is not "system" wide. Rather, discrimination surfaces in particular contexts and circumstances, such as regions of the country or in regards to specific kinds of crime. Discrimination does exist, but it is not so pervasive that context is irrelevant. If you want to treat discrimination, it stands to reason that you treat the contexts that give rise to it.

Finally, at the end of the continuum opposite to systematic discrimination is the notion of "pure justice." Those who believe "pure justice" exists, and there are not many who do, believe that there is no discrimination of any type affecting any group or groups at all—ever. This position on the continuum represents the ideal of American criminal justice. Again, few argue that it represents the reality. But, as the ideal, it is always the horizon toward which we should move.

It is debatable what role criminal justice profiling plays in fixing the criminal justice system somewhere on the above continuum. Some see profiling as evidence of systematic discrimination and as a tool of maintaining systematic discrimination. Others see profiling more as a manifestation of institutional or contextual discrimination. Still others argue that profiling simply is a symptom of where crime is and to not go where the crime is, through profiling or other means, is to unfairly leave vulnerable potential victims who live where the crime is—usually in lower-income, minority neighborhoods. By that logic, profiling is evidence of a desire on the part of the criminal justice system to protect all people, including the poor and minorities, and therefore reflects no discrimination. Whatever significance one places on criminal justice profiling in gauging the true level of fairness and equality in the United States, it clearly has become a cause célèbre—whether anecdotal or substantive—in the debate over "doing justice."

Applications of Criminal Justice Profiling

Profiling within the criminal justice system is most often associated with law enforcement. Most of the scholarly (and almost all of the popular) literature that focuses on criminal justice profiling emphasizes the law enforcement piece of the justice system.

Criminal justice profiling can and does take place at various stages of the criminal justice process including, but not limited to, police work. To the extent that profiling is defined broadly as the practice of justice officials directly or indirectly taking into consideration various characteristics of suspects or known offenders as they make decisions in their official capacity, profiling can occur in the law enforcement, prosecutorial, and judicial phases in the justice system.

Profiling by the Police

To place profiling by the police in context, we must at least consider what the goals of modern police agencies are. The police have three primary functions in American society: order maintenance, service, and law enforcement. Order maintenance refers to the prevention of behavior that disturbs the public peace. Service involves the provision by police of assistance to the public in matters unrelated to crime. Services the police may provide include medical assistance, helping citizens locked out of their vehicles, public relations activities, and so on. It is estimated that 80 percent of police calls do not involve crime (Roberg, Crank, and Kuykendall 2000). Finally, law enforcement refers to controlling crime by intervening in situations in which the law has been or is being broken and there exists a need to identify and apprehend those guilty of breaking it. It is this latter function of law enforcement that we have come to equate with the "profession" of policing. That has not always been the case. Policing as an occupation has come a long way.

The Origins of Police Institutions

From the late thirteenth century through the eighteenth century, England and its colonies utilized the parish-constable watch system of law enforcement (Samaha 1994). Under this system, each parish or town would appoint at least two unpaid constables, usually selected by lot. Constables in turn selected night watchmen to assist them in their duty. When a constable or night watchman, who later came to be called a "bailiff," would come across a crime in progress, the practice was to call out for help to any and everyone who could hear him. In fact, English law made it a crime for able-bodied citizens to ignore the "hue and cry" and required citizens to keep weapons in their homes for the purpose of rendering such assistance. These same citizens were also expected to join a posse, if necessary, to capture offenders. Posses were led by a leader of the shire—or county—in question. This leader was known as the shire reeve, from which the modern term *sheriff* is derived (Schmalleger 1993).

In the 1700s, particularly after the advent of gin, which was amazingly cheap for an intoxicating beverage, English urban areas became frequent sites of riots. Huge numbers of people living in London's industrial ghettos began binges of drinking and rioting to drown out their troubles. The night watchmen proved to be woefully incapable of dealing with the riots and, in fact, became targets of mob violence to the point of frequently being beaten for sport (Schmalleger 1993).

The alternative to the watchmen when things were out of control was to turn to the military. Under the English Riot Act, troops could be called out "in aid of the civil power" (Deakin 1988). In 1818, soldiers were called out to quell a riot in Manchester and in the process killed 11 and wounded over 500 in the crowd. After this incident and others with similar consequences, the notion of forming a police force to handle disorders became increasingly appealing to the British government. After all, the objection to creating a police force because it would constitute putting troops in the streets was negated by the fact that real troops were frequently put in the streets for lack of a police force.

Probably the single most significant event in police history was the passage of the Metropolitan Police Act of 1829. That piece of legislation, submitted to Parliament by Sir Robert Peel, created the first modern police force. Within a year of the act's passage, the Metropolitan Police force, commonly called the Met, employed over 1,000 officers. Officers were equipped with a uniform, a short baton, and a rattle, the latter being used to raise an alarm when necessary. Each constable, nicknamed a "bobby" in Peel's honor, was issued a number that he had to wear on his collar, making the bobbies immediately identifiable to the public (Peak and Glesnor 1996).

Although establishing a police force was controversial, as it resembled to some a standing army in the streets of London, the alternative of continuing to use the military was more problematic. The Met was created to keep the civil order without resorting to broadly administered violence wherever possible. The Met had a four-part mandate:

1. to prevent crime without using repressive force and to avoid calling out the military to control disturbances

2. to maintain public order by nonviolent means, using force only to obtain compliance as a last resort
3. to reduce conflict between the police and the public
4. to show efficiency through the absence of crime and disorder rather than through visible police actions

In the United States, modern police departments arose owing to circumstances remarkably similar to those that had existed in England. From the 1830s to the 1870s, there was an unprecedented amount of civil disorder occurring throughout the industrial United States. Very few cities escaped serious rioting and mob violence. The civil upheaval was often rooted in ethnic fighting due to the massive influx of immigrants during this time period. There was also violence rooted in economic issues, resulting in banks and businesses being ransacked by angry customers or employees (Walker 1977).

As had been the case in England, there was no continuous police presence in the urban centers of the United States in the early nineteenth century. The night watch was largely the only official mechanism in place, short of troops, to confront the frequent mob violence—and only then at night.

In one major city after another, the response was the same. Police departments began to be formed throughout the middle of the nineteenth century in America's urban centers to keep the peace. Policing in the United States paralleled policing in England. Some of the similarities between American and British police in the nineteenth century included (Uchida 2001)

- common legal tradition
- civilian workforce (not soldiers) with a military-style command structure
- crime prevention as the main mission
- random patrol of fixed beats as the main strategy against crime
- restrained police powers
- paid, uniformed police officers

Although police forces in the United States were modeled after London's metropolitan force, there were some significant differences between the English and American models.

Chief among the differences was the political orientation of the police. The Met was a creation of the national government in England, whereas in the United States police departments were installed by city governments. This made U.S. police officers much more a part of the political machinery than their London counterparts. Police officers were usually recruited by political leaders of a given ward or precinct and served at the pleasure of the political leadership. For example, in Cincinnati, after an election in 1880 changed the party in power, 219 of the 295 members of the police force were dismissed. Six years later, after another political power shift, 238 of the 289 patrolmen and eight of sixteen lieutenants were removed (Walker 1977).

Police in the United States in the nineteenth century were characterized by cronyism and endemic corruption and conducted themselves by a set of informal processes that had little to do with the official mandate of the police, namely to protect and to serve. But police were not up to no-good and nothing else. Police departments in that time period, commonly dubbed the political era of policing, spent much of their time engaged in services. Departments, as extensions of politics, were routinely tasked with providing ambulance services, running soup kitchens, running shelters, and other benevolent activities. American policing around the turn of the century was more oriented toward service than any other police function.

With the twentieth century came the Progressive Era. From 1900 to 1914, there were widespread reform efforts directed toward the criminal justice system. The reforms were consistent with efforts being made in government generally—namely, the depoliticization of the civil service and the birth of public administration as a distinct profession based on technical competencies and practices. The reforms directed toward police agencies included centralization of power by concentrating most authority in an autonomous chief; rational administrative procedures; upgrading personnel by means of selection, training, and discipline; and restricting the police role to enforcing the criminal law (Walker 1977; Samaha 1994).

Initially, the reform efforts toward the police were met with hostility from the police rank-and-file. They viewed reformers who sought to sever the police connection with political bosses as making their jobs more difficult, more dangerous, and less popular with the public. As one police scandal was publicly paraded after another, however, many officers began to see the police corruption and incompetence as conduits toward making all police-men laughingstocks; consequently, internal pressure began to swell for reform (Sparrow, Moore, and Kennedy 1990).

Gradually, over the years that followed the first decade of the twentieth century leading into the modern era, police departments around the country began to change. To be sure, corruption and incompetence plagued many agencies and in some cases exist systematically even today. But in totality, a genuine paradigm shift relating to policing began to take place in the collective and individual minds of officers, their managers, and the public. The quality and character of police officers began to matter as never before. For example, officers in departments undergoing reform were required to declare financial interests and remain debt free as a condition of employment, in order to minimize the temptation of corruption. Indeed, in an effort to ensure that bribery and protection rackets had seen their last day, many departments went so far as to forbid unnecessary or casual conversation with the public (Sparrow, Moore, and Kennedy 1990).

This obsolete rule has survived police culture in many cases to this day in the form of officer aloofness. In other words, the courteous but nonfriendly, businesslike demeanor we often observe in police officers as we try unsuccessfully to get out of a ticket does not necessarily originate in officer bias or rudeness. Rather, it is an unforeseen consequence of professionalization and countercorruption efforts.

Another reform in the police field was the use of motorized vehicles. This created an ability to cover more area of an assigned beat within a shift. This ability was further enhanced by the widespread use of radios in patrol cars by 1950. Reformers saw the radio-squad car as huge plus. Not only did the cars help keep officers separated from the public, thus minimizing the potential for corruption, but they gave officers the ability of preventive patrol and rapid response.

The "reform" or "professional" model of policing as it emerged during the first two-thirds of the twentieth century remains mostly intact today even as a new model—community policing—is championed in name. Modern police deeply resent political interference. They find their legitimacy and methods in the ideas of law enforcement and crime control, not community sentiment. And further, the ideas of professionalism have been reinforced through the advent of specialized police procedures and advanced forensic techniques.

Some developments in the professional era included the advent of the police code of ethics, merit selection and promotion, training standards, the use of management science, a new emphasis on impartiality in enforcing the law, advances in transportation, and scientific crime fighting. It is this last development that really serves as the parent of modern criminal profiling.

During the professional era, the primary mission of police departments became law enforcement, as opposed to service or even order maintenance. The supremacy in importance of fighting and solving crime was solidified in police culture. Additionally, isolation from the public was inevitable during this time period. The advent of the patrol car meant that officers were covering more ground while interacting less with the public.

It is this professional, crime-fighting model of policing that has by and large survived to this very day. Although police departments increasingly adopt community policing policies, which seek to form partnerships with the communities to solve rather than salve community problems, modern law enforcement still primarily serves as a reactionary, crime-fighting force.

In the professional model of policing, the overriding mission of law enforcement is to suppress criminal activity. Profiling, to the extent that it enables law enforcement to successfully identify potential criminal activity and perpetrators of such activity, is entirely consistent with the professional model. Perhaps this is why profiling has flourished in recent years and has been legitimized in law enforcement as a quasi-science through training and practice. The bottom line in the minds of many professionally oriented police officers is that profiling tends to work.

It also makes sense that with the growth of community policing, the comfort level of society with profiling is diminishing—particularly among citizens in the subcommunities most affected. Say those citizens: how can we partner with the police when they view us as potential violators based on objective criteria over which we have no control, such as our race?

Slave Patrols

The English origins of American policing serve as the primary source for understanding U.S. police history. The model for urban law enforcement given to us from the Met, or even the traditional notion of the office of county sheriff, derived from the British "shire reeve," who was responsible for tax collection and process service in the English countryside, does not, however, explain the police practices of the nineteenth-century American South.

Indeed, policing in the southern United States, particularly as policing related to black Americans, has a sad history of its own. Many historians recognize today that policing in the American South during the eighteenth century and first half of the nineteenth century was inextricably tied to slavery.

Owing to a fear of violent slave uprisings, along with fearing the lesser offenses of refusing to work, escape, killing livestock, and destroying equipment, formal slave patrols began to form in the Southern colonies (Samaha 2002).

South Carolina established the first slave patrol in 1704. Virginia followed in 1727 and North Carolina in 1753 (Hadden 2001). Those formal slave patrols established legislatively by the colonies constitute some of the earliest formal police operations in America. Patrollers were usually white men between the ages of sixteen and sixty. These men were often chosen from the rosters of the militia. They had three main duties: (1) searching slave quarters, (2) dispersing slave gatherings, and (3) safeguarding communities by patrolling the roads (Hadden 2001).

The slave patrols continued to exist throughout the South until the Civil War. In the wake of the Civil War and the emancipation of slaves, the slave patrols gave way to vigilante groups that continued to troll for blacks with an eye toward submission through intimidation at the least and downright terror for terror's sake at the worst. The Ku Klux Klan (KKK) was organized as one of these vigilante groups. Given the common heritage of organizations such as the KKK with elements of modern policing, it is little wonder that many African Americans have an antipathy for aggressive, contact-intensive police patrol tactics.

Emerging Theories of Crime and Profiling

Just as law enforcement, as an occupation and practice, has developed over time, so have the theories of crime often relied upon by the criminal justice system. There have been many theories advanced as to the cause of crime and criminality. Obviously, the same explanations people use to explain crime can be used to predict it as well. And people, once they believe themselves capable of predicting crime, will necessarily engage in profiling to do so. The degree to which race, ethnicity, gender, sexual orientation, or religion are pieces of those explanations relates to the degree that people will tend to be profiled along these lines.

As George Cole and Christopher Smith have noted, philosophies of crime in America and elsewhere in the West prior to the eighteenth century were inseparable from the prevailing theologies of the day. Under this worldview, mankind is fallen and inherently sinful. Crime is a natural manifestation of mankind's sinful nature. Formal indictments for criminal offenses in colonial times would include language such as "[John Doe] not having the fear of God before his eyes but being seduced by the instigation of the Devil, did commit [some offense]" (Cole and Smith 2001, 68).

The eighteenth century, however, ushered in rational approaches to explaining criminality in people. In particular, Cesare Beccaria (1738–1794) published *Essays on Crimes and Punishment* in 1764, which contained the tenets of what is now known as classical criminology. Beccaria claimed that the explanation for crime is not generally rooted in theology; rather, it is rooted in rational thinking. Becarria argued that when criminals commit crime, they do so out of their free will, having made a rational choice weighing the costs of possibly getting caught against the benefits of succeeding.

Beccaria's basic principles were

1. crime is caused by the individual rational exercise of free will
2. pain and pleasure are the two central determinants of human behavior
3. crime disparages the quality of the relationship that exists between individuals and society
4. punishment is a necessary evil and is sometimes required to deter criminal choices and serve as an example to others
5. crime prevention is possible through swift and certain punishment, which offsets any gains to be had through criminal behavior.

Although many in history have looked at Beccaria's principles as an excuse for harsh punishment, Beccaria himself was actually a staunch opponent of excess punishment.

The profiling implications of classical criminology are that crime may be predicted by identifying those most likely to find the benefits of committing a crime greater than the costs. If other people's rational choices regarding crime can be anticipated, then the criminal justice system may use that during enforcement to avert crime or during adjudication and sentencing to avert recidivism.

In the nineteenth century and first part of the twentieth century, another theory of crime became very popular. During that time, it was common to believe that crime was at least in part due to biology. In other words, adherents to this theory argued that some people are predisposed to committing crimes. That theory of crime—the theory that some people are born criminal—is the criminogenic theory of crime.

Criminogenics' most famous champion was Cesare Lombroso (1836–1909). Lombroso and others argued that people who were born criminal had some telltale biological and physiological features. For example, they claimed that criminals tended to have primitive physical features such as strong canine teeth, huge jaws, and high cheekbones. Indeed, the cartoon cliché of criminals having "slack jaws and beady eyes" came from this school of thought.

Lombroso's theory of crime was tied to naturalism and Charles Darwin's theory of evolution. If some people exhibited features that were common to a more primitive version of man, that is, a version appearing earlier in the evolutionary chain, then it was logical to assume that the behavior of those people would tend to be more primitive.

Although few serious scholars today advance Lombroso's criminogenic theories, many do believe that genetics, physiology, and heredity may play a part in determining criminal behavior. Studies continue to be done by biologists and research psychologists in attempts to identify genetic and physiological features that are associated with people who commit various types of crime—particularly violent crime.

The implications that the biological theories of crime have for profiling are plain. If criminals are likely to have certain physical features, then the criminal justice system, many would argue, should give proactive attention to people possessing those features before all others. Or, if criminals will likely have certain genetic features, then perhaps the criminal justice system should give proactive attention to those whose deoxyribonucleic acid (DNA) fits a certain profile.

For example, some researchers have published findings in mainstream scientific journals that sexual orientation has an association with pedophilia. In particular, it is claimed that homosexual men (generally assumed to constitute less than 3 percent of the total population) are responsible for a third of all child molestations. This disproportionate representation of homosexuals among sex offenders against children, if true, would have significant profiling implications. For example, people meeting the profile—namely, homosexual and male—might not be permitted to work unsupervised with children. Nor might they be permitted to adopt. Or, when male children went missing, homosexual males would be the first people law enforcement would look at for suspects.

Today, the most prevailing types of theories to explain crime are sociological ones. Sociological explanations of crime—and there are many—emphasize the role that society and social conditions (for example, poverty, prestige, family structure or lack thereof, role of institutions such as church, lack of education, and so on) have on individual offenders. Theorists along these lines claim that we are products of our environment. Consequently, treating undesirable social conditions is the best way to address criminality in our society.

Profiles that rely on sociological theories of crime would suggest that the criminal justice system could expect crime from those quarters of our society that are run-down, impoverished, lacking traditional family households, lacking socioeconomic opportunities, and so on. A profile of "typical" violent offenders in a particular city might be juveniles who have no father figures at home, who live in poverty with drug use all around them, and who receive no moral instruction from those over them.

Although many of the above profile's elements are associated with crime in America's urban areas, the practical application would require people to be treated differently on the basis of these conditions. This is a point already alleged by many—specifically, that the poor and minorities in this country are treated differently than others by the criminal justice system. As all are supposed equal before the bar of justice, inequitable treatment on the grounds of social status is offensive to most. Such profiling might be used, however, to identify needed points of intervention before the bar of justice is ever needed.

Common Police Profiles

Criminal justice profiling by law enforcement has been extensively represented and glamorized in books and film. Many Americans with no connection to criminal justice professions could tell you about common types of criminal adversaries that are targeted by profiling. David Harris, in his book *Profiles in Injustice* (2002), described three of the most common police profiles categories that have been used with regularity: (1) the hijacker, (2) the serial killer, and (3) the drug courier. None of the profiles is in essence about race, gender, religion, or sexual orientation, but some of these classifications carry weight within the profiles.

The Hijacker

Although much attention of law enforcement has been given to hijacking after the September 11 attacks, concern over the forcible commandeering of airliners has been with us for many years. In the late 1960s, U.S. airliners were successfully hijacked by the dozens. In 1968, eighteen American airliners were hijacked; in 1969, more than thirty airliners were hijacked (Harris 2002).

In an effort to put a stop to this epidemic problem of air piracy, U.S. authorities developed a profile of potential hijackers. It was hoped that hijackers would be spotted by alerted law enforcement officials before the hijackers ever got onto the airplanes.

The hijacker profile was behavior driven and relied on observations made by airline personnel, starting at the ticket counter. Those individuals who acted suspiciously or in some way met the profile would be screened in greater detail. The screening would involve having them pass through metal detectors and answer questions about their identity and destination.

Hijacker profiling had limited success, and by 1973, the Federal Aviation Administration scrapped the program and simply began to require all passengers to pass through metal detection devices. Many believe it is time, in lieu of searches of randomly selected passengers, to bring hijacker profiling back and concentrate our limited security resources at airports on those most likely to pose a threat.

The Serial Killer

The ability of law enforcement officials to profile serial killers and rapists is among the most glorified of law enforcement activities. Serial offender profiling is a relatively new police tactic that simply built upon the standard deductive reasoning process of traditional police investigations. Serial killer profiling really took root at the FBI Academy's Behavioral Science Unit. FBI special agent John Douglas and other FBI profilers became legendary in law enforcement circles for their ability to predict detailed characteristics about serial offenders based on patterns within the offenders' modus operandi (that is, the methods, times, locations, and victims drawn from in committing the offense).

As suggested earlier, profilers have generated much interest in the popular culture, thanks to fictional novel and motion picture portrayals of law enforcement profilers, as in Thomas Harris's *Red Dragon, Silence of the Lambs,* and *Hannibal* and in true crime reenactment television shows.

The premise of serial profiling is that much can be learned about violent serial offenders by talking to previously identified serial offenders. Through interviewing identified serial killers and sex offenders, patterns and themes have in fact emerged concerning the upbringing, general background, and modus operandi of these offenders. The information is then used to predict (although not prove) the types of people that offenders may or may not be. Today, the FBI and many large state and local police agencies employ profilers whose knowledge and expertise about violent serial offenders can be drawn upon whenever suspicions arise that a serial or bizarre offender has committed crimes in their respective jurisdictions.

Drug Courier

The development of drug courier profiles by our nation's drug enforcement agencies and police divisions in the 1980s war on drugs marked the beginning of widespread police profiling at the patrol officer level. After all, serial killings and hijackings are relatively uncommon criminal offenses, but drug trafficking is all around us. It was thought that if profiling as a police tool could be oriented toward drug traffickers, a significant dent in the drug trade through interdiction might be achieved (Harris 2002).

Drug courier profiles initially were utilized primarily in airports by drug agents. Law enforcement officials would use profiles, that is, characteristics commonly associated with drug couriers, in screening arriving and departing passengers. Those passengers who fit the courier profile would then be temporarily detained and questioned. The passengers would not be under arrest. Rather, the detention merely amounted to an investigatory stop.

The U.S. Supreme Court upheld the use of drug courier profiling at our nation's ports of entry in the case *U.S. v. Sokolow* (1989). In that case, the defendant paid for his ticket with cash; he traveled under a name different than that which was listed with his telephone number; he made a round trip to Miami; he stayed in Miami only two days, although the travel time alone took twenty-four hours; he appeared nervous; and he did not check any luggage. The Supreme Court recognized the right of the police to be drawn to the obviously suspicious circumstances of Sokolow's traveling.

In time, the drug courier profile no longer was confined to the nation's international airports. Law enforcement, having perceived a level of effectiveness in profiling drug couriers at the ports of entry, developed profiles of couriers and traffickers on the roadways. Law enforcement began to ask, "What are the similarities among those motorists who transport drugs on the highways?" Volusia County (FL) Sheriff Bob Vogel, who was instrumental in mainstreaming the practice of profiling on the highways in the 1980s, used the term *cumulative similarities* rather than *profiles*. These similarities will be discussed later, but suffice to say here that the perceived success of the practice of courier profiling on the highways led to law enforcement's widespread use of it, which in turn led to its widespread criticism and incumbent controversy.

Proactive and Reactive Profiling

Profiling by law enforcement officials can be thought of as either proactive or reactive, depending on the context. Proactive profiling occurs when officers on patrol utilize profiling as a tool to detect and prevent crime in the field. Reactive profiling is a tool used by criminal investigators to apprehend those who have already committed crimes. In other words, proactive profiling attempts to interdict and foil crime; reactive profiling seeks to solve crime.

Darin Fredrickson and Raymond Siljander defined proactive criminal justice profiling as the process whereby police officers "make judgements about another, relative to possible criminal activity, based on a number of overt and subtle factors which may or may not include things such as the person's race, manner of dress and grooming, behavioral characteristics, when and where the observation is made, the circumstances under which the observation is made, and relative to information the officer may already possess" (Fredrickson and Siljander 2002, 15).

When discussion is entered into about proactive criminal justice profiling done by patrol officers in the field, the discussion usually becomes one about racial profiling, as opposed to concern about other characteristics being singled out. This is because many of the voices of criticism concerning the tool of profiling come from community leaders in urban areas where the majority of inhabitants are racial minorities—African Americans, Hispanics, Asian Americans, and so on. In those urban areas, profiling is just one debate of many over various police strategies and practices that have been employed.

One especially controversial debate concerns that of the "broken windows" approach to patrol work. This approach, first proposed by James Q. Wilson and George E. Kelling, is based on the theory that if a neighborhood is allowed to run down, that situation breeds bigger problems. In fact, many crime prevention programs buy into the same assumptions. Vandalism, graffiti, broken windows in buildings, abandoned cars, and ill-kept properties are all thought to contribute to the image that people don't care in a particular neighborhood and that therefore crime can flourish. By contrast, neighborhoods that take care of the little things, such as running out the prostitutes and petty drug dealers, condemning drug houses and other substandard buildings, will broadcast a message that crime is not welcome here; take it somewhere else.

Broken windows, and its aggressive patrol tactics of questioning anyone raising suspicion and arresting people for minor offenses, was first practiced by the New York Transit Police and then later by the New York Police Department, both under the leadership of Bill Bratton. The use of broken windows policing is credited with dramatically reducing crime in the subway system in the early 1990s and then dramatically reducing crime in the City of New York in the mid- and late 1990s (Cleary 2000).

Critics of broken windows' zero tolerance approach to the minor offenses point out, however, that the strategy puts the officers in the position of an occupying military force. Police have little opportunity to form partnerships with the community and build trust among the residents when they are preoccupied with stopping every suspected minor offender with the hopes of turning the case into something bigger. These critics tend to view profiling, however successful it may or may not be in detecting crime, as ultimately counterproductive because it alienates the police from the community; it sets the police against the community by suggesting that people who fit a stereotype are probably up to no-good.

As mentioned earlier, uniformed officers who engage in profiling are frequently attempting to snare the drug offender. Profiling for drug offenders—particularly drug couriers—involves consideration of the race of the motorist, the gender, age, route of travel, and the vehicle being driven.

In the 1980s, law enforcement began to identify certain interstate highways from points of origin such as Miami that served as main arteries for transporting drugs up the East Coast and into the interior of the country. What's more, police officers noted that offenders were frequently minorities, were young males, and utilized rental cars. Rental vehicles were ideal in that they were mechanically reliable (Fredrickson and Siljander 2002). With the advent of computer terminals in squad cars, rental cars offered added protection against detection by the police in that a license plate check by officers while driving would show the registered owner to be the rental company, rather than the driver—who might or might not have a warrant or be suspended or revoked.

Indicators that a vehicle might be carrying drugs are many. In profiling, it is the totality of the facts that generates sufficient suspicion to warrant further inquiry by the officer. These indicators, with regard to the vehicle, include (Fredrickson and Siljander 2002)

- rear end riding low (because of the weight of the drugs)
- spare tire or luggage in the back seat to make room for drugs in the trunk
- tinted windows, or windows down during unusually hot or cold weather

- modifications or alterations to the vehicle
- very little if any luggage for out-of-state travelers
- "good guy" decals such as religious symbols, pro-police stickers, or antidrug stickers
- lifestyle statements, such as drug paraphernalia, decals of drugs, and decals of known drug-using rock bands
- multiple deodorants in the vehicle to mask the smell of drugs
- dirty vehicle with clean plates
- unusual driving . . . especially perfect driving or driving too slowly

Obviously, an individual may signal any number of these indicators and not actually be carrying drugs in his or her vehicle. But profiling plays the odds, and police note that the odds frequently pay off.

Profiling by patrol officers has frequently targeted other criminal activities as well. Profiling has been used very successfully to combat auto theft. Once again, race, age, and gender of the offender are pieces of a larger profile that also includes make of vehicle, number and type of occupants (a family, for example, would not fit the profile), direction of travel, and time of day.

The more glamorous and less controversial type of criminal justice profiling relates to reactive profiling—generally a tool of investigators rather than patrol officers. This type of profiling attempts to take facts and clues garnished from one or more crime scenes and develop a composite sketch of the likely type of person who committed the crime(s).

Specifically, criminal investigators who are profilers, such as those who work in the FBI's Behavioral Science Unit, perform their services in the pursuit of three goals (Holmes 1989):

1. to provide the criminal justice system with a social and psychological assessment of the offender
2. to provide the criminal justice system with a psychological evaluation of belongings found in the possession of the offender
3. to provide interviewing suggestions and strategies

The first goal relates to identifying the offender. The assessment will include basic information that is hypothesized about the offender in a particular case. The information will include a guess as to the offender's age, sex, race, religion, employment, marital status, education, and any other relevant factors that can be reasonably inferred.

The second and third goals of the criminal investigator/profiler are geared toward shoring up the case against a suspect once identified. Souvenirs and mementos taken from the victims and from other sources that are found in a suspect's possession can provide greater psychological insight as to what motivated the offender to offend in the way he or she did. Profilers will also help the primary investigators with strategies for questioning suspects. Based on the profile developed, it might be thought that certain points of conversation might be hot buttons worth pushing. Or it might be supposed that the suspect would love to tell his or her story, and therefore a more congenial approach would be fruitful.

Investigative profiling is generally reserved for the most serious types of offenses, such as rape and murder. Those who are experts in profiling are few and therefore their efforts tend to be channeled in that direction. As suggested earlier, criminal profiling is simply an extension of deductive reasoning utilized by police for ages. Some critics say that profiling murderers and rapists is a practice that requires no special expertise and exists as a science only in the minds of those who do it. One psychologist suggested that most profiles submitted for consideration in an investigation are either too vague and ambiguous to be useful or they are simple statements of common sense that did not require an expert from Quantico, Virginia, to make (Holmes 1989).

Prosecutorial and Judicial Profiling

Profiling is generally thought of as a law enforcement issue. There is growing attention, however, to profiling in prosecutorial and judicial venues of the criminal justice system as well. Although law enforcement has an argument that profiling is a tool that helps identify criminal suspects, there is significantly less rationale for considering race, gender, or other characteristics when it comes to prosecution decisions or rulings from the bench.

And yet, evidence does suggest that racial, gender, and other differences among people seem to matter as, in the aggregate, they are treated differently. In the next chapter, an examination of the discretion criminal justice officials have includes segments on prosecutorial and judicial discretion. Also, in a later chapter, summaries of several studies concerning real and alleged unequal treatment of various groups under the law by prosecutors and judges will be presented. You will have the opportunity to draw your own conclusions as to the legitimacy of charges of bias in the criminal justice system, whether it exists intentionally or not.

References

Carlson, D. P. 2002. *When Cultures Clash.* Upper Saddle River, NJ: Prentice Hall.

Cleary, J. 2000. *Racial Profiling Studies in Law Enforcement: Issues and Methodology.* St. Paul: State of Minnesota, House of Representatives Research Department.

Cole, G. F., and C. E. Smith. 2001. *The American System of Criminal Justice.* 9th ed. Stamford, CT: Wadsworth.

Deakin, T. J. 1988. *Police Professionalism: Renaissance of American Law Enforcement.* Springfield, IL: Charles C. Thomas.

Dye, T. R. 2001. *Politics in America.* Upper Saddle River, NJ: Prentice Hall.

Fredrickson, D. D., and R. P. Siljander. 2002. *Racial Profiling.* Springfield, IL: Charles C. Thomas.

Hadden, S. 2001. *Slave Patrols: Law and Violence in Virginia and the Carolinas.* Cambridge, MA: Harvard University Press.

Harris, D. A. 2002. *Profiles in Injustice.* New York: The New Press.

Hobbes, T. 1651. *Leviathan.* Reprint, London: J. M. Dent and Sons, 1965.

Holmes, R. M. 1989. *Profiling Violent Crimes.* Newbury Park, CA: Sage.

International Association of Chiefs of Police. 2003. Legislative Updates section. http://www.theiacp.org/leg_policy.

Mills, C. W. 1956. *The Power Elite.* New York: Oxford University Press.

National Commission on Crime Control and Prevention. 1994. *Final Report.* Washington, DC.

Peak, K. J., and R. W. Glesnor. 1996. *Community Policing and Problem Solving: Strategies and Practices.* Upper Saddle River, NJ: Prentice Hall.

Roberg, R., J. Crank, and J. Kuykendall. 2000. *Police and Society.* Los Angeles: Roxbury.

Samaha, J. 1994. *Criminal Justice.* 3rd ed. St. Paul, MN: West.

———. 2002. *Criminal Justice.* 4th ed. St. Paul, MN: West.

Schmalleger, F. 1993. *Criminal Justice Today*. 2nd ed. Englewood Cliffs, NJ: Regents/Prentice Hall.

Shott, R. G. 2001. "The Role of Race in Law Enforcement," *FBI Law Enforcement Bulletin*, November, pp. 24–32.

Sparrow, M. K., M. H. Moore, and D. M. Kennedy. 1990. *Beyond 911: A New Era for Policing*. New York: HarperCollins.

Uchida, C. 2001. "The Development of the American Police: A Historical Overview," pp. 18–35. In *Critical Issues in Policing*, 4th ed., ed. R. G. Dunham and G. P. Alpert. Prospect Heights, IL: Waveland.

Walker, S. 1977. *A Critical History of Police Reform*. Lexington, MA: Lexington Books.

Walker, S., C. Spohn, and M. DeLone. 2003. *The Color of Justice: Race, Ethnicity, and Crime in America*. Belmont, CA: Wadsworth.

2

Issues in Criminal Justice Profiling

Stereotyping and Profiling

Profiling is related to stereotyping but is not the same thing. Profiling is an act. In criminal justice, profiling involves the taking of some action by criminal justice officials based on observable conditions, behaviors, and activities. Stereotyping, on the other hand, is not action oriented; it is perception oriented (Lee, Albright, and Malloy 2001). Stereotyping is the ascription of characteristics to social groups or segments of society (Banaji and Bhaskar 2000).

That having been said, stereotypes help shape the meaning of the observations for the person doing the observing. Given the relationship of stereotyping to the formation of meaning and context for one engaged in criminal justice profiling, it is important to understand more thoroughly the concept of stereotyping.

Stereotyping is essentially a shortcut to perceiving people. Stereotypes can be rooted in truth or falsehood, or somewhere in between. But whatever their veracity, stereotypes allow people, including criminal justice officials, to start from somewhere other than zero when sizing up other people. Obviously in a criminal justice system such as ours, where all people are to be treated equally and are presumed to be law-abiding, stereotyping raises ethical quandaries apart from its utility.

Stereotypes can be thought of along two dimensions: accuracy and valance (Lee, Jussim, and McCauley 1995). Accuracy relates to the question of just how much the set of inferences in the mind of the perceiver matches the objectively measured (that is, actual) qualities of the group in question. A stereotype can be thought of as existing along a continuum ranging from completely accurate to completely inaccurate.

Although accuracy can be objectively measured, valance is more subjective. The dimension of valance relates to the degree that a stereotype is positive or negative. Sometimes the characterization of something as positive or negative depends on the perspective of the observer. One observer says: "Wow, that glass is half full!" A second says: "Darn, that glass is half empty." The first observer clearly is happy with as much in the glass as there is; the second is clearly disappointed. Both observers are accurate—the glass contains one half of its maximum capacity.

In the case of stereotypes, when we put the dimensions of accuracy and valance together (such as in the model in Figure 2.1), we can see four realms within which stereotypical perceptions are cast. Given that stereotypes shape context and meaning for an observer (to include criminal justice officials), understanding these realms becomes important.

As one can see in Figure 2.1, a stereotype can be accurate and positive, accurate and negative, inaccurate and positive, and inaccurate and negative. To the extent that stereotypes are drawn upon (and all humans draw upon them), the ideal is that a stereotype is accurate and positive. By contrast, clearly the worst kinds of stereotypes are those that are inaccurate and negative. Such stereotypes can be slanderous and vicious.

In the middle are those stereotypes that are inaccurate but positive and accurate but negative. For example, the stereotype that Asian Americans are really smart is positive. Who doesn't

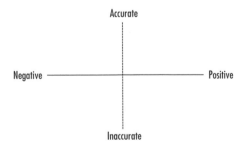

Figure 2.1   Intersection of Accuracy and Valance (Lee et al.)

want to be thought of as "smart"? The degree to which it is accurate—particularly for all Asian Americans—is debatable and subject to further evaluation. Maybe after looking at college entrance scores for Asian American high school students across the country and comparing them to other high school students, we might come to conclude that the stereotype is more accurate than not but fail to legitimately claim that it is completely accurate. Or we might not. But it is measurable; the accuracy is verifiable.

With regard to the issue of criminal justice profiling, and knowing that profiles are influenced, if not driven, by stereotypes, we can consider the combinations of accuracy and valance characterizing those stereotypes to help assess the legitimacy of a given profile.

Profiles rooted in a negative and inaccurate stereotype are unfair, unethical, immoral, and counterproductive (particularly due to the inaccuracy element). A stereotype that all urban African Americans are into drugs and crime is not only extremely negative and unfair to law-abiding African Americans, but it is wildly inaccurate, thereby resulting in false investigations and accusations of innocent people at the expense of more reasoned efforts against the genuinely guilty.

On the other hand, a stereotype that all Hispanic teenage males in particular Los Angeles neighborhoods who wear certain colored bandanas and have their pants hang low, exposing their boxer shorts, are gang members is one that is rooted in some truth. Although it would not be completely accurate (that is, true for *all* such persons), it may be largely accurate despite the negative connotation of being linked to gang membership. Law-abiding Hispanic teens wearing such clothing in the aforementioned way may find the negative stereotype offensive, but it largely works for law enforcement—thereby giving them a shortcut in making initial judgments of such people. When police officers in Los Angeles pay special attention to such people while ignoring others, all because of the relatively accurate stereotype, they have engaged in profiling.

In short, stereotypes that are positive and accurate are not controversial. Stereotypes that are positive and inaccurate are not useful. Stereotypes that are negative and inaccurate are harmful and not useful. Stereotypes that are negative and accurate are controversial. It is this realm that criminal justice officials, and particularly law enforcement officers, claim to occupy when they profile. They argue that it is unfortunate that this group or that group is subject to a negative stereotype, but the "shoe fits."

Community leaders, on the other hand, argue that the criminal justice system is too often in the realm of the negatively inaccurate. They argue that the culture of criminal justice in the United States perpetuates myths about groups of people—blacks, Hispanics, young males, gays—that are simply not true. Consequently, acting on those stereotypes predictably results in the harassment of the innocent and overreaction to the guilty.

Police Discretion

To the extent that criminal profiling by the police is a permitted and accepted practice in law enforcement, it is a manifestation of police discretion. Any discussion about reforming the use of profiling as a tool necessarily implies the need to curtail police discretion. Long before profiling was a current and controversial issue, politicians, academics, and practitioners were debating the appropriate limits of police discretion. So what is it?

Discretion exists when a public officer's effective limits on his or her power leave the officer free to make a choice among possible courses of action or inaction. It is worth noting that the emphasis is on the effective limits of the officer's power, not simply what is legal or what is authorized; the range of decisions available to an officer may include options that are illegal or of questionable illegality (Evans 1978). In light of this definition, police officer discretion might simply be paraphrased as an officer's having a choice in how to respond to a situation.

Discretion is what governs an officer's decision to pull over a traffic law violator or not, or to give him a ticket, or her a warning. It governs the detective's decision to work a particular case aggressively, or minimally, or whether to open the case to begin with. Discretion is everywhere in law enforcement; many police reformers and critics would like to rein it in.

Dean Champion and George Rush, in their book *Policing in the Community* (1997), presented a number of reasons that support the need for police officer discretion. The reasons include

- some laws are too vague to expect that they be enforced with regularity

- police have limited resources and therefore must pick their battles.
- enforcing all laws as written without discretion would cause community alienation
- discretion enables officers to individualize the law (for example, electing to take a juvenile vandal home to his parents when it is believed that this juvenile will be responsive to sanctions imposed by the parents)
- many violations are minor.

Advocates of giving police a wide berth in decision making point to these arguments and others. There are problems with police discretion as well. Samuel Walker noted that uncontrolled discretion can result in (Walker 1999)

- denial of due process for suspects
- denial of equal protection under the law
- poor police-community relations, particularly when most of the discretionary decisions to enforce the law are concentrated in particular communities or neighborhoods
- poor personnel management
- poor planning and policy development

Additionally, discretionary enforcement of the law can reduce the deterrent effect of the law and, because of discretion's hidden nature, can make officer decisions difficult to review (Brooks 2001).

There are four basic variables that influence police discretionary decision making. These are organizational variables, neighborhood variables, situational variables, and individual variables (Roberg, Crank, and Kuykendall 2000).

Organizational variables include things such as the bureaucratic nature of police departments and the criminal justice system. A growing number of police departments require that for every traffic stop, a form be completed to document the race and gender of the driver, as well as the reasons for the stop and outcome. Additionally, an officer would still be required to complete the initial contact report (ICR) and the citation or warning, if one is issued. For a number of officers, pulling over motorists for other than the most serious of violations is too much hassle. Consequently, the organizational variables—in this case paper-work—are an influence on officers' decisions to not pull people over (a decision within the realm of their discretion).

Neighborhood variables refer to the characteristics of a neighborhood that make policing it a unique experience. Things such as the racial and ethnic homogeneity or diversity of a community could be a factor in the decisions an officer makes. Likewise, the economy and business makeup of a community will have an impact as well. If the neighborhood being policed is a suburban residential community with little more than light industry and heavy commuter traffic, then traffic enforcement might be the normal operation for officers not responding to calls. A working-class neighborhood with numerous small shops and even some manufacturing facilities, however, may require that officers spend more time engaging in preventative patrol around those businesses to guard against break-ins or holdups; that would leave less time for traffic enforcement.

Situational variables refer to specific factors relating to an incident to which the officer is responding and/or which the officer is resolving. Factors that are situational include how the officer came into the situation (was the officer dispatched or did he or she just happen along), the demeanor and attitude of the parties involved, the gender of the parties involved, the relationship between the complainant and the suspect, the type of offense, the location, and the presence of others.

For example, if an officer happens upon a dispute between neighbors, he or she might choose to handle it less formally than if the officer had been dispatched. Or if an officer responds to a misdemeanor assault, the officer may be more inclined to make an arrest in lieu of a citation if the parties have an "intimate" relationship (ironically, officers were more likely to have exactly the opposite reaction only a few years ago—prior to heightened attention given to domestic violence). Still another example of situational variables includes the demeanor of the suspect. If a motorist carries on with outrage about being stopped for speeding, he will almost certainly receive a citation. If a motorist is polite and apologetic, and the offense wasn't too serious, many officers would be inclined to give a warning instead. A bad attitude is not illegal; yet those people with bad attitudes frequently receive harsher treatment from agents within the criminal justice system. Whether that's fair or not, it is obvious evidence of discretion.

The final variable is officer individuality. In other words, this variable is specific to the officer and includes the officer's education, experience, age, race, gender, and career ambitions. Officers with less experience will make different discretionary decisions than those with more experience. Officers who treat their job as just a job, or who are cynical, will make different decisions than those who view law enforcement as their life's calling and approach their occupation with passion. Officers who are members of an ethnic or racial minority may be more sympathetic with others from that group and more understanding of their culture and their plight. Perhaps female officers may be more diplomatic than many male officers. All these factors can and do impact the decisions police officers make in the field on a daily, and hourly, basis.

Charging Decisions

Prosecutors throughout the United States have considerable discretion in determining who is going to be charged and with what. Clearly, things such as race or ethnicity should not enter into the decision making about what charges, if any, should be brought against one subject or another. Yet there have been studies that suggest that prosecutors tend to be lenient in their decisions toward female offenders and more likely to prosecute racial minorities over whites (Schmalleger 1999) or to upgrade charges against minorities while downgrading them for whites (Robinson 2002).

But prosecutors must consider some screening factors to help them determine which cases are worthy and which are less of a priority. The U.S. Department of Justice offers guidelines to federal prosecutors to gauge whether a particular case should be pursued or not. The guidelines ask prosecutors to consider (Cole and Smith 2001)

- federal law enforcement priorities of the day
- the nature and seriousness of the offense
- the deterrent effect of prosecution
- the person's culpability in connection with the offense
- the person's criminal history
- the person's willingness to cooperate in the investigation

- the probable sentence or consequences if the prosecution is successful

Nowhere among the consideration criteria is there listed race, gender, sexual orientation, or other factors not related to the criminal activity itself.

In criminal justice literature, three decision-making models have emerged to help explain how prosecutors accept or decline individual cases: legal sufficiency model, system efficiency model, and trial sufficiency model (Jacoby 1979). The three models vary according to how strong the case must be prior to acceptance for prosecution.

The legal sufficiency model requires only the minimum level of legal elements necessary to prove a case against a suspect. Prosecutors operating under this model will tend to accept virtually all cases given to them by the police, knowing that the majority of them will be plea-bargained away before ever reaching trial. That outcome is fine with them because many of these cases are questionable as to whether proof beyond a reasonable doubt (the standard for a conviction) could be demonstrated in court. Attorneys operating under this model are comfortable with the fact that many of these cases will eventually be dismissed.

The system efficiency model is a little more stringent in standards. The weak cases are screened out upon receipt from law enforcement. Then, of those that remain, the majority are disposed of outside of court. Fewer cases are expected by the prosecutor to be dismissed altogether, however, because the truly lousy cases are not pursued from the start. Although these cases are stronger, there is still an emphasis on plea bargains and diversions, given the volume of cases and the time it takes for a prosecutor to try a case.

The trial sufficiency model is the most stringent in screening cases. Prosecutors operating according to the trial sufficiency model will only accept cases that clearly have enough evidence to win at trial. In other words, the outcome of getting a conviction upon trying the case, whether before a judge or a jury, is not in doubt in the prosecutor's mind. With such cases, plea-bargaining is not common. If plea-bargaining does take place, the terms will be especially favorable to the prosecutor.

Given the volume of cases generated in the urban areas, prosecutors are frequently overwhelmed with case decisions. Urban prosecutor offices often follow one of the first two models and emphasize plea-bargaining as a means to dispose of cases. Plea bargains mean convictions. Given that urban areas have large minority populations, it is not surprising to see large numbers of minority convictions.

But is it fair?

In 1886, the Supreme Court addressed the question about the legality of racial motivation in bringing charges against suspects. The Court said clearly in *Yick Wo v. Hopkins* that it was impermissible for racial discrimination to be a motive in charging decisions. Since then, however, the Supreme Court has upheld in case after case the right of prosecutors to decide who and how to charge, short of breaking the law (McCoy 1998).

In making the decision to prosecute or not, prosecutors may consider factors outside the strict merits of the case, such as community sentiment. Consider the case against the police officers who had beaten Rodney King in 1992. They had been tried for and acquitted of criminal assault against King. Customarily, the U.S. Justice Department does not retry cases that were lost at the state level unless there was a substandard prosecutorial effort made at the state level. That was certainly not the case regarding the effort of the Los Angeles County District Attorney's Office. Even so, the community's sentiment cried out for another prosecution, and the U.S. Justice Department obliged.

In Court

The entrances and hallways to courtrooms across the United States are frequently adorned with icons of equal justice for all, such as pictures or statues of Lady Justice, blindfolded and holding her scales. Indeed, the emphasis on formal procedures to ensure due process and equal protection would make one think that profiling, that is, classification consciousness, would have no place there; regardless of how one comes to be there, all are equal upon stepping into the courthouse. Even in the courthouse, however, there has historically been a place for profiling by class (race, gender, and so on). The courthouse activity most touched today by the practice of profiling is the jury selection process.

Jury selection is one area in the trial process where attorneys have some latitude in their ability to discriminate. Through voir dire, which refers to the questioning of prospective jurors by the prosecution and defense attorneys to screen out individuals the attorneys believe are biased or incapable of delivering a fair verdict, attorneys can have jurors stricken from the jury pool (Cole and Smith 2001).

During the voir dire process, prosecutors and defense attorneys are granted the ability to make a limited number of peremptory challenges and an unlimited number of challenges for cause. Peremptory challenges traditionally meant that an attorney could disqualify a potential juror for any reason or for no reason at all. The attorney needed only to feel uncomfortable with that juror, and he or she would be excused jury duty in that case. There are limits to the number of peremptory challenges attorneys can exercise. The precise number depends on the jurisdiction, but customarily, the defense has more preemptory challenges than does the prosecutor.

Challenges for cause are when either the prosecutor or the defense attorney can convince the judge, based on objective evidence, that a prospective juror is likely incapable of rendering a fair verdict and therefore must be removed. A potential juror whose husband was killed in a robbery might be fine as juror in a tobacco lawsuit but is too likely to be biased against the defendant in a robbery or murder case. In such a case, the judge would strike the juror from service, and neither side would lose one of its peremptory challenges.

Historically and through legal imposition, juries consisted of white men. Over time, the laws changed to allow women and minorities to serve on juries. What was permissible under the law, however, was not always seen as desirable by attorneys trying the cases. Indeed, through peremptory challenges and through challenges for cause based on flimsy rationales of jury bias offered to sympathetic judges, women and minorities continued to be discriminated against when it came to jury duty.

The U.S. Supreme Court has a track record of eyeing discriminatory jury pools and peremptory challenges with suspicion when a particular race or group of people is excluded from jury duty. As far back as the 1879 case of *Strauder v. West Virginia,* the Court said that a defendant who is a racial minority is deprived of equal protection under the Fourteenth Amendment when members of his or her race are purposefully excluded from the jury. The law in place that was struck down by the Court was West Virginia's 1873 law concerning who could serve on juries. It read: "All white male persons who are twenty-one years of age and who are citizens of this State shall be liable to

serve as jurors, except as herein provided." The persons ex-
cepted were state officials.

As David Cole noted in his book *No Equal Justice* (1999), the
Court in *Strauder* recognized that race matters. Strauder was
denied equal protection through the exclusion of black jurors
because there was an assumption that black and white jurors,
especially in the post–Civil War era, would evaluate a black
defendant differently.

Ironically, the practice of excluding jurors on the basis of race
would be challenged 100 years later relying precisely on the opposite conclusion—namely, that there should be no presumption
that one race is inherently biased against the other and is incapable of rendering a fair verdict. If that were true, say some, then
the Supreme Court erred in *Strauder* in its reasoning by assuming
that an all-white jury could not fairly evaluate Strauder.

Despite the *Strauder* case, discrimination against minorities
who would serve on juries continued for decades with the
Supreme Court's blessing via its upholding of convictions. In
Smith v. Mississippi (1896), the Court upheld a conviction of a
black man convicted by an all-white jury, despite the fact that
there were 1,300 black voters and only 300 white voters in the
county and that no blacks had ever been selected to serve as
jurors in that county since their emancipation (Cole 1999).

In the case of *Neal v. Delaware* (1881), however, the U.S.
Supreme Court was compelled to find in favor of a black defendant because the lower courts (in particular, the Delaware
Supreme Court) actually put to paper their unfettered bias
against blacks. Even though the State of Delaware had a population of less than 150,000, whereas its black residents totaled over
26,000, and had never had a black citizen serve as a juror in the
history of the state, the Delaware Supreme Court upheld the bias
against black jurors and therefore the conviction against Neal by
an all-white jury, stating in part: "That none but white men were
selected is in nowise remarkable in view of the fact that—too
notorious to be ignored—that the great body of black men resid-
ing in the State are utterly unqualified by want of intelligence,
experience, or moral integrity to sit on juries. Exceptions there
are, unquestionably, but they are rare. . . ." (103 US 370)

Even in 1881, the U.S. Supreme Court could not let that one
go. In the Court's words, such a rationale excluding blacks from
jury duty amounted to a "violent presumption" about the fitness
of blacks to engage in jury service. Despite *Strauder* and *Neal*,

however, the Supreme Court, with rare exception, let stand numerous convictions rooted in all-white juries for decades to come (Cole 1999). It was not until the latter part of the twentieth century that the Supreme Court began to consistently afford relief to defendants convicted by juries derived from suspect pools or by suspect challenges.

In *Batson v. Kentucky* (1986), the Supreme Court overturned a conviction because prosecutors had used the peremptory challenge to exclude black jurors, and the trial judge did not require a rational explanation for the exclusions.

In 1991, the U.S. Supreme Court heard the case of *Powers v. Ohio*. In that case, the Supreme Court declared that it was unconstitutional to issue preemptory challenges in a criminal case if the challenge was based on race. The court declared that

> the very fact that [members of a particular race] are singled out and expressly denied . . . all right to participate in the administration of the law, as jurors, because of their color, though they are citizens, and may be in other respects fully qualified, is practically a brand upon them, affixed by the law, an assertion of their inferiority, and a stimulant to that race prejudice which is an impediment to securing individuals of that race equal justice which the law aims to secure to all others (499 US 400).

Later in the same term, the U.S. Supreme Court declared that racially motivated peremptory challenges were likewise unconstitutional in civil cases. The Court said in *Edmonson v. Leesville Concrete Company, Inc.* (1991), that "it is clear that neither prosecutor nor civil attorneys in the future will be able to exclude minority potential jurors consistently unless they are able to articulate clearly credible race-neutral rationales for their actions" (500 US 614).

Then, in the case of *J.E.B. v. Alabama* (1994), the U.S. Supreme Court extended the logic against racially motivated peremptory challenges to those challenges motivated by gender. Gender discrimination was very common in peremptory challenges, as women were often seen by prosecutors as less likely to grant the death penalty in capital cases and, ironically, as harsher critics of female victims of sexual violence who are perceived to have contributed to their victimization by their lifestyle choices.

The Supreme Court wrote in *J.E.B.*:

The Equal Protection Clause prohibits discrimination in jury selection on the basis of gender, or on the assumption that an individual will be biased in a particular case solely because that person happens to be a woman or a man. Respondent's gender-based peremptory challenges cannot survive the heightened equal protection scrutiny that this Court affords distinctions based on gender. Respondent's rationale—that its decision to strike virtually all males in this case may reasonably have been based on the perception, supported by history, that men otherwise totally qualified to serve as jurors might be more sympathetic and receptive to the arguments of a man charged in a paternity action, while women equally qualified might be more sympathetic and receptive to the arguments of the child's mother—is virtually unsupported and is based on the very stereotypes the law condemns. The conclusion that litigants may not strike potential jurors solely on the basis of gender does not imply the elimination of all peremptory challenges. So long as gender does not serve as a proxy for bias, unacceptable jurors may still be removed, including those who are members of a group or class that is normally subject to . . ."rational basis" review and those who exhibit characteristics that are disproportionately associated with one gender. (000 US U10411)

The dissenting justices in the *J.E.B. v. Alabama* case, observing that a growing number of preclusions were cropping up to the historically absolute right of peremptory challenges, noted that "the core of the Court's reasoning [to ban preemptory challenges when based on discrimination against a protected class] is that peremptory challenges on the basis of any group characteristic subject to heightened scrutiny are inconsistent with the guarantee of the Equal Protection Clause. . . . Since all groups are subject to the peremptory challenge . . . it is hard to see how any group is denied equal protection."

Despite the decisions in *Batson v. Kentucky, Powers v. Alabama, Edmonson v. Leesville Concrete,* and *J.E.B. v. Alabama,* discrimination against potential jurors, and by extension, defendants, did not end. As the Court said in *Edmonson,* the attorneys would have to articulate clearly credible race-neutral (and later, gender-neutral) rationales for their actions. But what is "credible"?

The lower limits of the term were put to the test in the 1995 case of *Purkett v. Elem*. In this case, prosecutors removed jurors of one particular race. The trial judge, according to the *Batson* ruling, asked the prosecutor to provide nonracially motivated reasons for removal of the prospective jurors.

The prosecutor responded:

> I struck [juror] number twenty-two because of his long hair. He had long curly hair. He had the longest hair of anybody on the panel by far. He appeared to not be a good juror for that fact, the fact that he had long hair hanging down shoulder length, curly, unkempt hair. Also, he had a mustache and a goatee type beard. And juror number twenty-four also has a mustache and goatee type beard. Those are the only two people on the jury . . . with facial hair. . . . And I don't like the way they looked, with the way the hair is cut, both of them. And the mustaches and the beards look suspicious to me. (000 US U10277)

The U.S. Supreme Court, in a vote of seven to two, upheld the striking of those prospective jurors, despite the objectively silly reasons offered by the prosecutor, because the trial judge asked for, received, and accepted the nonracially motivated explanation for the exclusions. The Supreme Court left in place the use of peremptory challenges. Had it ruled otherwise, it effectively would have left only those challenges that were based on reasonable concerns about juror fitness, which is the definition of challenges for cause.

One interesting fact about the legal and illegal profiling that takes place by both prosecuting and defense attorneys during voir dire is that the prevalence of it has not drawn that much attention. Scholars who spend time exploring the fairness of the criminal justice system are certainly aware of the jury selection issue, but it has not captured the public's attention, nor that of their elected representatives, as the issue of police profiling has.

Perhaps one explanation is that police profiling involves encounters between the system (in the form of the police) and citizens, guilty and innocent. By contrast, at least in the public's eye, profiling in court only affects the guilty. "Why else would they be in court if they weren't guilty, after all?" The subtlety of this profiling, coupled with its belated position along the criminal justice chain of events, means it will likely remain an issue of interest to academic types and activists, but few others.

At Sentencing

Still another point in the criminal justice process where profiling of a sort can occur is at the sentencing phase. Many scholars have examined sentencing for different types of bias. The overwhelming majority of reports and studies suggest that criminal sentences handed down in the United States are replete with evidence of bias. Scholars point to disparity of sentences between those received by blacks and whites, Hispanics and whites, men and women, minority juveniles and white juveniles, male juveniles and female juveniles, and so on.

The assertion of many of these studies, or at least the implication of them, is that the sentencing process is unfair in light of the statistics that emerge. If the sentencing patterns are disparate, that is, if they do indeed reflect a bias, then is it a result of some sort of judicial profiling, or do other explanations prevail? If it is profiling at the heart of many of these disparities, then it must be judges and juries who are doing so. How can this be when procedures are supposed to be in place to ensure fairness and neutrality? Is it really possible that judges may consider things such as race or sex of the convicted when passing on a sentence?

Some inferences might be drawn from the studies highlighted later in this handbook. But first, to put those studies in context, one must understand how sentencing in the United States works. Keep in mind that differences do exist from state to state. Even so, there are some basic commonalities among most sentencing procedures in criminal courts across the country.

Upon conviction, punishment is doled out to the offender. There are many goals of punishment. One goal is retribution, that is, punishment for punishment's sake because it is deserved. Another goal of punishment is deterrence; it is hoped that being punished will deter that individual offender from offending again (specific deterrence) and will be a lesson to the rest of us not to engage in that same criminal behavior (general deterrence). A third goal of punishment, especially involving incarceration, is that of incapacitation. In other words, through punishment, the public will be protected from the offender for at least the duration of the punishment. A final goal of punishment is rehabilitation. This last goal is not about being punitive to the offender, but rather restorative. Rehabilitation seeks to treat the underlying causes of criminal behavior in the offender and then restore that person to society as a constructive and law-abiding member.

Depending on the circumstances of the case, a judge may seek to achieve any one or more of these goals in handing down a sentence. And it is the judge who is responsible for sentencing. In states where juries make recommendations as to sentence, the judge has the ultimate responsibility of deciding whether to follow the jury's recommendations or to do something different. In fact, in the very recent U.S. Supreme Court case of *Ring v. Arizona* (2002), the Court ruled the death sentences imposed by juries in Arizona and several other states were unconstitutional, as that duty should belong to the judge.

This does not mean that judges have absolute, unrestrained discretion in their sentences. Sentencing for crimes is usually broadly (but sometimes specifically) proscribed in the penal codes of each state. There are three types of sentences in the United States: indeterminate, determinate, and mandatory (Cole and Smith 2001).

Indeterminate sentences are sentences for an indefinite period of time that specifies a minimum and maximum period to be spent incarcerated. This type of sentencing is generally associated with rehabilitation because it allows for an offender to be paroled and released at such time within the minimum and maximum sentencing range that the offender is sufficiently treated and reformed to return to society. Over two-thirds of the states permit judges to set indeterminate sentences for at least some offenses.

Determinate sentences are those that set a specific period of time to be served. Fourteen states require determinate sentences in lieu of indeterminate ones. Even though the judge must prescribe a specific sentence with determinate sentencing, the judge often still has discretion. Determinate sentencing relies on sentencing guidelines passed by the legislature that list presumptive sentences for offenses (that is, the sentences the judge should give to the offender absent some reason not to). An upward or downward departure from that presumptive sentence is permitted by the judge as circumstances warrant. The judge need only be prepared to explain the departure from the guidelines.

Finally, all states use mandatory sentencing for at least some offenses. A mandatory sentence is one that is required by law to be imposed upon conviction of a particular offense. For example, in many states, a first degree murder conviction requires that the offender be sentenced to life without parole. In cases involving mandatory sentences, judges have no discretion at the sentencing phase.

Other than in mandatory sentencing circumstances, the sentences received by offenders who commit the same crime may vary even within the same jurisdiction. How is that so? It is because judges are often permitted to consider aggravating and mitigating factors (Schmalleger 1999). Aggravating factors work against the offender and include such things as

- the defendant induced others to participate in the commission of the offense
- the offense was particularly heinous or cruel
- the defendant was armed with or used a deadly weapon while committing the crime
- the offense was committed to obstruct justice or avoid arrest or escape
- the offense was committed for hire
- the offense was committed against a law enforcement officer performing his or her duties
- the offense was motivated by hatred of a protected group.

In considering aggravating factors, judges may lengthen a sentence or even invoke the death penalty in some states because of them.

Judges may also consider mitigating factors in their sentences. Mitigating factors work in the defendant's favor and include

- defendant has no prior criminal record
- defendant has already made restitution
- defendant is a person of good character and of good reputation
- defendant aided in the apprehension or prosecution of others
- defendant acted under strong provocation

- the offense was committed under duress, coercion, threat, or compulsion at a level that reduces but not completely absolves the defendant's culpability
- the defendant was suffering a mental or physical condition that reduces but not completely absolves the defendant's culpability.

The net effect of aggravating and mitigating factors is that convicted offenders are treated differently by judges who must assign—sometimes subjectively—weight and value to these factors in determining a sentence. Race, gender, sexual orientation, and religious affiliation are neither legitimate aggravating nor mitigating factors in any state's sentencing guidelines. Therefore, one would not expect to see profiling by the judiciary along these lines. Profiling critics note, however, that some legitimate factors may be disproportionately associated with race, gender, and so on and therefore result in de facto profiling. For example, having small children who rely on you may be a mitigating factor; that factor will favor female offenders more often than male offenders. Or committing a crime motivated by hate is an aggravating factor in many jurisdictions and might be more associated with certain racial groups or religious beliefs over others.

In looking at sentencing patterns, some caution must be injected into assumptions based on numbers alone. The numbers may be indicative of judicial profiling, or they may be indicative of other things that happen to also correspond to groups of one kind or another. Profiling in law enforcement and even in jury selection has its defenders. But few would argue that taking into consideration race, gender, sexual orientation, or religion has any place in the activity of an unbiased and neutral judge. As profiling by the judiciary is the least defensible, we should be very aware of possible alternative explanations.

Constitution and Civil Rights

It is important to remember that criminal justice profiling does not occur in a legal vacuum. There are parameters within which profiling may legitimately occur; profiling outside of those parameters can trigger a variety of ethical, moral, statutory, and constitutional violations.

We can be grateful that the United States is a country that does impose limits on how government relates to its citizens, even while pursuing justice. Chief among our protections is the Constitution of the United States. This document contains the Bill of Rights, which is the first ten amendments to the Constitution and was ratified in 1791. The Bill of Rights was added to the original constitutional document to ensure that individuals' liberties were protected in their dealings with the government. Several of the first ten amendments have specific relevance to the criminal justice system and are worth mentioning below:

First Amendment:
Congress shall make no law respecting the establishment of religion, or prohibiting the free exercise thereof; or abridging the freedom of speech, or of the press; or the right of the people peaceably to assemble, and to petition the Government for a redress of grievances.

Fourth Amendment:
The right of the people to be secure in their persons, houses, papers, and effects, against unreasonable searches and seizures, shall not be violated, and no Warrants shall issue, but upon probable cause, supported by Oath or affirmation, and particularly describing the place to be searched, and the persons or things to be seized.

Fifth Amendment:
No person shall be held to answer for a capital, or otherwise infamous crime, unless on a presentment or indictment of a Grand Jury, except in cases arising in the land or naval forces, or in the Militia, when in actual service in time of War or public danger; nor shall any person be subject for the same offense to be twice put in jeopardy of life or limb; nor shall be compelled in any criminal case to be a witness against himself; nor be deprived of life, liberty, or property, without due process of law; nor shall private property be taken for public use, without just compensation.

Sixth Amendment:
In all criminal prosecutions, the accused shall enjoy the right to a speedy and public trial, by an impartial jury of the State and district wherein the crime shall

have been committed, which district shall have been previously ascertained by law, and to be informed of the nature and cause of the accusation; to be confronted with the witnesses against him; to have compulsory process for obtaining witnesses in his favor, and to have the Assistance of Counsel for his defense.

Eighth Amendment:

Excessive bail shall not be required, nor excessive fines imposed, nor cruel and unusual punishments inflicted.

As worthwhile as these protections are, they did not widely protect citizens from state and local government historically. In fact until the last half of the twentieth century, the Bill of Rights served primarily to protect citizens from federal abuses alone. It is true that state constitutions had similar bills of rights contained in them, but their interpretations were subject to the whims of local judicial politics.

On the heels of the Civil War, the Fourteenth Amendment was ratified in 1868. Section One of this amendment sought specifically to protect individuals from state and local governmental abuses of power. The Fourteenth Amendment (Section 1) reads as follows:

All persons born or naturalized in the United States and subject to the jurisdiction thereof, are citizens of the United States and of the State wherein they reside. No State shall make or enforce any law which shall abridge the privileges or immunities of citizens of the United States; nor shall any State deprive any person of life, liberty, or property, without due process of law; nor deny any person within its jurisdiction the equal protection of the laws.

Primarily in the last four decades, through a series of U.S. Supreme Court cases, the Bill of Rights in the Constitution has also come to be applied directly to state and local governments by way of a process called "incorporation." Essentially, the Supreme Court has determined that the protections of the First, Fourth, Fifth, Sixth, and Eighth Amendments apply to state and local governments because of the due process and equal protection provisions of the Fourteenth Amendment. In other words, the Fourth Amendment has been "incorporated" into the Fourteenth, and so has the Fifth Amendment, the Sixth, and so on.

In addition to protections of the Constitution by way of evolving interpretations by the courts, the Congress of the United States and state legislatures throughout the land have passed civil rights legislation affording additional protections to "protected classes." In the Civil Rights Act of 1964, the U.S. Congress outlawed discrimination in housing, employment, and other areas on the basis of race, ethnicity, religion, and gender. Discrimination legislation relating to age and disabilities was passed later. Many state legislatures have also passed civil rights laws that prohibit discrimination on the basis of sexual orientation.

Many would argue that criminal justice profiling violates these various constitutional safeguards. People who are subject to a traffic stop because they fit a profile that includes race as a prominent factor might claim that their Fourth Amendment right to be free from unreasonable searches and seizures as well as their Fourteenth Amendment right to be treated fairly under the law was violated by officers. Or, an offender receiving the death penalty might claim his or her Sixth Amendment and Fourteenth Amendment rights were violated when a prosecutor successfully excluded all but the most hawkish of females from the jury.

To be sure, when the criminal justice system breaches potential constitutional liberties, the bar is high for the government to justify its actions. At a minimum, whenever the criminal laws and the actions the government takes to enforce them touch on constitutionally protected interests, the government must show that the laws and actions are rationally related to furthering a legitimate government interest.

Criminal laws that directly infringe upon fundamental rights found in the Bill of Rights are subject to more stringent evaluation, however. Such laws receive "strict judicial scrutiny," which means that the law is presumed by the court to be unconstitutional absent the government's ability to show a "compelling government interest" (Scheb and Scheb 1999). Likewise, enforcement actions that directly challenge our civil liberties in a way that is not explicitly endorsed by the Constitution are likely to be viewed as unconstitutional as well.

The debatable question about criminal profiling is: does profiling rise to a level of patent unconstitutionality absent the high standard of a "compelling government interest," or is it adequate for government to show that profiling as practiced is rationally related to the legitimate government interest of fighting particular crimes, for example, drug trafficking, hijacking, and so on?

Elsewhere within these pages some attention has been paid to relevant court cases concerning profiling in court—particularly during the voir dire process. As suggested earlier, however, there is currently no more controversial manifestation of profiling than that which is done by police patrol officers against suspected drug traffickers, gang members, and others thought to be possibly up to no-good.

Many people are confused as to what is exactly required for a police officer to pull a motorist over. Some people believe officers can stop people on gut feelings or hunches alone. Sadly, some officers believe that as well. But the standard is higher. Specifically, police officers may pull over motorists if they have reasonable suspicion that a legal violation—traffic or criminal—has taken place. Reasonable suspicion is an accumulation of observations, along with an officer's informed experience, that leads one to reasonably believe a motorist has committed a violation (Klotter 2002). With reasonable suspicion, an officer may stop and temporarily detain a person to investigate further those suspicions.

Investigative stops are rooted in the landmark case of *Terry v. Ohio* (1968). In that case, the U.S. Supreme Court explained the limits of detention for investigative purposes. In that case, a plainclothes Cleveland, Ohio, police officer was walking his beat in downtown Cleveland when he saw three individuals acting suspiciously. In particular, he saw the three men peering into a store window, walking down the street a short distance, and then coming back to peer through the window again. The officer suspected that the suspects might be casing the store in preparation for holding it up.

The officer approached the subjects, identified himself as a police officer, and asked their names. The responses by the suspects were muted, and the officer decided to pat one of the suspects down. In doing so, he felt a pistol in the pocket of the suspect's overcoat. The other two suspects were also patted down for weapons and an additional revolver was found.

The Supreme Court upheld the detention and search for weapons by the officer. It said that police officers may approach and detain people for the purposes of investigating possible criminal activity when the officers can reasonably conclude, in light of their experience, "that criminal activity may be afoot." And in *Delaware v. Prouse* (1979), the threshold of reasonable suspicion has also been extended to the stopping and searching of suspects in motor vehicles.

The outcome of that investigative stop is to either develop the probable cause (if it does not already exist at the time of the stop) necessary to take action—such as write a ticket or make an arrest—or to set the person free.

An example of this would be if an officer hears of a report that a bank robbery just took place involving two men who left the scene in a blue Camaro. Not far from the scene, the officer sees a blue Camaro with two occupants and pulls it over. The officer at this point does not have probable cause to make an arrest. The officer cannot say in court that those particular occupants in the Camaro the officer is trying to catch up to in order to initiate a stop are the bank robbers. But it is certainly reasonable to investigate the possibility.

After the officer stops the vehicle, realizes the two occupants are husband and wife with a previously unseen child in the backseat, and verifies that these people do not fit the description of the robbers and therefore lets them go, the stop in retrospect was no less reasonable—even though probable cause for an arrest did not develop. That's the purpose of an investigative stop.

With exception of truly random checkpoints in certain cases, traffic stops that are based upon anything less than reasonable suspicion are unconstitutional. Obviously, if an officer observes the subject vehicle committing a violation, then reasonable suspicion and even probable cause exist that a violation occurred and a stop is clearly warranted.

Once a vehicle is stopped, there is also some confusion—inside policing and out—of just when an officer may search a vehicle. The Fourth Amendment generally requires that the police have a search warrant if they want to search someone's belongings and possibly seize them for evidence. The U.S. Supreme Court, however, has crafted several exceptions to the search warrant requirement that police officers may use in searching a motorist's vehicle.

1. Consent—Consensual encounters are those interactions between the police and the citizens that are voluntary and require no legal basis for the interaction to occur. Citizens may break off the encounter with the officer at

any time and may choose to forego interaction with the officer altogether. The courts have consistently held that searches of vehicles when the motorist in control of the vehicle gave consent to do so are valid searches, even if the motorist was not expressly told of his or her right to refuse to consent. Rather, the courts have looked at the degree to which a reasonable person would know that they were free to refuse the search. An officer asking permission to search a vehicle suggests to a reasonable person that the answer could be "no."

2. Terry Search—Police officers may search the passenger compartment of a vehicle for weapons if the officer has reasonable suspicion to believe weapons may be present. This is only a search for weapons. Opening a film canister or reading documents strewn about the car floor would not be permitted in a Terry search.

3. Plain View—Police officers who observe evidence or contraband in plain view may seize that evidence. In order for the search to be valid, officers must have the legal justification to be where they were when the evidence was observed, and it must be apparent that the object observed constitutes evidence of a crime. If an officer on a traffic stop sees drug paraphernalia sitting in the cup holder of the vehicle, that evidence can be seized. If it can be shown that the traffic stop was without merit, however, then the officer had no right to be where he or she was when the observation was made, and the evidence would become inadmissible.

4. Carroll Search—The most sweeping warrantless search authority given to police officers is that granted to them by the Supreme Court in *Carroll v. United States* (1925) and reiterated in *Chambers v. Maroney* (1970). The Supreme Court essentially ruled that because vehicles are mobile, obtaining actual search warrants in a timely manner from a judge back at the courthouse is not always realistic or possible. Therefore, officers may search a vehicle for evidence without a warrant, bumper to bumper, if they have sufficient probable cause as to warrant a search warrant should they have sought one. There is still a preference for a warrant if there is time and means to get one, but it is not required when dealing with motor vehicles.

It is important to note that refusal to give permission for a search does not constitute probable cause that there is evidence of a crime in the vehicle despite certainly arousing the suspicions of the police officers. Many officers will utilize drug dogs to stiff around the vehicle, however. If the dog detects a "hit," then most officers will conclude they have probable cause that drugs are in the vehicle and conduct a Carroll search. Further, most courts will uphold that belief by the officers. Still others will develop probable cause after finding evidence during a more limited search—for example, a Terry search for weapons.

Another very important Supreme Court case that relates directly to the authority officers have in the field to engage in profiling is *Whren v. United States* (1996). This case addressed the frequent complaint of black motorists that police officers use incredibly minor offenses as the basis for their stops, knowing full well that they are looking for more serious offenses. Critics further argue that black motorists are being stopped far more often for these minor offenses then white motorists and that therefore illegal race-based profiling is taking place. In other words, minor violations are being used as a pretext for stopping African Americans and other minorities.

For example, it has been alleged that a disproportionate number of minorities are pulled over on the New Jersey Turnpike by troopers for speeding, even though virtually everyone exceeds 55 miles per hour. And, in Maryland, a study showed that blacks constituted 73 percent of the motorists who are stopped and searched along I-95, even though they make up only 14 percent of the motorists (Roberg, Crank, and Kuykendall 2000).

In the *Whren* case, the Court addressed head-on whether pretextual traffic stops—that is, those with an objective basis for the stop but actually rooted in ulterior motives of the officer—are constitutional.

In the *Whren* case, police officers who were patrolling in a "high drug area" of Washington, D.C., observed a vehicle stopped at a stop sign for an unusually long period of time, then suddenly turning without signaling. The vehicle was stopped purportedly by the officers to warn the driver about traffic violations. Upon approaching the vehicle, however, the officers observed in plain view plastic bags of crack cocaine.

The suspects in the case, James Brown and Michael Whren, were convicted of federal drug crimes. They challenged their convictions because the officers did not have reasonable suspicion or probable cause that they were trafficking in drugs, and the traffic violation was just a pretext to stop them. After all, the officers had been in civilian clothes and an unmarked squad car; traffic enforcement was obviously not the officers' number one priority, said the defendants.

Whren and Brown relied in part on the Court's decision in *Delaware v. Prouse* (1979). In that case, a police officer stopped a motorist without observing a traffic or equipment violation. Rather, the officer contended he simply wanted to check the driver for a valid license and proper vehicle registration. The stop resulted in the officer's arresting Prouse for driving after revocation and, incident to that arrest, finding marijuana on his person. The Supreme Court in *Prouse* said "the permissibility of a particular law enforcement practice is judged by balancing its intrusion on the individual's Fourth Amendment interests against its promotion of legitimate governmental interests"(440 US 648). In the *Prouse* case, the government's legitimate interests were deemed to be outweighed by Prouse's Fourth Amendment interests, and therefore the conviction was overturned.

Whren and Brown were hoping for a similar decision on the part of the Supreme Court regarding their case. After all, a pretextual stop based on a petty, generally unenforced traffic law is little more than the hunch the officer had in *Prouse*. Furthermore, the Court in *Florida v. Wells* (1990) had indicated that an inventory search prior to a vehicle's being towed must not be used as a pretext for a search for incriminating evidence. The decision in that case suggested, at least to Whren and Brown, that the court looked disapprovingly at "police attempts to use valid bases of action against citizens as pretexts for pursuing other investigatory agendas" (517 US 806).

The Supreme Court in *Whren*, however, cited other cases where the motives of the officer did not adversely affect the objective basis for action. In the end, the Court ruled in *Whren* that as long as an objective basis for a traffic stop exists, including minor equipment and moving violations, then there is no unreasonable seizure in violation of the Fourth Amendment. The convictions were upheld. The Court did reiterate that stops may not be based on race or some other similarly illegal factor. But if they are, the relief is found in the Fourteenth Amendment, not the Fourth Amendment.

Justice Scalia, writing for the majority, said:

We think these cases [cited in the *Whren* opinion] foreclose any argument that the constitutional reasonableness of traffic stops depends on the actual motivations
of the individual officers involved. We of course agree
with petitioners that the Constitution prohibits selective
enforcement of the law based on considerations such as
race. But the constitutional basis for objecting to intentionally discriminatory application of laws is the Equal
Protection Clause, not the Fourth Amendment. Subjective intentions play no role in ordinary, probable-cause
Fourth Amendment analysis" (517 US 806).

Pros and Cons of Criminal Profiling

Arguments against Profiling

There are many arguments that can be made against criminal justice profiling. One argument against profiling is really a counter-
argument to those who argue for profiling. Many proponents of
profiling suggest that some groups more than others—certainly
men more than women and often minorities more than whites—
commit a disproportionate share of crime. In support of this,
many statistics are presented that show, for example, that blacks
are arrested per capita far more often than whites.

Jim Cleary and others have noted, however, that this reasoning is circular. They claim it is precisely because blacks are targeted disproportionately by law enforcement that they are
arrested disproportionately by law enforcement. In other words,
racial profiling helps create its own justification (Cleary 2000).

Harvard professor Randall Kennedy, on the other hand, conceded that blacks and other minorities are committing greater
numbers of crime and also conceded that most profiling is done
by criminal justice officials who are well intentioned and are not
racists. But he remains firmly against criminal justice profiling on
principle when it is based even partly on race or some other protected classification (Kennedy 2000).

Kennedy argued that profiling results in a downward spiral
of relations between criminal justice officials and members of the
community. Well-meaning and courteous police officers will
eventually pull over individuals who themselves had always

been supportive of law enforcement but have grown tired of being stopped. When they lash out against the officers out of resentment of their plight, the officer will likely defend himself or herself, but the spiral begins. Eventually, after a number of similar encounters, the regard held by officers and citizens for each other will inevitably be low.

Kennedy's ultimate criticism of profiling is not rooted in the practical effects on police-community relations; it is rooted in principle. Regardless of the odds of a black man committing a crime compared to a white woman or some other breakdown, Kennedy posited that people should be judged solely by their individual conduct. Factors such as race or gender should not even partly be used to form opinions or suspicions about other people. The use of profiling, however successful it may be, undercuts this principle and therefore should be discarded, said Kennedy. Success is not an argument. Think how safe and crime free we would be if we dismissed the Fourth Amendment requirement against unreasonable searches and seizures. But we don't, because principle trumps even safety and success.

Still another argument against profiling is the potential harm it causes individual law-abiding citizens who fall subject to it. This harm includes mental anguish and emotional distress from the degradation of a confrontational and accusatory encounter with the police. Consider the following testimony given in March 2000 by an African American to the U.S. Senate's Judiciary Committee, which was investigating the occurrence of racial profiling by law enforcement.

> My name is Master Sergeant Rossano Gerald. I am glad to have an opportunity to talk with you today about my experience in Oklahoma.
>
> The issue of racial profiling is a serious problem in this country today and I am glad to see that the Senate is beginning to take a look at it. I am coming forward to tell my story to try to prevent this from happening again. I don't want anything like this to happen to my son again.
>
> In August of 1998, I was driving in Oklahoma on my way to a family reunion. At that time I was a Sergeant First class in the Army stationed in Fort Richie. My 12-year-old son Gregory was with me. As soon as we crossed the border from Arkansas, I noticed patrol cars

in the area and began driving even more carefully than usual. Within minutes, an officer pulled me over for "following another car too closely." He did not give me a citation.

Soon after, we stopped to buy gas and use the restroom. After our break we continued driving. Having been stopped once already, I was driving particularly carefully. I was in the right hand lane when I saw two patrol cars approach on the ramp. I signaled, then pulled over to let them in. I said to my son, "Watch this, I bet they'll stop me again." Sure enough, I was pulled over again.

An officer walked to the rear of my car and told me to get in the patrol car. I later learned that his name was Trooper Perry. Once he had me in the car and started questioning me, I told him that my son was still in my car. He left and got Gregory and frisked him before putting him in the back of the patrol car.

He told me that I had changed lanes without signaling. I told him that I had signaled, and asked how he would have been able to see from his vantage point on the ramp.

Trooper Perry started writing me a warning ticket and asking me questions. He asked me why I was nervous. I told him that I was not nervous, but upset because I had just been stopped by another trooper. He then asked me more questions about my destination, my point of origin and my military assignment.

Trooper Perry informed me that he had just made a drug bust and asked to search my car, and I said no. I asked him to call my Commanding Officer, Captain Rhodes, because it is standard operating procedure for the army. He refused. He would not let me call Captain Rhodes on my cell phone. I asked him again later to call my Commanding Officer and again he refused. Trooper Perry gave me the warning ticket but told me that I was not free to go.

Trooper Perry continued asking me questions. He badgered me about why I would not let him search my car if I had nothing to hide. I was polite but would not let him search my car. He asked me if I was carrying any weapons or contraband and I informed him that I was not. Trooper Perry then stated that it was legal for him to search my car without my consent.

Trooper Perry called for the K-9 unit from the second patrol car. I said I wanted to watch the search and we got out of the car. The dog walked around the outside of the vehicle. The dog did not "alert." He did not bark, scratch, whimper or sit down, although the trooper kept patting certain areas of the car and would not let the dog walk away. Even though the dog did not alert, the second trooper patted the right wheel well and claimed that the dog had alerted. He said he would conduct a full scale search now. I have been trained in using dogs and thought that the search was highly improper and unusually suggestive.

Trooper Perry ordered Gregory and me to get back into the car. At this point, I became really worried that the Troopers were going to plant illegal contraband in my car. Trooper Perry then got the drill and took over the search. He began drilling under the carpet at the feet of the passenger side. Trooper Perry came back to the car and stated that he had found "something." The two troopers spoke privately. I was then accused of having a secret compartment in my car that had drug residue in it. This compartment was actually a footrest that was a feature of the car.

I was then handcuffed by Trooper Perry who man-handled me, thrust me into his car and then strapped me in. He turned off the on-board camera and took out the tape. The second trooper continued the search of my car. At one point, Trooper Perry and the other officer lifted the hoods of their patrol cars, an action that had no obvious purpose. I was worried that they were trying to obstruct my view so that they could plant contraband in my car.

During the search we overheard Trooper Perry on the radio with another trooper. He told the other trooper that he was turning up nothing. The other trooper told him to keep searching and asked if he needed back up. By this point a third unit had appeared.

This trooper moved Gregory into his car and asked him questions without me being present. The second trooper brought the drug dog to the car that Gregory was in and asked him some of the same questions. The dog kept barking at Gregory, who was afraid it would bite him.

The troopers put our luggage on the ground and had the dogs sniff it. They found airline tickets, one of which was to Chicago. When the trooper asked me about it, I answered that Gregory had flown out of Chicago. Because he had again asked me about drugs, I informed him that my car had passed inspection and received military clearance and that because of my military assignment, I was subject to random urinalysis tests and would never do drugs. Trooper Perry was angry that I would not give him details about my classified assignment. I suggested that he contact my Commanding Officer.

At 3:45 P.M. the Troopers let me go with nothing more than a warning ticket. I was told that I was being let go because I was "behaving myself now." I complained that my car and baggage were a mess and Trooper Perry said, "We ain't good at repacking." Trooper Perry had removed parts of the headliner, floorboards, carpet and other areas. There was over one thousand dollars of damage.

As soon as we were released, I called Captain Rhodes. He advised me to go to Fort Sill where the Director of Public Safety searched my vehicle in case drugs were planted in my car. An Army-certified narcotic working dog did not find any drugs or contraband.

This experience was very traumatic for Gregory. Throughout the interrogation, he was frightened and crying. Even before he was removed from my presence he was nervous, crying and hyperventilating. I had to watch while my son suffered tremendous physical discomfort from the heat. Trooper Perry had turned off the air conditioning when he put us in his car, despite the ninety degree heat.

Before we were finally released, one of the troopers asked who would come get Gregory if they arrested me. This remark made Gregory more nervous and upset. He was crying and wondering what would happen to him and I tried to calm him down. He was scared for the rest of the trip. My son has since become afraid of dogs. He continues to ask his mother why his father was treated this way.

I was very humiliated by this experience. I was embarrassed and ashamed that people driving by would think I had committed a serious crime. It was particularly horrible to be treated like a criminal in front of my impressionable young son.

I never thought I would find myself in the position of suing police officers. I am an authority figure myself. I don't want my son thinking that this kind of behavior by anyone in uniform is acceptable. I hope that by coming forward to tell my story it might prevent other people of color from being treated this way. (United States Senate Judiciary Committee Hearing, Subcommittee on the Constitution, March 30, 2000)

Sergeant Gerald was only one of several who testified or submitted statements for the record concerning their brushes with profiling. The witnesses included not just African Americans, but Hispanics, and included people from all walks of life, including a prominent attorney pulled over on the way home from a family member's funeral. In all cases, the testimony reflected deep resentment at having their privacy invaded and being suspected of wrongdoing without any basis. It is clear that these occurrences create lifelong memories of unpleasant and, from their perspectives, unfair encounters with the criminal justice system.

A final argument raised with frequency today in opposition to criminal justice profiling, particularly by the police, is that it is inconsistent with the new law enforcement paradigm of community policing. Many definitions of community policing exist, but they all tend to have the common theme of partnership between the police and the community. Community policing can be defined as a philosophy of law enforcement, based on the concept that police officers and citizens working together in creative ways can help solve contemporary community problems related to crime, the fear of crime, social and physical disorder, and neighborhood decay (Trajanowicz and Bucqueroux 1990). This definition has serious ramifications for police-community relationships and leaves little room for preemptive, adversarial profiling of community members.

The Police Executive Research Forum is a think tank organization dedicated to improving police practices. It notes that community-oriented policing requires departments to change their thinking by asking questions relating to five dimensions of police work (Police Executive Research Forum 1996):

1. Deployment—how can more officers be moved closer to the citizens?
2. Community revitalization—how can officers help prevent neighborhoods from deteriorating and instead create conditions that result in less fear of crime?
3. Problem solving—how should officers identify and analyze problems and then develop solutions and assess their success?
4. Customer—how can officers be more responsive to citizen needs and open up lines of communication?
5. Legitimacy—how can officers gain credibility with the public in the notion that the police are fair and equitable in the provision of service?

The answers to most of the above questions leave little room for aggressive police tactics and criminal justice profiling in particular. Critics point out that profiling is a tool of the professional policing era. In the community policing era, officers need not and should not go it alone—them against the community. Rather, officers should seek to build relationships in the community that will yield dividends in the future.

Arguments for Profiling

There is frankly no contest to the assertion that some groups of people commit disproportionate shares of crime. African Americans, for example, constitute 13 percent of the nation's population and yet represent 43 percent of persons arrested for serious violent crimes and 32 percent of persons arrested for serious property crimes nationwide (U.S. Department of Justice 2003a). In Virginia, although only 20 percent of the state's population, African Americans represented 51 percent of those committing Part I felonies (most serious offenses) and 40 percent of Part II felonies (remaining felonious crime). Although some critics, such as Jim Cleary, have argued that profiling is self-perpetuating, the fact that there is a disproportionate number of minorities arrested for the most serious offenses mitigates that criticism. The serious felonies are investigated until suspects, whatever their race, materialize. Investigating a homicide or armed robbery is not driven by a bias against one race or another. The crime occurred.

What's more, the statistics are bound by context and do not only affect African Americans. All races are subject to light shed by statistical realities. Most individuals trafficking illegal aliens on the southern border are likely to be of Hispanic origin (Kennedy 2000). Statistically, a stop of a van driven by a Hispanic male will more likely yield smuggled drugs or aliens than would a stop of a van driven by an apparent soccer mom in the same border vicinity.

Besides race, observations about gender jump out in association with criminal activity. Of the nearly six million violent crimes committed in the United States in 1999, 80 percent were committed by men, 19 percent by women, and 1 percent remained unknown (U.S. Department of Justice 2003b). An officer responding to a violent crime, while not ruling out anything, can at least know that odds are the perpetrator is a man. Is that bias or merely a recognition of a statistical reality?

In addition to the statistical argument, supporters of profiling point out that it is common sense. Johnny Hughes of the National Troopers Coalition, a retired major in the Maryland State Police, testified to the U.S. Senate in 2000 that criminal profiling is a good, effective, and commonsensical law enforcement tool. Police trainees are taught to observe the individual characteristics or indicators for drug-courier activity and other crimes in progress. These observations are based on reason, said Major Hughes, not race (or any other class per se). He argued that common sense dictates that preventing and investigating crime in minority areas are necessarily going to involve the interaction of police with predominantly minorities (National Commission on Crime Control and Prevention 1994).

A white male in an urban black neighborhood late at night with license plates that register to the suburbs is quite possibly in the area to purchase drugs. The race of the suspect, in this case Caucasian, cannot help but be noticed. To completely ignore that aspect of an overall profile or observation is to unrealistically hamper law enforcement from thinking.

Finally, some defenders of criminal justice profiling note that public safety and the community are benefactors. It is argued that to avoid using good and proven police techniques in the detection and prevention of crime is to do so to the detriment of the community. Doing so unnecessarily leaves the public vulnerable to criminals who might have otherwise been apprehended. The very public harmed when profiling is disallowed are usually minorities and the poor, as it is their neighborhoods that are often overrun with the criminal element. To leave law-abiding minorities—which are the majority in such neighborhoods—to stew in a crime-ridden environment could itself be considered racist or classist. Minorities have the right to be safe too.

For example, studies show that blacks are far more likely than whites to be victims of serious crime. In 1993, black males between the ages of twelve and twenty-four were murdered at a rate of 115 per 100,000; the murder rate for white males in the same age group was 12 per 100,000. Blacks were four times more likely than whites to be victims of gun violence (DeLisi and Regoli 1999). We know that 80 percent of black victims of violent crime are victimized by blacks (U.S. Department of Justice 2003b). Given that violent crime tends to be intraracial, one can argue that it is minority communities who are served by effective criminal justice profiling.

Remedies

There are two primary remedies that citizens can pursue when they feel they have been illegally profiled or in some other way discriminated against by the criminal justice system. One route is to involve the U.S. Department of Justice (DOJ), Civil Rights Division. The other route is to pursue civil litigation.

The DOJ Civil Rights Division maintains a section devoted to special litigation, which includes the responsibility of suing local and state law enforcement agencies. Under authorities given to DOJ under the Civil Rights of Institutionalized Persons Act (CRIPA), violations of the civil rights of those who are incarcerated can be investigated, civilly litigated, and even prosecuted by the Department of Justice.

Additionally, under authority of the 1968 Omnibus Crime Control and Safe Streets Act, DOJ's Civil Rights Division has the authority to initiate civil litigation to remedy patterns of racial, ethnic, gender, or religious discrimination by law enforcement agencies that receive federal funds. The Violent Crime Control and Law Enforcement Act of 1994 further empowers DOJ to conduct similar investigations and seek similar remedies from agencies administering juvenile justice that demonstrate patterned illegal conduct.

A common tactic for the DOJ in recent years has been to enter into consent decrees with targeted criminal justice agencies. In exchange for the dropping of the federal lawsuit against them, agencies and departments under investigation for discriminatory conduct consent to an agreement whereby a multitude of things will be done by that department, depending on the areas identified by DOJ as needing improvement. Typically, the departments agree to things such as (U.S. Department of Justice 2003b):

- revising policies concerning citizen encounters
- instituting a reformed training program
- changing supervisory practices and protocols
- implementing systems to receive and investigate citizen complaints
- greater emphasis on minority recruiting/promotions

In 1997, the police departments of Pittsburgh, Pennsylvania, and Steubenville, Ohio, entered into consent decrees with the Department of Justice to avoid federally spearheaded lawsuits alleging pervasive racial discrimination in the departments.

In 1999, a consent decree was entered into between DOJ and the New Jersey State Police owing to complaints of racial profiling. The year 2000 saw a similar agreement between DOJ and the Montgomery County, Maryland, Police Department. In 2001, agreements were entered into with the police departments of Los Angeles, Washington, D.C., and Highland Park, Illinois. All of these consent decrees were rooted in complaints of racial discrimination and profiling. Other types of violations by law enforcement officers and departments, such as sexual harassment and coercive sexual conduct, are also being investigated.

In 2002, the DOJ and the Cincinnati, Ohio, police department entered into a consent decree with each other. Cincinnati had been plagued by horrible relations between the police and the black community there. This relationship deteriorated into riots following a shooting by an officer of a wanted, but unarmed, African American. The officer was prosecuted in the death of the suspect but was acquitted. With the growing national attention on Cincinnati, the DOJ took a closer look. According to a DOJ press release, among the terms agreed to by both parties were the following things that the city and the police department (CPD) would do:

- enhance policy requirements and limitations on the use of force by officers, including the use of firearms, beanbag shot guns and 40 millimeter foam rounds, chemical irritant and canines;
- improve supervisory oversight of use of force incidents; supervisors will document and investigate each incident giving rise to a use of force for compliance with CPD policy and to evaluate the tactics used by the officer;
- implement policy revisions and training which will emphasize that de-escalation techniques, such as disengagement, area containment, surveillance, waiting out a subject, summoning reinforcements or calling in specialized units may be an appropriate response to a situation;
- enhance and expand its risk management system that will provide CPD managers with information necessary to better supervise officers and groups of officers;
- analyze trends in uses of force, searches, seizures, and other law enforcement activities that create a risk of officer misconduct;
- create a cadre of officers who are specially trained to intervene in situations involving people with mental illness;
- improve the procedures for investigating allegations of misconduct and uses of force by CPD officers and to complete the investigations in a more thorough, fair, and timely manner;
- publicly report important data regarding CPD use of force incidents and civilian complaints; and
- implement a variety of changes in the procedures used for receiving, investigating, and resolving misconduct complaints. CPD will make complaint forms and informational materials more widely available at a variety of public locations. (U.S. Department of Justice 2003a)

Currently, the DOJ Civil Rights Division is participating in a program entitled the Police Misconduct Initiative. The DOJ is on the record as favoring the tool of consent decrees and expects to enter into many more agreements with state and local criminal justice agencies in the future.

The other common remedy available to citizens when they believe their civil rights have been violated by law enforcement or some other criminal justice entity is to pursue civil litigation themselves.

Although there has long been the right to sue certain criminal justice officials, including police officers, for violating one's civil rights, the practice has become increasingly common in recent years. In the 1960s, there was an average of 6,000 such civil cases each year against law enforcement. By 1976, the number was 13,400. And recent figures have shown more than 30,000 cases each year against the police (Kappeler 2001).

The ability to sue the police and other state-level criminal justice officials is rooted in the Civil Rights Act of 1871, which was codified in Title 42 of the United States Code, Section 1983. To win a "1983" action, the plaintiff (that is, the one bringing the suit) must show that (Kappeler 2001):

- the officer was acting under the color of law
- the violation was a constitutional or federally protected right
- the violation was sufficiently serious enough to reach a "constitutional" level.

The requirement that an officer acted under the color of law simply refers to the idea that the officer used or in some way implicated his or her status as a criminal justice official during the incident that violated the plaintiff's rights. Usually, showing that the officer acted under the color of law is not difficult for profiling cases. The facts that the officer was in uniform, in a squad car, filed official documents on the case, displayed or was obviously armed with a weapon, and was working with the department's authorization are all evidence that the officer acted under the color of law.

The most common violations raised in 1983 actions are alleged violations of the First, Fourth, Fifth, Sixth, Eighth, and Fourteenth Amendments, along with the Civil Rights Act of 1964 and subsequent amendments.

Although a technical violation of one's civil rights may have occurred, the courts have been reluctant to uphold civil rights lawsuits if the offense is not sufficiently serious. Although exactly how serious the violation has to be is an issue that has been back and forth in various district and appellate courts, most would agree, for example, that an officer telling a jabbering suspect in the backseat of the squad car to "shut up" does not constitute a serious violation of the First Amendment free speech right.

Generally, 42 USC 1983 allows private citizens to sue individual officers who violate civil rights. If it can be shown, however, that the department acted with "deliberate indifference" in regulating the conduct of its employees, then the department could be liable as well. To link an employee's misconduct to the department at large, a plaintiff would need to show things such as (Kappeler 2001)

- the frequency of violations
- extent to which the violations were routine for other employees
- extent to which the practice was accepted by supervisors
- number of employees involved in violation in question
- retention of, failure to discipline, and failure to investigate employee
- failure to prevent future violations
- failure to train employees adequately, properly, or at all

Although there have been a growing number of lawsuits against officers for unlawful profiling and other alleged civil rights violations, the cases usually do not succeed for the plaintiffs. Only about 8 percent of civil cases brought against officers and departments are won (Kappeler 2001). Officers do have defenses they can rely on. If they can demonstrate they acted in good faith (that is, they could not have known at the time that their conduct was illegal), then they will prevail. Likewise, if it can be demonstrated that their conduct was "objectively reasonable" at that time—in other words, a reasonable officer in the same situation with the same amount of information would have acted similarly—the officer will win the case.

Some think the laws should be loosened up further to make it easier to win and sustain convictions against criminal justice officials thought to be engaging in discriminatory conduct. Others, however, point to the fact that criminal justice employees are usually just doing the best they can. To extend greater liability to them—people who are earning working-class wages at best and often enjoy no widespread public appreciation—will only make recruitment of decent officers tougher, and that is a problem that itself can cyclically contribute to the very problem of misconduct that so many criminal justice professionals, politicians, and citizens are trying to alleviate.

Profiling after 9/11/01

It is impossible to ignore the effects that the catastrophe that was September 11, 2001, brought to the issue of profiling in criminal justice. Prior to 9/11, it was difficult to find public officials who would defend profiling under any circumstances. As William McDonald noted, profiling had developed a "broad and almost unchallengeable public antipathy" (McDonald 2003, 232). Governors, presidential candidates, and FBI director Robert Mueller, when a candidate for his job, all decried profiling—particularly racial or ethnic profiling—as obscene in relation to the Constitution and generally unfair and immoral.

But on September 11, 2001, nineteen males of Middle Eastern descent, most of whom were from Saudi Arabia, killed approximately 3,000 people in the United States. Had law enforcement and intelligence officials ignored the obvious commonality in race among the assailants, they would have been properly accused of gross incompetence or negligence. There are certain people currently at war with the United States, and their last names are *never* Jorgesen or Smith. But the opposite is true as well. Not *all* men named Mohommad are at war with the United States. Many so named are Americans and love America. So what is law enforcement to do?

In examining current federal policy, one sees a tiered approach to the use of profiles, be they based on race, ethnicity, religion, or gender. In June 2003, the U.S. Justice Department issued new policy guidelines to all of federal law enforcement that banned the use of racial and ethnic profiling. Doing so was consistent with President Bush's proclamation in February 2001 that racial profiling was "wrong and we will end it in America" (U.S. Department of Justice Guidance Regarding Use of Race by

Federal Law Enforcement Agencies, 2003, 1). At that time, President Bush directed the Justice Department to look at the use of race and ethnicity by criminal justice agencies and to craft policies to curtail their use.

The policy does indeed ban the use of racial profiling, absent specific suspect information that would implicate race, in traditional law enforcement activities. Such activities include general patrol functions for uniformed police services, drug investigations, and other general crimes. The policy is more permissive, however, where national security and border integrity are concerned.

Regarding traditional law enforcement activities, the policy reads:

> In making routine or spontaneous decisions, such as ordinary traffic stops, Federal law enforcement officers may not use race or ethnicity to any degree, except that officers may rely on race and ethnicity in specific suspect description. This prohibition applies even where the use of race or ethnicity might otherwise be lawful.
>
> In conducting activities in connection with a specific investigation, Federal law enforcement officers may consider race and ethnicity only to the extent that there is trustworthy information, relevant to the locality or time frame, that links persons of a particular race or ethnicity to an identified criminal incident, scheme, or organization. This standard applies even where the use of race or ethnicity might otherwise be lawful. (U.S. Department of Justice 2003b, 2–4)

The standard articulated above for traditional law enforcement activities is more stringent than the Constitution requires. Indeed, the Supreme Court has made it clear that the Constitution does not concern itself with the motives of officers where an objective offense is observed; nor does the Constitution prohibit profiling for particular offenses, such as drug trafficking, where race of the suspect is one of many factors in the profile. But now, using race as a factor or acting on an observation of an actual offense when the officer is personally more inclined to do so when committed by members of a particular race is prohibited practice for federal law enforcement.

The policy might have stopped there but for 9–11. The policy goes on to state that the above standards do not affect current Federal policy with respect to law enforcement activities and other efforts to defend and safeguard against threats to national security or the integrity of the Nation's borders. . . . In investigating or preventing threats to national security or other catastrophic events (including the performance of duties related to air transportation security), or in enforcing laws protecting the integrity of the Nation's borders, Federal law enforcement officers may not consider race or ethnicity except to the extent permitted by the Constitution and the laws of the United States. (U.S. Department of Justice 2003b, 8)

It is worth noting that even where the potential harm is catastrophic, the policy pays homage to the Constitution. Even so, race and ethnicity (and by extension, religion and gender) may indeed be used as factors in developing profiles of those who might do the United States significant harm.

In short, federal policy bans profiling—usually. This policy is a stark example of the dilemma inherent to profiling generally. If we concede that profiling does prevent some crime (and many say it does not), we must also acknowledge that it does so at a cost—particularly for those innocents who are subject to it. In the weeks following 9–11, many Middle Eastern men were asked to disembark from commercial airliners because passengers and pilots refused to fly with them aboard. These individuals were demeaned, inconvenienced, and embarrassed. If it turns out that just one of the dozens this happened to actually intended to do a flight harm—perhaps by blowing it up with a shoe bomb—would we say it was all worth it? And if it *is* worth it in airline security, is it not likewise worth it to get a murderous, drug-dealing gang member off the streets of Chicago?

One thing is absolute after 9–11: far fewer people are absolutely against criminal profiling than were before.

References

Banaji, M., and R. Bhaskar. 2000. "Implicit Stereotypes and Memory: The Bounded Rationality of Social Beliefs." In *Memory, Brain and Belief*, ed. D. L. Schacter and E. Scarry. Thousand Oaks, CA: Sage, 139–175.

Brooks, L. W. 2001. "Police Discretionary Behavior: A Study of Style." In *Critical Issues in Policing*, 4th ed., ed. Roger G. Dunham and Geoffrey P. Alpert. Prospect Heights, IL: Waveland, 117–131.

Champion, D. J., and G. E. Rush. 1997. *Policing in the Community*. Upper Saddle River, NJ: Prentice Hall.

Cleary, J. 2000. *Racial Profiling Studies in Law Enforcement: Issues and Methodology*. St. Paul, MN: State of Minnesota, House of Representatives Research Department.

Cole, D. 1999. *No Equal Justice*. New York: New Press.

Cole, G. F., and C. E. Smith. 2001. *The American System of Criminal Justice*. 9th ed. Stamford, CT: Wadsworth.

DeLisi, M., and B. Regoli. 1999. "Race, Conventional Crime, and Criminal Justice: The Declining Importance of Skin Color." *Journal of Criminal Justice* 27 (November):549–557.

Evans, M., ed. 1978. *Discretion and Control*. Beverly Hills, CA: Sage.

Jacoby, J. 1979. "The Charging Policies of Prosecutors." In *The Prosecutor*, ed. W. F. McDonald. Beverly Hills, CA: Sage, 75–97.

Kappeler, V. 2001. *Critical Issues in Police Civil Liability*, 3rd ed. Prospect Heights, IL: Waveland.

Kennedy, R. 2000. "Suspect Policy." In *Criminal Justice*, ed. Joseph Victor. Guliford, CT: Dushkin/McGraw-Hill, 102–106.

Klotter, J. C. 2002. *Legal Guide For Police*. 6th ed. Cincinnati, OH: Anderson.

Lee, Y. T., L. Albright, and T. Malloy. 2001. "Social Perception and Stereotyping: An Interpersonal and Intercultural Approach." *International Journal of Group Tension* 30, no. 2., 183–209.

Lee, Y. T., L. Jussim, and C. McCauley. 1995. *Stereotype Accuracy: Toward Appreciating Group Differences*. Washington, DC: American Psychological Association.

McCoy, C. 1998. "Prosecution." In *The Handbook of Crime and Punishment*, ed. M. Tonry. New York: Oxford University Press, 457–473.

McDonald, W.F. 2003. "The Emerging Paradigm for Policing Multiethnic Societies: Glimpses from the American Experience." *Police and Society*, No. 7:232–249.

National Commission on Crime Control and Prevention. 1994. *Final Report*. Washington, DC.

Police Executive Research Forum. 1996. *Themes and Variations in Community Policing*. Washington, DC.

Roberg, R., J. Crank, and J. Kuykendall. 2000. *Police and Society.* Los Angeles: Roxbury.

Robinson, M. B. 2002. *Justice Blind?* Upper Saddle River, NJ: Prentice Hall.

Scheb, J. M., and J. M. Scheb II. 1999. *Criminal Law and Procedure.* 3rd ed. Belmont, CA: Wadsworth.

Schmalleger, F. 1999. *Criminal Justice.* 3rd ed. Upper Saddle River, NJ: Prentice Hall.

Trajanowicz, R., and B. Bucqueroux. 1990. *Community Policing: A Contemporary Perspective.* Cincinnati, OH: Anderson.

U.S. Department of Justice, Bureau of Justice Statistics section. *http://www.ojp.usdoj.gov/bjs,* accessed in 2003.

U.S. Department of Justice. 2003a., Civil Rights Division section. *http://www.usdoj.gov/crt,* accessed in 2003.

U.S. Department of Justice. 2003b. *Guidance Regarding the Use of Race by Federal Law Enforcement Agencies.* Washington, DC.

Walker, S. 1999. *The Police in America.* Boston: McGraw-Hill.

3

Global Perspectives on Profiling

The balancing act concerning profiling—weighing its useful-
ness in criminal justice against its unfairness toward individuals—is not one unique to the United States. Nor is it even
unique to Western democracies. Profiling in one fashion or
another can be observed in criminal justice systems all around
the world.

That having been said, the issue of profiling has not been
confronted in other countries exactly the same way it has been in
the United States. It couldn't be. The U.S. Constitution is unique,
and America's constitutional and legal development over the
decades is even more so. As U.S. courts and legislatures came to
develop theories, philosophies, and practices relating to profiling
and relating to the larger issue of equal justice for all under the
law, they did so within the context of American institutions, cultural development, demographic conditions, and the like.

Likewise, as other countries have grappled with fairness
issues balanced against effective law enforcement practices, they
have done so without the benefit of the U.S. Constitution.
Instead, they did so under their own constitution or under no
constitution at all. Consequently, and not surprisingly, countries
around the world treat the issue of profiling with varying
degrees of acceptance or aversion, as the case may be.

Four Legal Traditions around the Globe

To better understand how the issue of profiling manifests itself
around the world apart from the United States, one must have an

understanding of the main legal traditions that give birth to the world's criminal justice systems. Comparative criminal justice scholars, such as Philip Reichel, commonly identify four main legal traditions: civil, common, socialist, and Islamic (Reichel 2002).

Civil Law Tradition

The tradition most identified with Western nations is the civil tradition. This tradition can be traced back to the Roman Empire. It is the tradition that emphasizes the need for laws and regulations to be written down in a systematic manner by some political authority (Mukherjee and Reichel 1999). Typically, the political authority is a legislative body. In such systems, the legislature is generally considered the source of all law. The importance of writing down the law is found in the need for all citizens to know what the law is, to know what their rights are, and to know what is expected of them.

There have been variations of the civil tradition over time. The Romans as far back as 450 B.C. codified a collection of laws into what was known as the Twelve Tables. These laws contained specific rights for all Roman citizens (Reichel 2002).

More recently, in the early nineteenth century, France codified its laws into a single set of laws known as the Napoleonic Code. This code was composed of many previously existing French laws as well as some new ones. Despite part of the code's consisting of older French laws, the validity of all aspects of the code was based in the fact that it had been enacted once again in this single code. What had been before was not relevant. What "is" was all that mattered.

The *Code Napoléon* was extremely influential in the development of legal systems throughout Europe and Latin America. The code, and its successors in other countries influenced by it, made it possible for average citizens to know where they stood under the law. It also provided for a separation between those who made law and those who would apply and interpret it. The role of courts under the civil tradition, particularly as influenced by the Napoleonic Code, is inherently restrained. Judicial activism, that is, making laws from the bench, has no place in the true civil law tradition.

Common Law Tradition

The common law tradition differs from the civil law tradition in that the customs of the people are the sources of law, not what some legislature has written down. Although the customs are eventually put into written form, this fact does not detract from the source of the law: the people's customary behavior and attitudes of what is right and wrong.

For this reason, the common law tradition is associated with jury-based judgments. It is not judges who decide if one behaved appropriately or reasonably given a set of circumstances. Instead, juries of peers are placed in the position to judge the actions of others.

Further, under common law, judges were expected to follow the people's leading by relying on precedent. This notion of relying on the interpretation and application of common law in the past is called stare decisis. For judges to give great deference to precedence is a hallmark of the common law tradition.

Because the written codes, to the extent the laws are written down, are mere reflections of the higher common law, there is great room for judges to interpret and apply the law according to their read of precedence and according to their understanding of common law, that is, the customs and sensibilities of the people with regard to what is reasonable.

The written law is not the final authority under the common law tradition. Rather, the law only receives ultimate legitimacy after judicial review (Mukherjee and Reichel 1999). And even then, the law's legitimacy must receive periodic approval. This is why the First Amendment of the Constitution, for example, seems to permit a government-owned nativity scene on display at Christmas one year and then prohibits it the next, despite the unchanged wording of the amendment. The understanding of the wording, particularly within the context of an increasingly secular culture, has been changed by the courts.

America's legal system and that of its parent nation England hail from the common law tradition. It is no wonder, then, that so much change socially in the United States has taken place as a result of court decisions. Likewise, the practices of the U.S. criminal justice system have been profoundly impacted by the judicial review process.

Socialist Law Tradition

The socialist law tradition is the newest of the major legal traditions recognized by scholars. The roots of this tradition can be traced to the legal system of the Soviet Union; virtually all socialist societies in existence today borrowed significant elements from the Soviet legal model (Reichel 2002).

At the heart of socialism is the philosophical position that the law is merely a tool to be utilized by man. Socialists believe that within nonsocialist countries, the law is used by those in power—particularly the wealthy—to keep power and hold the working class down. Socialists say by contrast that socialist systems use the law for the benefit of the common man. To this end, the law is not seen as a higher value that checks the behavior of all people, including rulers. Instead, it is a tool to accomplish a particular end. The law's validity is not verified by the courts; the law is by definition valid because the people, through the legislature (or through a dictator for that matter), have put the law in place in support of some policy; the law is subordinate to policy (Mukherjee and Reichel 1999).

Islamic Law Tradition

There are approximately a billion Muslims in the world. Millions of Muslims live in countries where Islam is not the predominant religion, such as the United States. Millions more live in countries where Islam is predominant, but the government is secular. A good example of this is Turkey. And still millions more live in countries that rely on the tenets of Islam in all facets of life, including public law. In such countries—Iran is a good example—the legal system's authority is rooted in divine authority—namely, Allah's.

The word in Arabic for Islamic Law is *Shari'a*. Shari'a is not in place to only govern religious facets of life. For nations who follow Islamic law, Shari'a is what governs all facets of life. There is no compartmentalization allowed. A believer either follows Shari'a entirely, or not. Likewise, a nation is either truly Islamic by following Shari'a, or it is not. For many Muslims, a nation that is secular in its public law system and fails to adhere to Shari'a is an ungodly and damned nation at best.

As Philip Reichel noted (1999), Shari'a law is primarily articulated in the Quran and the Sunna. The Quran is the holy book of Islam. It is the Muslim's Bible. According to Islamic tradition, the Quran was handed down to the prophet Muhammad by the angel Gabriel. The Sunna is a supplement to the Quran and is considered a written record of the statements and deeds of the prophet Muhammad.

Although the Quran and the Sunna do contain rules governing people's relations and interactions with one another, they do not collectively make up a comprehensive criminal code. Consequently, they are augmented by the reasoning and rulings of religious scholars and leaders. These augmentations fill in the details that are sometimes lacking from the broader proclamations of the Quran and the Sunna.

Legal Processes

When considering the criminal justice systems around the world, in addition to the legal traditions that exist, one must also consider the legal processes that generally exist. In examining legal processes, one does not speak so much of the authority of the law, which goes to the legal tradition prevalent in a country. Rather, one speaks of the relationship of the participants in the justice system to the system and to each other, that is, the accused, the victims, the state, and so on.

Scholars regularly identify three basic types of processes contained in the world's legal systems. These are the inquisitorial process, the adversarial process, and the informal process. These categories are identified for conceptualization purposes. In fact, justice systems around the world commonly contain mixtures of each, much like the fact that legal traditions are blended in many countries. But the categories of legal process serve to develop an appreciation for the fact that similar offenders, for example, may be handled differently from one nation to another—sometimes even when legal traditions are shared.

The inquisitorial process is often associated with the crime control model of criminal justice, which appeared earlier in this book. The crime control model emphasizes the need to process offenders efficiently through the system. The more quickly bad people are off the streets, the more quickly crime is thereby controlled, and we are presumably safer for it.

The inquisitorial process—as the word suggests—is focused on the offender. What did the offender do? Where and when did he or she do it? The goal of the process is to get to the truth by inquiry. In its purest form, such a process is not totally concerned with fairness because sometimes leveling the playing field defeats finding truth and securing justice.

The adversarial process, on the other hand, is concerned about fairness. This process is generally associated with the due process model of criminal justice. The due process model, also addressed earlier in the book, emphasizes the need of protecting the accused, lest people be wrongly convicted. In this model, it is better that society allow a guilty person to go free rather than risk a miscarriage of justice by punishing an innocent.

For adherents of the due process model, freedom is paramount, and the reasons for taking freedom away must be overwhelmingly compelling. The reasons must be so compelling, in fact, that those reasons are apparent even when an unmitigated advocate of the accused presents evidence to the contrary.

This is the sum and substance of the adversarial process. Adversarial processes are intentionally built into many of the world's justice systems, including that of the United States, precisely to give every bit of benefit of the doubt to the accused but not yet convicted. Through the adversarial process, the state must work hard to convince judges and juries that the criminal justice system has treated an accused person fairly and that despite that fair treatment—that benefit of the doubt—it still remains clear that a crime was committed and the accused committed it.

Should the state fail to make a case in the face of an adversary vigorously defending the accused, then the accused must be set free without regard for whether the accused actually did it. The question "Did he do it?" sums up the inquisitorial process. The question "Can procedural hurdles be overcome to prove it?" sums up the adversarial process.

A third category of processes can be labeled the informal process. Reichel (1999) noted that the Shari'a provides for the use of informal processes to deal with criminal offenders. The Islamic legal tradition in fact encourages informal approaches for dealing with individual misconduct. In many cases, if a property crime occurs, and even with some types of violent crime, offenders are given the opportunity to reconcile with their victims through compensation. If compensation is satisfactory to the victim, then their desire to pursue retribution under the Shari'a may be deterred. In such cases, police records may not even be created, and criminal charges may never actually be formalized.

This is not unlike some of the restorative justice efforts being attempted in various U.S. jurisdictions. The difference is that even restorative justice programs in the United States involve formal processes with formal consequences.

Profiling around the World

Just as in the United States, criminal justice profiling in other countries is, by definition, group conscious. Therefore, it makes sense that profiling is a more pressing issue in countries where, as in the United States, different groups reside.

In the United States, racial minorities are frequently the subjects of criminal justice profiling. This book has already considered some of the reasons for this, ranging from the notion that criminal justice officials are racist to the proposition that minorities tend to commit more crimes and therefore more readily draw the attention of the justice system.

These very same issues are debated hotly in other countries where racial and ethnic minorities are present. To survey profiling around the globe, countries will be examined in the following sections. What is especially interesting is the fact that so many issues that are integral to a discussion of American criminal justice profiling are likewise implicated when examining justice systems abroad. One gets the sense that politics is politics, people are people, and criminal justice practices are criminal justice practices, wherever one finds oneself in the world.

In 1995, the United Nations released the results of a study concerning the incarceration rates of ethnic minorities around the world and the crimes for which they were incarcerated. In the Netherlands, for example, minorities made up 9 percent of the total population and yet accounted for 40 percent of the prison population. What's more, half of these were incarcerated for property and drug offenses that, for most others, typically result in diversionary sanctions short of imprisonment. The pattern seen in the Netherlands plays out in virtually every other country profiled by the study.

The United Nations findings suggest that the problems and issues facing the criminal justice system in the United States concerning treatment of minorities is not America's problem alone. These issues are recurrent around the globe. In the remainder of this chapter, we briefly examine six countries for similarities and differences where treatment of ethnic and religious minorities by the criminal justice system is concerned. As we will see, there are far more similarities than differences. Many of the criminal justice themes and controversies are the same as are present in the United States.

Australia

In discussing criminal justice in Australia, one cannot ignore the fact that the nation itself started off as a penal colony. Its very existence, historically, is anchored in criminal justice. Originally, England utilized the colony of Australia as a place to which to banish criminals. As far back as 1598, the British Parliament authorized the transportation of criminals to far-off places so as to rid the British Isles of their presence (Reichel 1999).

The American colonies were among those that regularly received British convicts. With the Revolutionary War and the ousting of Britain from America, the British needed a new place to which to transport its convicts and found such a place in Australia. From the late eighteenth century to the middle of the nineteenth century, 160,000 prisoners arrived in Australia. Beyond mere banishment, most prisoners also had an obligation to work off their sentences. By 1868, the practice of prisoner transportation to Australia was over (Hughes 1987).

Despite its rather unique beginnings, Australia is a country with many similarities to the United States. It is a nation whose origins are found in Great Britain. It is a nation whose frontier has been historically to the West. The country is known for its rugged individualism. And, like the United States, it was inhabited by indigenous people before Europeans ever arrived.

Despite being a relatively small country in population, the diversity of Australia is remarkable. Australia has a population of nearly twenty million people. Approximately four million of these people were born abroad in more than 200 other countries. Ninety-two religious denominations are represented in the country along with 170 languages. Two and a half million Australians speak something other than English in the privacy and routine of their homes (Leong 2001).

Much of this diversity comes from immigration. The nation has been a popular destination for immigrants from all over the world, including English-speaking Great Britain, Canada, and the United States. A little more than a third of a million of Australians are indigenous to the nation-continent, however. Their ancestry predates all others; these are the Aborigines. Aborigines total approximately 1.7 percent of the total Australian population but 19 percent of the Australian prison population (Broadhurst 1996).

Today, Australia is a federalist nation; consequently, there are semi-independent criminal justice systems in all six Australian states and two territories. And of course, there is a national justice system as well. A common criticism of Australian criminal justice is that there is a huge discrepancy in justice practices and services from one state or territory to another.

Some of this is unavoidable and explained by demographics. The state of Western Australia and the Northern Territory, for example, are both incredibly sparse. It is impossible, say justice officials, to provide the same level of professionalism and service in the Outback as in Sydney or Melbourne. The critics respond, however, that many of Australia's problems where criminal justice is concerned—especially unfair profiling—actually take place in the more populated states and urban centers where one would otherwise expect more professional service.

In Australia, the relationship between the criminal justice system and minorities invariably is reduced to consideration of the relationship between the police and Aborigines.

Proponents of the notion that Aborigines are treated unfairly point to the incarceration rates as proof positive. As Camp and Camp (1997) noted, African Americans constitute 13 percent of the U.S. population and 47 percent of the prison population. As disparate as this figure is, Aborigines are much worse off by the numbers. With only 1.7 percent of Australia's total population, and donating enough of its members to make up 19 percent of the Australian prison population, Aborigines can rightly be considered the most incarcerated people in the world (Reichel 1999).

In Australia, policing is largely the responsibility of the states. The authority that law enforcement has is generally the same throughout the country, however. For example, the opportunities police have to make an arrest typically fall under the following circumstances (James 1994, 31):

- when an offender is caught in the act of committing an offense
- when an offender is caught after having committed an offense

- when a person is found on the premises that were searched under a search warrant and the person is linked to the evidence seized
- when there is a belief that a warrant exists for the person's arrest
- when a person who loiters at night is suspected with reasonable cause of committing an offense

It is the last provision that gives police ample opportunity to focus on particular groups known to the police for criminal conduct. When an officer finds a young, male Aborigine or other minority loitering about outside a convenience store or a tavern, it often doesn't take very much to develop reasonable cause that the loiterer has been up to some kind of no-good.

Germany

The country of Germany has over eighty million inhabitants. The governmental system in Germany is federal. In modern Germany, there are sixteen states with their own semiautonomous governments—similar to the federal system in the United States. Although there does exist a powerful German constitution that gives considerable authority to parliament, the implementation of Germany's laws and the function of law enforcement are conducted for the most part at the state level (Albrecht and Teske 2000). This means that decisions about the enforcement and prosecution of various crimes are made by locally accountable officials rather than nationally accountable ones, thus allowing for different standards from one part of the country to another.

The decentralization of criminal justice in Germany is but one mitigating factor in how people are treated by the justice system. Events of post–Cold War history have also had an impact. Two such events are the unification of Germany and the embrace by Germans of the European Union.

Throughout the Cold War, Germany actually existed as two countries—the Federal Republic of Germany (commonly known as West Germany) and the German Democratic Republic (commonly known as East Germany). But with the collapse of the Soviet Union and the demise of compulsory communism in Eastern Europe, Germany was reunited on October 3, 1990, under one government and one constitution.

Immediately, the criminal justice resources of a unified Germany were strained. East Germany was incredibly poor compared to the west. Workers in the east were largely unemployed. Many of the skilled workers were educated or trained at substandard levels and were not easily absorbed into the west's modern and free-market economy.

East Germany donated poverty and broken infrastructure to the new, unified Germany, whereas West Germany donated freedom and due process. No longer were German citizens, even in the east, to be rounded up on mere suspicion of criminal violations. No longer would fear of the famed East German secret police, known as the Stasi, keep economically depressed peoples in check. In a unified Germany, socioeconomic disadvantage for Germans and nonethnic Germans alike could be outwardly expressed without fear of brutal reprisals. This created a serious challenge for the German criminal justice system.

Germany's membership in the European Union (EU) also poses challenges for Germany's criminal justice efforts. In 1992, the Maastricht Treaty forged a formalized unified Europe. As a part of the treaty, coordination among member nations was required in areas of border controls, immigration, and criminal justice. Despite being a federalist society with considerable state-level authority, Germany as a nation became bound by certain rules and conventions as a part of a united Europe, including practices governing the fair and equitable dispensing of justice (Schulte 2001).

The free-flowing travel of people and goods into Germany as a result of its membership in the EU has given birth to new forms of criminal activity. Organized crime involving many different ethnic groups has skyrocketed. Extortion rackets have emerged. Instances of trafficking in stolen goods, drugs, and even human beings have become common types of criminal cases for law enforcement. Prostitution, money laundering, and illegal immigration are all up (Schulte 2001).

In Germany, more than eight million people—or approximately 10 percent of the population—are foreign born. Many of these immigrants come from developing, non-Western areas of the world. This is a change from only 1 percent foreign born in the 1950s (Albrecht 1997). For example, two million ethnic Turks live in Germany today. Among them are a couple hundred thousand ethnic Kurds. Long-standing disputes between Turks and

Kurds that have nothing to do with Germany have been imported into the country, along with the violence that has historically characterized those disputes.

In Germany today, there are approximately 7,000 activists of the Kurdish Workers Party, a Marxist terror organization that targets Turks anywhere in the world. German criminal justice officials have been thrust into this conflict by virtue of Germany's changing demographics. When responding to these new threats, German authorities have not always been well received by the ethnic minorities they try to police.

As Albrecht noted, there have been some trends in the criminal justice system that would suggest Germany has a problem with how it deals with minorities. Statistics relating to the German prison population showed that ethnic Germans were being imprisoned at lesser rates than they had been in the past. Ethnic minorities—and particularly foreign-born nationals—were being put in prison at far greater rates, however, than in the past. In fact, foreigners in the 1990s accounted for more than three times the number of arrests in Germany that one would expect given their representation in the population (Albrecht 1997).

As in the United States, the 1980s and 1990s saw an increase in the use of incarceration for violent offenders. This seemed to correspond to an increase in violent crime. Again, changing demographics and absorption of increasing numbers of poorer people tend to be associated with increases in crime rates generally in any country. Germany was no exception.

This has resulted in a belief—sometimes but not always spoken—among many Germans and certainly among German criminal justice officials that the growing crime problem is due to "outsiders" (Albrecht and Teske 2000).

Many criminologists and policymakers in Germany do attribute certain kinds of crime directly to the nation's growing foreign-born population. Those offenses are not the serious and violent ones that Germans tend to be most anxious about, however. Rather, studies have shown that the influx of migrant workers, asylum seekers, and other immigrants is most associated with petty offenses, such as shoplifting. Between 1989 and 1990, for example, reports of shoplifting in Berlin went from 36,000 cases to 60,000 cases; conventional wisdom in Germany attributed this to the opening of borders (Albrecht and Teske 2000). In any case, it gives ammunition to those in the criminal justice system who prefer to "keep an eye" on foreigners because of the odds.

France

Like Germany, France is a charter member of the European Union. Also like Germany, France has faced dramatic increases in immigration in the past several years from economically depressed areas in Eastern Europe and the Middle East. In fact, France played a major role, along with England and Russia, in colonizing and influencing the Middle East—particularly after World War I. North African countries such as Algiers and Morocco were dominated by the French for decades; the historical connection between North African Arabs and France has made the country a particularly hospitable place to migrate to—at least procedurally.

Despite the common roles as leaders in the EU and despite many of the same demographic phenomena taking place, France and Germany are decidedly different in many key areas when it comes to criminal justice. Chief among the differences is the centrality of police services in France, compared to the more decentralized federal system in Germany.

In fact, France offers perhaps the best example of centralized policing in Western Europe. As such, many critics have noted that the interests of the state, that is, France, too often trump the interests of the individual (Loveday 1999). Some have gone so far as to say that France's system of policing produces as close to a totalitarian form of government as any Western country can (Loveday 1999).

Although there is no federalist system of checks and balances on law enforcement in France, there are checks and balances nonetheless through the existence of two somewhat competing and generally noncooperating national police forces. The first is aptly known as the National Police and is housed in the Interior Ministry. It is more often associated with traditional policing activities such as uniformed patrol and emergency response—particularly in urban areas.

The more prestigious Gendarmerie is also a national law enforcement agency with both uniformed and plainclothes officers. Its function is to perform police duties in rural France and in communities of 10,000 or less. Given the relatively low number of urban areas in France, 95 percent of French territory and approximately 50 percent of the French population fall under the Gendarmerie's responsibility (Reichel 2002). In addition to general law enforcement duties, the Gendarmerie is also responsible for dignitary protection—a duty it wrestled away from the National Police in 1987. This transfer of responsibility is one of many high-profile developments that have typified these two agencies, both of which seem to take great pride in upstaging the other and even, when possible, arresting scandalized officers from the other (Loveday 1999).

It is also worth mentioning that relatively recent French legislation has made it possible for local municipalities to create their own police forces. The authority of the national forces is not diminished, but nevertheless many small governments have sought to have a greater connection to the law enforcement and crime prevention activities in their communities. This has been accomplished in many cases through the creation of municipal police departments. And, in the end, such autonomous municipal departments are ultimately linked in their training, appearance, and practices to the National Police force. Citizens have a hard time distinguishing the two. Consequently, most communities have not bothered to burden themselves with their own locally controlled department (Reichel 2002).

Although other countries explore the ages-old Robert Peel model of bringing the police closer to the public and in partnership with the public as community policing doctrine advocates, the French model of policing does not lend itself to such reforms and innovations (Brogden 1999). By definition, the role of the French police forces emphasizes public order above all else, including personal freedom. Therefore, the police in France tend to have a fairly free hand to pursue justice and order as they see fit, sometime even at the expense of whole groups of people.

Charting the experiences of minorities in France with the police and the larger criminal justice system is difficult, despite the centrality of the system. This is because France does not recognize the existence of minority groups per se. The nation keeps no official tabulations on minorities who are citizens of France. Rather, the government simply notes who is a citizen and who is not. Officially, France does not recognize that French citizens who are first- or second- or even fifth-generation immigrants or descendants of immigrants may not be fully assimilated into French society and therefore may be treated differently (Jackson 1997).

Studies have shown that the largest groups of foreign workers living in France who are not actual citizens come from the countries of Algeria, Morocco, Portugal, Spain, Tunisia, Turkey, and Italy. A survey of urban mayors in France showed that children from these groups—particularly from the North African countries—have trouble succeeding in school, frequently have run-ins with the law, and generally exhibit a great deal of hostility toward their adopted host nation and its people (Jackson 1997).

Immigrants from North African countries such as Algeria, Morocco, and Tunisia make up the largest share of noncitizen, migrant groups in France. Their estimated share of the total French population is 3 to 5 percent. In some municipalities, however, they make up as much as 47 percent of the total population. They are overwhelmingly Muslim (in an overwhelmingly Catholic country). They frequently have dark complexions and therefore are visibly recognizable. They are often employed as low-skilled migrant workers, if employed at all. They tend to be poor. All these factors create ripe conditions for discrimination and, for better or worse depending on one's perspective, profiling by criminal justice officials concerned first and foremost with public order.

In France, the national crime rate in 1990 was about 62 crimes per 1,000 people. In regions of France with large representations of immigrant groups (such as along the Mediterranean Sea), the crime rate was 124 per 1,000 people (Jackson 1997). Similar trends are observed in sections of urban areas dominated by immigrants. It appears that higher crime rates do correlate with France's immigrant population.

An examination of the French criminal justice system's response to immigrants living in France suggests that considerable discrimination takes place. For example, one study showed that if individuals eventually imprisoned for their offenses were French nationals, they were held in pretrial detention at a rate of 75 percent. Immigrants meeting the same criteria were held in pretrial detention at a rate of 90 percent. Most of these detentions were actually effected by the decision of magistrates as opposed to law enforcement officers (Robert 1995).

The use of detention without the determination of guilt for immigrants is seen as a necessary evil despite concerns about individual rights because such practices are seen by French society as indispensable for maintaining public order. Also suspicious to critics of the French justice system is the fact that so many foreigners, once convicted, are sentenced to prison at greater rates than others. Even as far back as 1990, foreigners constituted 30 percent of the total prison population. The percentage is higher today (Jackson 1997).

With regard to law enforcement, there is little doubt that the social and economic marginalization of foreigners—particularly Arab Muslims—has fostered hostility between Arab groups and the police. Police stand expectant of rioting and lawlessness. Arab immigrants find solace and reinforcement in themselves as a group set opposed to law enforcement. According to French social scientist Michel Wievorka (1992), the French police admittedly develop some racist language and behaviors toward specific groups while adhering to the general principle of equal application of the law for all. The "us versus them" mentality has come to drive the actions of police and migrants alike. When that happens, abuses in profiling are generated.

China

China is a country of 1.3 billion people. The nation's landmass covers 3.7 million square miles, encompassing all types of terrain. Much of China is rural and underdeveloped. Only about 20 percent of China's population lives in urban areas.

There are fifty-six ethnic groups in China, but one group stands out as the overwhelming majority: the Han Chinese. They constitute about 94 percent of China's population. Most of the remaining 6 percent live outside of the developed urban areas, instead living in the rural west and northwest regions (Gaylord 2000).

As most people know, China is a communist country with a powerful central government. There is no tradition of individual liberties in China. The state, representing the people collectively, is supreme. Certainly, a significant duty of the criminal justice system in China, as in any totalitarian regime, is to quell dissent. Groups and individuals who are thought to be subversive, including ethnic and religious minorities seeking greater freedoms for themselves, become frequent targets of government intervention.

This is not to say that general, nonpolitical crime gets a pass in China. In fact, owing to the increasing liberalization of the economy (as opposed to politics), financial corruption has become routine at all levels of bureaucracy and business. As legitimate economic opportunities increase in China, so do illegitimate ones; it is considered axiomatic that crime grows with the economy (Gaylord 2000). The public is keenly aware of the corruption and expects the government to deal with it.

General crime in China has been on the rise since the mid-1980s. For example, in just four years, from 1984 to 1988, crime rates went from 40 per 100,000 people to 77 per 100,000 (Bakken 1993). The increase in crime has been attributed to a variety of factors, chief among them the growing population of young people. In the 1950s and 1960s, crime committed by offenders aged fourteen to twenty-five consistently accounted for 20 to 35 percent of total crime. In the 1980s and 1990s, 60 to 75 percent of total crime was committed by offenders in that age group (Gaylord 2000). Despite the rising crime figures in China, perspective is still in order. The fact is that studies show Western nations have crime rates as much as 140 times that of China.

Today in China, the criminal justice system's greatest priority is organized crime and low- to mid-level corruption. Although corruption is also widely known to exist at high levels of government and in the Communist Party, for obvious reasons little enforcement has been directed there. Most justice officials want to continue to be justice officials.

For rudimentary criminal matters, China's criminal justice system is actually rather informal. According to Reichel (2002), China frequently relies on the informal mechanism of People's Mediation Committees (PMCs) to deal with disputes. There are about one million PMCs throughout China, organized at the workplace, in neighborhoods, and at schools. Each PMC is composed of ten to twenty citizens. The PMCs adjudicate wide varieties of alleged offenses through questions and discussion. Officially, PMCs operate under the authority of local government, but their policies and standards are set at the national level. For more serious offenses in China, the justice system uses four levels of "People's" courts. Given that the system is more inquisitorial, as one would expect in a totalitarian government, trials tend to be simply continuations of the investigation (Reichel 2002).

The police in China are known as the People's Public Security Forces. There are approximately 1.4 million civil police personnel in China. They are augmented by 600,000 members of the Armed Police Forces, who are organized under military command but have a civil police function (Shaowen 2001).

The stated mission of the police forces in China is to prevent, frustrate, and investigate criminal activity; maintain social security and order; curb behavior thought damaging to social security; control traffic; control the borders; protect dignitaries and important facilities; manage demonstrations; manage computer security; and monitor and control social organizations (Shaowen 2001). Clearly, the police in China have not prioritized the need for solid community relations and partnerships along the lines of the Peel model. Social control is paramount, not individual rights.

With the introduction of economic and trade reforms in the last couple of decades, China has seen an increase in offenses such as drug trafficking, alien smuggling, fraud, organized crime, and technology crime. Given the system in place, the police have had a free hand to tackle these problems as they see fit—which often includes targeting ethnic and philosophical minorities, as well as foreigners, all of whom are perceived as commonly implicated in these types of crimes.

Outrage at criminal justice profiling in China is a nonstarter within the country. Most Chinese lament the safety, security, and order that existed prior to the implementation of economic reforms. Cracking down on minorities who are believed to be responsible for disorder is not an unpopular activity of government. Dismay over China's lack of civil rights and selective prosecution of minorities—especially religious and political ones—is generally held on to primarily by China's critics in the West.

The economic ties that the United States and other Western countries have forged with China make it difficult, however, for those nations to impose any consequences. In December of 2001, the United States granted China permanent Most Favored Nation (MFN) trading status in spite of a widely acknowledged downturn of civil liberties in that country. The most serious consequence China seems to face for its practices is typically a harsh speech or two by American legislators on the Senate and House floors.

Japan

Japan is a nation of 124 million people. It is a nation of several islands, but its population is primarily located on four of them. For a democratic and free country, it has one of the lowest crime rates in the industrialized world (Leishman 1999).

Japanese law enforcement is both centralized and decentralized. It is centralized in the sense that there exists a National Police Agency (NPA), the duties of which are to oversee law enforcement functions throughout the country. It is decentralized, however, in the sense that most actual law enforcement activities take place among the nation's seven regional police bureaus and the metropolitan police departments such as in the capital city of Tokyo.

Police officers and other criminal justice officials in Japan are held in high regard by the public. The police are considered to be the experts in law enforcement, and so the public defers to them greatly without a lot of second-guessing. In return for this deference, the police in Japan likewise hold the public in high esteem. The notion of "service to the public" is embedded in Japan's police culture.

Interestingly, Japan's police agencies have long maintained a collaborative atmosphere among the police personnel and with the public. Empowering individual officers to work with one another and with management to solve problems is a tenet of American community policing, which arrived in the United States about ten to fifteen years ago. Japan, on the other hand, has been doing this for decades. One criticism, however, of this style of policing in Japan is that the deliberative nature of addressing problems fosters a slowness to act in responding to major crimes and incidents (Leishman 1999).

Japanese policing is extremely community oriented. Police officers in urban and rural areas alike are expected to blend into the community and simply be of service. Officers frequently find themselves being consulted on family and personal matters, as well as taking the customary complaints and responding to accidents (Leishman 1999).

Like most countries in the developed world, Japan's crime rates have been inching up. They are still considered low by Western standards, however, with a victimization rate 10 percent lower than that in Europe (Mayhew 1994).

To the extent that Japan's crime rates have gone up and are gaining public attention there, the crimes of particular concern are those committed by organized crime syndicates and gangs, foreigners, and terrorists. As these criminal elements are frequently the target of investigators as opposed to uniformed patrol officers, it is worth delineating the privileges that detectives have in Japan.

Although policing in general is very community centered, observers of the criminal justice system there note that detectives conduct their work in a very enabling legal and cultural environment (Leishman 1999). Where criminal investigations are concerned, the importance of individual liberty and civil rights is subordinated to the public need for safety and social order.

In Japan today, the most serious transnational crime problems are weapons and drug smuggling. These offenses are commonly associated with illegal immigration and foreigners—particularly Koreans, Filipinos, and Chinese. This leads to the temptation to treat legal and illegal visitors differently from the citizenry. Interestingly, to do so would be a violation of Japan's Police Code of Ethics. Among the provisions of that code, officers promise to respect human rights and perform their duties with courtesy and impartiality (Ueno 1994). In fairness, though, Japanese law enforcement has been fairly successful in its pursuit of professional, impartial policing. But the temptation for differential treatment is clearly there and requires official concerted effort to resist.

Law enforcers in Japan, as in the United States, are given considerable discretion. They are not expected to enforce the law mechanically. In the United States, critics have noted that discretion is frequently associated with partiality. Consequently, many justice pontificators in America argue for diminishing police discretion.

In Japan, however, most observers agree that police use their discretion to the benefit of the public. Police are taught that some people, including offenders, are weak and should be subjected to empathy and understanding. Heavy-handedness is frowned upon by the public and therefore frowned upon by police leadership. Law enforcement in Japan is truly conscious of its public image. Law enforcement in Japan doesn't work to counter or deflect criticisms from the public, including its sizable minority communities. Instead, it works very hard to have no critics.

India

With over one billion people, India has historically been considered the second most populated country on earth. Current estimates are that now India has overtaken China as the most populated country. The nation is extremely diverse. Its citizens speak eighteen languages with hundreds of dialects. Hindu is the predominant religion, but all major faiths are represented among the populace.

India is credited with being the world's largest democracy. A former British colony, it won its independence in 1947 and became a republic in 1950. Although independent, India's criminal justice system—and particularly its constabulary—is still reflective of British influence.

India is made up of twenty-five states and seven territories. Much of the nation's criminal justice activities are engaged at the state level. Even so, India's national government also provides police services dedicated to border security, industrial security, and significant criminal investigations. About three-quarters of India's two million law enforcement officers work for state police forces. Approximately 600,000 work for the federal government.

India is a nation that has been particularly plagued by terrorist gangs seeking to make political and religious strides through violence. For example, in the state of Punjab, Sikhs, who are a religious minority in India, have been fighting for an independent state since India's inception. Through the backing of Sikhs in wealthy western countries such as the United Kingdom, the United States, and Canada, violent Sikh organizations have been able to sustain ongoing attacks against government interests. Likewise, Islamic extremists have sought to undermine and overthrow Indian rule in Kashmir and Jammu. Attacks against Indian governmental infrastructure as well as against civilians have made terrorism a pressing concern for Indian criminal justice and public safety officials.

The illicit drug trade is also of considerable concern to India's law enforcement. With over three-quarters of India's population living in rural areas, and given the size of India (3.2 million square kilometers), the ability of drug traffickers to grow opium, heroin, ganja, and cannabis is largely unchallenged.

Law enforcement in India, as in some parts of the United States and unlike most parts of Japan, is maligned by the public for being corrupt, heavy-handed, unfair, and inefficient. Public opinion surveys in India show that the public frequently lacks confidence in its police forces to discharge their duties properly. This has resulted in a decided lack of cooperation with the police by the public and a siege mentality among officers. In fact, police are deemed so unreliable and untrustworthy that admissions of guilt made by offenders to police officers have generally not been admissible as evidence (Diaz 1994).

India has a long cultural tradition of subordinating the rights of individuals in favor of the social order of things. Much of this has to do with the Hindu-rooted caste system. Historically, Indian society has existed within five castes. The caste one belongs to determines one's station in life. The highest caste consists of priests; the lowest caste is made up of various "untouchables." Most Indians are somewhere in between. Castes are not classes, because in a class-oriented society, one can move up or down. With a caste system, people are born to their caste and remain there all their lives.

In the last few decades, India has shifted away from the caste system to a class form of social order (Vincentnathan 2000). A diminished view of the value of those trapped in the lower echelons of society remains pervasive, however, in Indian culture.

India does pride itself as a nation ruled by law. It has a strong constitution and a court system that was set up to embody justice and fairness—particularly for those accused of crimes.

Despite its large population and its democratically enshrined freedoms, India has a relatively low crime rate, thereby relegating the criminal justice system to step in as a last resort where family, religion, and other informal social controls fail to stem criminal activity. In the mid-1990s, India had a property crime rate of 47 per 100,000. This compares quite favorably to the rate per 100,000 in the United States (4,814), Germany (4,824), Canada (4,883), France (4,137), and Japan (1,019).

Given the relatively low crime rate in India overall, coupled with a lack of partnership with the public, India's criminal justice system is very susceptible to focusing on those more serious matters such as civil unrest and terrorism in the regions of the country heavily populated by minorities. Civil rights watch groups warn that Muslims in the Kashmir and elsewhere along the border of hated Pakistan, Sikhs in the Punjab, and Christians in the rural interior may all be subject to hostile treatment by justice officials who would preempt potential problems through aggressive enforcement against them or a lack of enforcement against those in the majority who would transgress against the minority.

Summing Up

For those living in the United States, it is probably easier to forget the rest of the world than it is for people living anywhere else. In America, everything needed is at hand. Additionally, there is no long tradition of global awareness and certainly no widespread tradition of global travel or language and cultural proficiency. Consequently, it is tempting to fail to realize that many of the issues that confront and confound criminal justice officials and civil rights advocates in the United States are alive and well all over the earth.

The United Nations has recognized the potential dangers of biased treatment, mistreatment, and maltreatment directed toward minority groups by the world's criminal justice systems wherever they may be. The fact that the United Nations annually studies criminal justice efforts on a worldwide scale demonstrates the interest in notions of equality and justice held by most of the international community.

In 1990, the United Nations expressed the weight it gives to these notions by declaring, among other things, that mistreatment by the police of the policed, including minorities, should be a criminal offense—particularly when force is used. For many countries, such an idea is absurd. For most countries, it's a reality.

And for the United States, there is solace in knowing that it is not alone in tackling such heated criminal justice issues and is not necessarily behind in the effort; and there is disillusionment in knowing that inequitable treatment of people is so ingrained in human nature that there are precious few places on the planet one can go to avoid it.

References

Albrecht, H. J. 1997. "Minorities, Crime, and Criminal Justice in the Federal Republic of Germany." In *Minorities, Migrants, and Crime*, ed. Ineke Haen Marshall. Thousand Oaks, CA: Sage, 86–105.

Albrecht, H. J., and R. Teske. 2000. "Germany." In *Crime and Crime Control: A Global View*, ed. G. Barak. Westport, CT: Greenwood Press, 29–48.

Bakken, B. 1993. "Crime, Juvenile Delinquency and Deterrence Policy in China." *Australian Journal of Chinese Affairs* 30:29–58.

Broadhurst, R. 1996. "Aboriginal Imprisonment in Australia." *Overcrowded Times* 7(3): 5–8.

Brogden, M. 1999. "Community Policing as Cherry Pie." In *Policing across the World*, ed. R. I. Mawby. New York: Garland Publishing, 167–186.

Camp, C. G., and G. M. Camp. 1997. *The Corrections Yearbook*. South Salem, NY: Criminal Justice Institute.

Diaz, S. M. 1994. "Police in India." In *Police Practices: An International Review*, ed. D. Das. Lanham, MD: Scarecrow Press, 181–229.

Gaylord, M. 2000. "China." In *Crime and Crime Control: A Global View*, ed. G. Barak. Westport, CT: Greenwood Press, 13–28.

Hughes, R. 1987. *The Fatal Shore*. New York: Alfred A. Knopf.

Jackson, P. I. 1997. "Minorities, Crime, and Criminal Justice in France." In *Minorities, Migrants, and Crime,* ed. Ineke Haen Marshall. Thousand Oaks, CA: Sage, 130–147.

James, S. 1994. "Police in Australia." In *Police Practices: An International Review,* ed. D. Das. Lanham, MD: Scarecrow Press, 1–122.

Leishman, F. 1999. "Policing in Japan: East Asian Archetype?" In *Policing across the World,* ed. R. I. Mawby. New York: Garland Publishing, 109–125.

Leong, M. 2001. "Australia." In *International Police Cooperation: A World Perspective,* ed. Daniel Koenig and Dilip Das. Oxford, UK: Lexington Books, 113–120.

Loveday, B. 1999. "Government and Accountability of the Police." In *Policing across the World,* ed. R. I. Mawby. New York: Garland Publishing, 132–150.

Mawby, R. I., ed. 1999. *Policing across the World.* New York: Garland Publishing.

Mayhew, P. 1994. *Findings from the International Crime Survey: Home Office Research and Statistics Paper No. 8.* London: Home Office.

Mukherjee, S., and P. Reichel. 1999. "Bringing to Justice." In *Global Report on Crime and Justice,* ed. G. Newman. New York: Oxford University Press, pp. 65–88.

Newman, G., ed. 1999. *Global Report on Crime and Justice.* New York: Oxford University Press.

Reichel, P. 1999. *Comparative Criminal Justice Systems: A Topical Approach,* 2d ed. Upper Saddle River, NJ: Prentice Hall.

———. 2002. *Comparative Criminal Justice Systems: A Topical Approach,* 3d ed. Upper Saddle River, NJ: Prentice Hall.

Robert, P. 1995. "A Lawmaker's Headache: Pretrial Detention." *Penal Issues: Research on Crime and Justice in France,* Volume 6, March: 3–5.

Schulte, R. 2001. "A German Perspective on Future European Security Needs." In *International Police Cooperation: A World Perspective,* ed. D. Koenig and D. Das. Oxford, UK: Lexington Books, 141–157.

Shaowen, Y. 2001. "International Police Cooperation in China." In *International Police Cooperation: A World Perspective,* ed. D. Koenig and D. Das. Oxford, UK: Lexington Books, 129–140.

Ueno, H. 1994. "Police in Japan." In *Police Practices: An International Review,* ed. D. Das. Lanham, MD: Scarecrow Press, 231–283.

Vincentnathan, S. G. 2000. "India." In *Crime and Crime Control: A Global View,* ed. G. Barak. Westport, CT: Greenwood Press, 65–82.

Wievorka, M. 1992. *La France Raciste.* Paris: Seuil.

4

Chronology

The purpose of this chapter is to provide a time line of significant events that relate directly or indirectly (but significantly) to the issue of criminal profiling. Many elements of the time line also appear elsewhere in this book. Even so, events are presented here with brief explanations in order to present an overall, albeit abbreviated, picture of the relevant history behind profiling.

1704 South Carolina legislatively establishes the first slave patrol in the American colonies. The slave patrols serve in a law enforcement capacity with the primary duties of searching slave quarters for contraband, dispersing slave gatherings, and generally safeguarding communities from marauding slaves by patrolling the roads.

1727 Virginia legislatively establishes a slave patrol similar to South Carolina's.

1753 North Carolina legislatively establishes a slave patrol similar to South Carolina's.

1764 Cesare Beccaria publishes *Essays on Crimes and Justice*, which articulates the themes of what is now known as classical criminology. The thrust of this criminological theory is that people commit crimes after making rational choices; consequently, swift and certain punishment must result from criminal deeds in order to deter people, through rationalization, from choosing criminal behavior.

1800   Franz Joseph Gall develops "phrenology," as published in his work *Anatomy and Physiology of the Nervous System, and of the Brain in Particular.* Phrenologists believe that mental functions, including deviant thoughts and behavior, come from localized parts of the brain. Consequently, phrenologists of the day believe an examination of one's skull can predict inferiority among races of people and propensities to commit crime.

1829   Phrenology becomes a widespread theory in the United States to help explain deviance; the acceptance of the theory is due to the work of Gaspar Spurzheim, a former student of Franz Joseph Gall's.

The Metropolitan Police Act passes in the British Parliament, creating the Metropolitan Police of London. The force, known as the "Met," is headed by Sir Robert Peel and is the first modern civil police organization. It is mandated to emphasize crime prevention, community relations, maintaining order without violence to the extent possible—many of the themes of modern-day community policing.

1850s–   Political era of policing. Law enforcement in the United
1910s   States during this time is largely a tool of the political machines in power in any given city. Police officers are hired and promoted based on who they know politically and what they have done for the political bosses, whether it be financial donations, getting out the vote efforts, or similar activities. Much of the effort of law enforcement during this period is devoted to service-related duties, such as soup kitchens, driving ambulances, and so on, as these activities are politically popular.

1857   *Dred Scott v. Sandford.* The U.S. Supreme Court rules that blacks whose ancestors were brought to America as slaves were not included in the Constitution when it mentioned the "people of the United States" or "citizens." Because they were a "subordinate and inferior class of beings, who had been subjugated by the dominant race . . . they had no rights or privileges" under the Constitution, even in slave-free territories and states.

1866   Ku Klux Klan (KKK) is formed as a fraternal organization in Pulaski, Tennessee. Its members are former officers of the Confederate Army. In short order, the group gains popularity and membership grows. The scope of its purpose also grows beyond the bounds of fraternity. The KKK becomes a group of marauders who intimidate, assault, terrorize, and murder newly freed blacks.

1868   The Fourteenth Amendment to the Constitution of the United States is ratified, thus giving all people born or naturalized in the United States the rights of citizenship. States are prohibited from depriving any person of life, liberty, or property without due process of law.

1871   The Ku Klux Act passes in the U.S. Congress and is signed into law. The law calls for civil and criminal sanctions against any persons who would infringe upon another's civil rights and gives the government the authority to use force to intervene against those who would deny others their civil rights.

1875   The Civil Rights Act of 1875 passes in the U.S. Congress and is signed into law. This law makes it a criminal and civil offense to deny other people, regardless of race or previous condition of servitude, full and equal enjoyment of public accommodations, advantages, facilities, theaters, public conveyances on land and water, and other places of amusement. The law also prohibits discrimination in jury selection for state and federal courts on the basis of race and color. The law is to be enforced by U.S. marshals and violations prosecuted in federal courts.

1876   Cesare Lombroso publishes *Criminal Man* and presents the theory of atavism. This theory argues that criminals are born to be criminals because of primitive and savage biological traits. This Darwinian theory was widely accepted in the United States in the late nineteenth century and the first half of the twentieth century and was

1876, used by some in criminal justice to justify oppressing cer-
cont. tain peoples, such as African Americans, to prevent their
inevitable criminal deeds.

1879 *Strauder v. West Virginia.* The U.S. Supreme Court rules
that a criminal defendant who is a racial minority is
denied his equal protection rights under the law when
members of his race are purposefully excluded from the
jury. The West Virginia law that says only white males
can serve as jurors is declared unconstitutional because
of the racial litmus test of being white. Not addressed is
the issue of whether limiting jurors to males is permissible. The court's silence on the issue allows that practice
to continue.

1886 *Yick Wo v. Hopkins.* The U.S. Supreme Court rules that
prosecutors may not consider the race of a criminal suspect when deciding whether to charge someone. Prosecutors maintain discretion in charging decisions and are
permitted even some degree of caprice in their decisions,
as long as race in no way enters into the decision-making
process.

1860s– Laws emerge throughout the South in the United States
1950s to keep blacks and whites separated. State legislatures
throughout the former Confederacy pass laws requiring
dining facilities, recreational facilities, public transportation seating, bathrooms, drinking fountains, and a host
of other accommodations to be separated for use according to race. Blacks are not permitted to use "whites only"
accommodations, nor are whites permitted to use "colored" accommodations, although there is rarely a desire
for the latter, since accommodations for blacks are
always substandard. These laws requiring separate
accommodations are known as "Jim Crow" laws.

1896 *Plessy v. Ferguson.* The U.S. Supreme Court rules that Jim
Crow laws are constitutionally permissible as long as the
separate accommodations for blacks are equal to those
for whites. Further, the Court rules that the Fourteenth
Amendment's Equal Protection Clause does not require

social equality among the races; it only requires political equality.

1905   August Vollmer becomes town marshal, and then police chief, for the city of Berkeley, California. He is widely regarded as the father of professional policing in the United States. Vollmer is among the first law enforcement administrators to require formal academic police training for rank and file officers. He is also known for putting his officers in patrol cars, and later, putting radios in those patrol cars, to enhance police presence and response times.

1910s–   Progressive era of policing. Law enforcement in the
1960s   United States during this period largely moves away from overt political influence in favor of reforms that are taking place in government generally. In particular, police organizations begin to move autonomous authority into the position of police chief, personnel are selected and promoted on the basis of merit, professional training is required of officers, and the emphasis for police becomes law enforcement rather than service.

1920   The Nineteenth Amendment to the U.S. Constitution is ratified, granting women the constitutional right to vote in federal, state, and local elections.

1940   *Cantwell v. Connecticut.* The U.S. Supreme Court rules that the criminal prosecution and conviction of three Jehovah's Witnesses for sharing the faith without a solicitation license and for breaching the peace is unconstitutional. The court rules that criminal laws, when applied to constrain legitimate religious practice, violate the First Amendment's No Establishment Clause.

1942   In the wake of war declared against Japan by the United States, President Franklin Roosevelt issues an executive order authorizing the creation of military zones that persons of Japanese descent may not enter. These military zones cumulatively include the entire West Coast of the United States to a depth inland of about forty miles. Dur-

1942,   ing the war, approximately 112,000 persons of Japanese
cont.   descent are involuntarily relocated from the West Coast
      to war relocation camps run by the U.S. military.

1944   *Korematsu v. United States.* The U.S. Supreme Court rules
      that the prosecution of a U.S. citizen of Japanese descent
      for entering a prohibited military zone—in this case,
      Korematsu's home—was constitutional. Korematsu's
      rights under the Fourteenth Amendment were not vio-
      lated by his prosecution. The court also rules, however,
      that once Japanese Americans' loyalty to the United
      States can be ascertained, they may no longer be held
      involuntarily in the military relocation camps.

1947   A report is published by President Harry Truman's Com-
      mittee on Civil Rights. The report declares that every cit-
      izen, regardless of race, is entitled to four basic rights: to
      be safe and secure in their person, to freely exercise the
      privileges of citizenship and civic duty, to be free in con-
      science and expression, and to have equal opportunity.
      The committee goes on record to acknowledge that the
      first right—to be safe and secure in one's person—is
      severely threatened, particularly for minorities, by the
      practices of arbitrary arrest and police brutality.

1954   *Brown v. Board of Education of Topeka.* The U.S. Supreme
      Court rules that "separate but equal" is inherently
      unequal and therefore unconstitutional. This ruling
      reverses the precedent set in *Plessy v. Ferguson,* which
      upheld racial segregation law in the South. In this case,
      the Court determines that even when facilities, opportu-
      nities, curriculum, and other amenities are in fact equal
      in quality, which is rare, there is still inequality because
      of the social harm minorities succumb to that is caused
      by segregation.

1957   Civil Rights Act of 1957. This, the first civil rights act to
      be passed by Congress since 1875, creates the U.S. Com-
      mission on Civil Rights. The purpose of the commission
      is to investigate voting rights violations and denial of
      equal protection under the law. The act also clarifies the
      qualifications to be a federal juror, reinforcing the fact

that race, ethnicity, and religion should have no part in disqualifying one for jury duty. Finally, certain criminal penalties are prescribed for violating the act.

1961 *Hoyt v. Florida.* The U.S. Supreme Court rules that a Florida law that systematically excludes women from becoming jurors does not invalidate the murder conviction by an all-male jury of a female accused of killing her husband. The Court is asked by Hoyt to apply the standard of "strict scrutiny" to Florida's law—customary when a "suspected class" is involved—but it refuses. Instead, the Court applies only the "ordinary equal protection scrutiny" standard. Hoyt's conviction is upheld.

Mapp v. Ohio. The U.S. Supreme Court rules that evidence obtained by police without a search warrant, when such a warrant is required, must be excluded from use at trial. Thus, the exclusionary rule now applies to all levels of law enforcement, not just to federal law enforcement as it had since the 1920s. Exemplifying the dramatic impact of this case on police practice, in the year prior to *Mapp,* New York City police officers do not bother to obtain even one search warrant. In the year following *Mapp,* the same department obtains over 800 warrants.

1963 Martin Luther King Jr. delivers his famous "I have a dream" speech from the steps of the Lincoln Memorial in Washington, D.C., to over 200,000 people in attendance. In his speech, he references the police brutality suffered by blacks in the South as well as in the urban North.

1964 The Twenty-Fourth Amendment to the U.S. Constitution is ratified. This amendment outlaws any poll tax or other tax imposed on prospective voters for the right to vote. Leading up to this amendment, poll taxes had been an effective means in southern states for excluding blacks, who were generally poorer than whites, from voting.

Freedom summer. Civil rights activists from college campuses in the North, along with black activists living in the South, seek to educate eligible black Mississippi

1964,
cont.
voters on how to vote and get them registered to vote. A massive voter registration campaign is waged. Early in the campaign, three civil rights workers—Michael Schwerner, Andrew Goodman, and James Chaney—are arrested by local law enforcement in Neshoba County, Mississippi. They are released after posting bond and disappear. The Federal Bureau of Investigation later finds their fire-scorched vehicle and their murdered bodies in a rural swamp. The murders are the work of the local Ku Klux Klan. The sheriff and a deputy are among those charged with violating the civil rights of Schwerner, Goodman, and Chaney. The sheriff is eventually acquitted; the deputy and other local Klan members are convicted.

The Civil Rights Act of 1964 passes in the U.S. Congress and is signed into law by President Lyndon Johnson. The purpose of the act is to eliminate racial segregation and other forms of discrimination. The act addresses discrimination in voting, employment, education, and segregation in public facilities. The act authorizes the U.S. attorney general to take legal action on behalf of individuals who are discriminated against. The act also prohibits federal funds from going to any organization that discriminates. Finally, the act creates the Equal Employment Opportunity Commission to ensure that the right to fair employment is not infringed upon because of one's race, color, religion, sex, or national origin. Hiring and firing decisions based on these criteria are outlawed. Exceptions exist for religious and Indian organizations.

1965
Griswold v. Connecticut. The U.S. Supreme Court rules that a right to privacy exists in the U.S. Constitution despite not being expressly mentioned therein. The Court reasons that a right to privacy can be found in the "penumbra" of the Fourteenth Amendment's rights of due process and equal protection. In this case particularly, the court finds that a state law making it a crime to prescribe or use contraceptives is unconstitutional. The Court says married couples have a right to privacy with respect to their sexual and reproductive choices.

1968 *Terry v. Ohio.* The U.S. Supreme Court rules that it is permissible for police officers to temporarily stop and detain persons, without a warrant, when an officer has reasonable suspicion that a particular person is engaged in, or about to be engaged in, committing a crime. This investigatory detention must be brief unless probable cause is developed through the encounter so that an arrest can be made. The Court also rules that a pat down of the suspect for weapons is permissible without warrant if reasonable suspicion exists that the suspect is armed.

The Omnibus Crime Control and Safe Streets Act of 1968 is passed in the U.S. Congress and signed into law. This legislation, among many other things, authorizes the U.S. attorney general to pursue civil litigation against those persons or organizations, including state and local governments, who discriminate against others on the basis of race, color, national origin, gender, or religion. The act also establishes the Law Enforcement Assistance Administration, which over time provides more than $7 billion to police agencies and institutions of higher education to research and develop better, more professional police practices.

Late   U.S. airlines and law enforcement team up to develop a
1960s profile of potential air hijackers, or "skyjackers." The need for developing such a profile is great during this time as a rash of hijackings take place. In 1968, 18 U.S. airliners are hijacked. In 1969, more than 30 U.S. airliners are hijacked. The federal government also creates its Air Marshal program to put armed law enforcement officers on board selected flights to deal with hijackings should they arise.

1972 *Yoder v. Wisconsin.* The U.S. Supreme Court rules that a state law requiring school attendance for children through the twelfth grade is unconstitutional in that it unlawfully requires Amish children to attend. The Court rejects a lower court decision that requires a practice of a religious group to be central and inseparable in that group's theology before First Amendment protections

1972, would kick in. A lower court has said that for the Amish,
cont. having children not attend school after the eighth grade
is essentially a community lifestyle issue, not an inherently religious one. The Supreme Court, however, simply
says a practice must be "rooted in religious belief," as is
the Amish's communal and simple lifestyle, to be protected by the First Amendment.

Eisenstadt v. Baird. The U.S. Supreme Court rules that the
constitutional right to privacy afforded to a married couple in *Griswold v. Connecticut* extends to unmarried heterosexual couples as well.

1975 Freda Adler publishes *Sisters in Crime,* which is the major
early work in feminist criminology. This publication sets
out to explain the differences in crime rates between men
and women. Adler explains the differences as largely
being due to the lack of opportunity for women in society. Just as women are denied equal access to legitimate
endeavors, likewise the same lack of access throughout
society inhibits their ability or desire to pursue illegitimate endeavors.

Taylor v. Louisiana. The U.S. Supreme Court rules that the
jury selection laws in Louisiana, which require women to
register an interest in being considered for jury duty
whereas men are simply drawn from the county rolls, is
unconstitutional as it has the effect of systematically
excluding women. This decision effectively reverses
Hoyt v. Florida.

Late The community policing model of law enforcement
1970s emerges to compete with, if not replace, the professional
model of policing. With community policing, an emphasis is placed on building relationships between police
officers and members of the community being policed.
Partnership is a key concept, as opposed to the more
standoffish and neutral approach to the public inherent
to the profession model. An additional emphasis is
placed on problem-solving by officers and community
members; abandoned is the strictly reaction orientation
of the professional model.

1979   *Delaware v. Prouse.* The U.S. Supreme Court rules that the decision to stop a black motorist without observing a traffic or equipment violation is unconstitutional under the Fourth Amendment's protection against unreasonable searches and seizures. In this case, the Court declares once and for all that stopping people for reasons ranging from an officer's outright racial bias to an officer's legitimately felt hunch is unacceptable absent an objectively observable violation.

1982   James Q. Wilson and George Kelling, both criminologists, publish *Broken Windows*, which theorizes that visible urban decay fosters criminal activity. Consequently, if one wants to deter and reduce crime in one's neighborhood, one needs a neighborhood that appears to care. Broken windows need to be fixed; abandoned vehicles need to be towed; garbage needs to be picked up. And police need to aggressively pursue nuisance offenders, such as prostitutes, truants, vagrants, panhandlers, and petty drug dealers.

1985   Crack cocaine explodes on the scene as the illegal drug of choice in New York City. It is a smokable form of cocaine that is cheap and very addictive. In the coming months and years, crack use and addiction spread throughout the United States—particularly in the urban inner cities.

1986   The Anti-Drug Abuse Act is passed by the U.S. Congress and signed into law by President Ronald Reagan. This legislation signals the beginning of the War on Drugs. Drug dealers and drug cartels become federal law enforcement's public enemies number 1. The act devotes nearly $2 billion to fight the drug epidemic. It allocates nearly $100 million to build new prisons, $200 million for drug education, and $241 million for drug treatment programs. The act creates mandatory minimum federal prison sentences for drug offenses. Crack cocaine, used more by minorities and the poor, draws stiffer penalties than powder cocaine, used more commonly by the white middle and upper class. The federal prison population grows exponentially in the coming years as a result of

1986, low-level drug offenders being sentenced to mandatory
cont. federal prison terms.

Bowers v. Hardwick. The U.S. Supreme Court upholds the
conviction of two homosexuals who were charged with
sodomy. The Court refuses to extend the Fourteenth
Amendment's implied right of privacy from *Griswold v.
Connecticut* to consenting adults engaged in sodomy.

Batson v. Kentucky. The U.S. Supreme Court overturns the
conviction of a black defendant because the prosecutor
had used his right of peremptory challenges to exclude
blacks from the jury. In this case, the prosecutor fails to
articulate that there is some other reason besides the race
of the prospective jurors that causes him to exclude all
blacks. The Court states that although peremptory challenges can be based on almost any reason, race cannot be
a factor in peremptory challenges.

1989 Volusia County, Florida, sheriff Bob Vogel establishes the
Selective Enforcement Team to interdict drug trafficking
on Interstate 95, which runs north/south through the
county and connects Miami, Florida, to the Mid-Atlantic
and Northeast. In three years, the team seizes $8 million
in forfeitable cash from drug offenders and untold scores
of drugs heading for market. Vogel and his Selective
Enforcement Team are controversial, as almost immediately after the team is created, there appears to be racial
bias against blacks and Hispanics in the decision by officers of whom to stop.

U.S. v. Sokolow. The U.S. Supreme Court rules law
enforcement's development and use of drug courier profiles is permissible in developing reasonable suspicion to
warrant an investigatory detention. The Court states that
profiles consisting of many factors, and not based solely
or primarily on race, are constitutional.

1991 *Powers v. Ohio.* The U.S. Supreme Court rules that a
racially discriminatory use of peremptory challenges to
exclude blacks from a jury is unconstitutional even when
the accused on trial is white. Racially motivated peremp-

tory challenges are unconstitutional regardless of the similarity or difference in race between those prospective jurors excluded and the person on trial. Powers's murder conviction is reversed, and he is granted a new trial.

Motorist Rodney King flees from the California Highway Patrol and the Los Angeles Police Department in a motor vehicle at speeds of over 110 miles per hour. His vehicle is cut off by squads and the chase ends. During the attempt to subdue King, Los Angeles police officers Lawrence Powell, Theodore Briseno, and Timothy Wind and Sgt. Stacey Koon are videotaped delivering more than fifty baton blows before handcuffing King.

1992   The four Los Angeles police officers in the Rodney King beating are tried in California district court for use of excessive force and assault against King. Sgt. Stacey Koon and Officers Timothy Wind and Theodore Briseno are acquitted on all charges. Officer Lawrence Powell is acquitted on all but one charge, about which the jury could not reach a decision. The acquittals lead to a race riot in South Central Los Angeles. The riots result in the deaths of 52 people, 7,000 arrests, and more than $1 billion in damaged property.

1993   Los Angeles police officers Lawrence Powell, Timothy Wind, and Theodore Briseno and Sgt. Stacey Koon are tried in federal court for violating Rodney King's civil rights. Sgt. Koon and Officer Powell are convicted and sentenced to thirty months in federal prison. Officers Wind and Briseno are acquitted.

1994   Rodney King sues the City of Los Angeles and officers Powell, Wind, and Briseno and Sgt. Koon in civil court for violating his civil rights. The city of Los Angeles stipulates liability and is ordered to pay King $3.8 million. The civil jury finds none of the four officers liable and awards King zero dollars in damages from each officer.

J.E.B. v. Alabama. The U.S. Supreme Court extends the logic the Court articulated in Batson v. Kentucky to the issue of gender. The Court rules that, just as race cannot

1994, be used as a basis for peremptory challenges to prospec-
cont. tive jurors, neither can gender.

The Violent Crime Control and Law Enforcement Act
passes the U.S. Congress and is signed by President Bill
Clinton. The act is a sweeping omnibus crime bill with a
wide range of provisions including enhancing the federal death penalty, enhancing the protection of women
against domestic violence, fine-tuning antiterrorism
laws, establishing the Police Corps training program,
allocating grants for community policing initiatives, and
strengthening the U.S. Department of Justice in addressing the issue of police misconduct. In particular, the Special Litigation Section of the Justice Department is
empowered under Title 42 to pursue civil relief when
police officers individually or collectively as a department engage in a pattern and practice of misconduct and
civil rights violations.

1995 Five Philadelphia police officers are convicted of fabri-
cating evidence against African Americans in that city.
The convictions call into question approximately 1,500
prosecutions involving those officers.

1996 *Romer v. Evans.* The U.S. Supreme Court rules that
Amendment 2 to Colorado's constitution, which prohibits governmental bodies from adopting special laws
protecting homosexuals from discrimination, violates
the Equal Protection Clause of the Fourteenth Amendment of the U.S. Constitution. The Court finds that sin-
gling out a group, in this case homosexuals, and banning
them from seeking additional protections while all other
groups may still lobby for additional protections is
unconstitutional.

Whren v. U.S. The U.S. Supreme Court rules that the
motives of police officers for stopping a motorist are
irrelevant if an actual violation of the law, no matter how
minor, is observed. In other words, police may use traffic
and equipment violations as bases for a stop, even
though the police may have little interest in traffic
enforcement and may be fishing for more serious offend-

ers. The Court refuses to adopt a standard for officers that would require no pretext before a stop could be made.

New Jersey Superior Court judge Robert E. Francis throws out nineteen drug-possession cases, concluding that state troopers patrolling the New Jersey Turnpike had improperly singled out and stopped black motorists.

1997   Under the authority granted to it in the Violent Crime Control and Law Enforcement Act of 1994, the U.S. Justice Department, Special Litigation Section, enters into consent decrees with the following police agencies in order to monitor reforms to which the police agencies agree: Steubenville, Ohio, Police Department; Pittsburgh, Pennsylvania, Police Department. In agreeing to the conditions of the consent decree, the police departments avoid further litigation against the federal government.

1998   Four African American males driving a rented van on the New Jersey Turnpike are pulled over by state troopers. During the traffic stop, the troopers open fire on the van, wounding three, two critically. No drugs or contraband are found, and no charges are filed against the four occupants of the van. The state awards the four occupants nearly $13 million in a civil settlement. The troopers involved in the incident are convicted of making an unlawful stop. The troopers go on record, saying that racial profiling is the policy of the New Jersey State Police.

1999   The New Jersey state legislature passes a resolution asking for the U.S. attorney general to investigate allegations of racial bias and profiling by the New Jersey State Police. The resolution notes that the New Jersey attorney general's office is not in a position to be impartial, thus requiring federal review.

The U.S. Department of Justice settles a lawsuit against the New Jersey State Police, resulting in a consent decree whereby a federal monitor oversees the effort by the

1999,   state police to implement ninety-seven agreed-upon
cont.   reforms, including providing additional training to
troopers on civil rights, installing computer tracking systems for tracking traffic stop data, and installing video
cameras in every squad car.

The Traffic Stops Statistics Study Act is introduced in the
Senate and the House. The bill requires the U.S. attorney
general to conduct a nationwide study of traffic stops by
law enforcement officers. The study would seek to identify the violations for which motorists were stopped,
motorist identifier information (race, gender, ethnicity,
and approximate age), number of occupants in vehicles
stopped, whether searches were conducted by the officers, duration of the stops, and disposition of the cases.
Federal funds would be appropriated to help state and
local governments pay for the study. The bill does not
pass.

2000   New Jersey governor Christine Todd Whitman causes
some controversy when she is photographed frisking a
black man while out on patrol with a state trooper. The
black man has been stopped for suspicious activity but is
not ultimately arrested as no law has been violated.

U.S. Department of Justice, Special Litigation Section,
enters into a consent decree with the Montgomery
County, Maryland, Police Department in order to monitor reforms to which the agency agrees. In agreeing to the
conditions of the consent decree, the police department
avoids further litigation against the federal government.

The U.S. Senate Judiciary Committee holds hearings to
investigate the issue of racial profiling and its pervasiveness in American society. Senator John Ashcroft, who
later becomes the U.S. attorney general, chairs the hearings. Victims of racial profiling are called to testify, as are
police officers and other law enforcement officials with
varying views on the issue.

2001   President George W. Bush, in his first address to a joint
session of Congress, decries the practice of racial profil-

ing by law enforcement officers. He further pledges to help end the practice of racial profiling in the United States.

A Cincinnati police officer shoots and kills Timothy Thomas, an unarmed nineteen-year-old black man. The city erupts into rioting. Later, Officer Steve Roach is charged with the death of Thomas but is acquitted. The incident sparks a U.S. Justice Department investigation.

U.S. Department of Justice, Special Litigation Section, enters into consent decrees with the following police agencies in order to monitor reforms to which the agencies agree: Highland Park, Illinois, Police Department; Washington, D.C., Metropolitan Police Department; Los Angeles Police Department. In agreeing to the conditions of the consent decree, the police departments avoid further litigation against the federal government.

Four U.S. airliners are hijacked. Two airliners are flown into the twin towers of the World Trade Center in New York City, one airliner is flown into the Pentagon, and one airliner crashes in rural Pennsylvania when passengers attempt to retake the jet. It is believed that the last jet was heading for the White House or the U.S. Capitol building. Nineteen men of Arab descent accomplish the four hijackings. In the wake of this disaster, Americans begin to question the wisdom of disbanding racial profiling. In the days, weeks, and months following the tragedy, Arab visitors, immigrants, and Arab Americans are scrutinized by law enforcement and intelligence officials, as well as by regular (and now wary) Americans.

The U.S. Patriot Act passes both houses of Congress and is signed into law by President George W. Bush. The law, among other things, makes it easier for federal law enforcement officers to conduct covert surveillance operations against suspected terrorists. Civil liberties groups decry the law and predict that the government will use it to infringe upon the rights of Arab Americans and Muslims. Supporters of the law respond that Americans will not tolerate another 9–11 and that the law is not race- or

2001, religion-specific. Further, supporters note that it would
cont. be unreasonable to ignore the fact that those who
attacked the United States on 9–11 were all indeed Arab
and were all Muslims.

2002 U.S. Department of Justice, Special Litigation Section,
enters into consent decrees with the following police
agencies in order to monitor reforms to which the agencies agree: Detroit Police Department; Buffalo, New
York, Police Department; Columbus, Ohio, Police
Department; Cincinnati, Ohio, Police Department. In
agreeing to the conditions of the consent decree, the
police departments avoid further litigation against the
federal government.

2003 *Lawrence v. Texas.* U.S. Supreme Court rules that consenting adults have a constitutional right to sexual privacy.
This applies to heterosexual and homosexual conduct.
The ruling overturns the long-standing decision in *Bowers v. Hardwick.* In doing so, the antisodomy laws of thirteen states are invalidated.

The Department of Justice issues a policy for all of federal law enforcement that bans criminal justice profiling
that is based solely or primarily on race or ethnicity—
even where such profiling would otherwise be permitted
by the Constitution and by laws. Although the Supreme
Court in *Whren* said that motives of officers do not matter, this directive requires federal law enforcement officers to act according to pure and racially neutral motives.
Using race or ethnicity by federal officers absent specific
and trustworthy information that a suspect of a particular race or ethnicity is involved in a crime, or operating
while holding to generalized racial or ethnic stereotypes,
is forbidden.

The University of Minnesota School of Law releases a
landmark study. The study involves the tracking of traffic stop information from sixty-five urban, suburban,
and rural Minnesota law enforcement agencies. The
study shows that white motorists are stopped less frequently than black, Hispanic, or Native American

motorists. White motorists who are stopped, however, more frequently possess drugs or other contraband than do minorities. These findings hold true for urban, suburban, and rural contexts. Although debate rages around the methodological soundness of the study, it goes a long way toward dispelling the notion that minority motorists are stopped more because they more often than whites are in possession of contraband.

5

Biographical Sketches

In this chapter, personalities are introduced who directly or indirectly have played a significant role in relation to the issue of profiling. Few, if any, individuals of notoriety have focused their lives on the issue of profiling. Many people, however, have concerned themselves with the issue of profiling within the context of their broader life's work. Many of the individuals listed below have served in the larger cause of civil rights for groups traditionally discriminated against, and confronting the issue of profiling is simply a manifestation of the larger cause to which they are dedicated. Others listed below have served in law enforcement or in the judiciary—particularly the U.S. Supreme Court. These individuals, in their professional capacities, have been connected to the issue of profiling and have wielded influence in one way or another with regard to this issue. Still others listed were theorists or philosophers whose ideas, passed on through history, had and have an impact on the debate over profiling.

The list of individuals below should not be construed as complete or absolute. Countless others have weighed in on the issue of profiling, and many have worked all their adult lives as proponents of equal treatment under the law while achieving justice. A cursory examination of the individuals listed here provides the reader with at least a start in compiling biographies of people who have influenced the debate over profiling.

Freda Adler (1933–)

Freda Adler is one of America's most well-known criminologists, past or present. Acclaim for her work and theories first emerged in 1975 when she published *"Sisters in Crime,"* which set out to explain female criminal behavior from a feminist perspective. This has come to be known as the liberation theory of criminology. Adler's work consistently rejected the notion that women commit crime or not because of biological or psychological determinants. Instead, Adler suggested that women commit crime in proportion to their decreasing oppression in society. Adler said that as women are increasingly liberated from society's traditional notions of womanhood, and thereby are free to pursue legitimate economic, social, and political advancement, so are they increasingly empowered and are in a position to pursue illegitimate gains in these same areas. According to Adler, women are no longer confined to the most menial of offenses; rather, they are capable of being world class in their criminality just as men can be. Adler continues today to be an influential member of academia as a proponent of feminist criminology.

Harry A. Blackmun (1908–1999)

Harry Blackmun was born in southern Illinois in 1908. His family moved to Minnesota, where he grew up. In fact, a childhood friend in grade school was the future chief justice Warren Burger. Blackmun attended Harvard University and received his B.A. in 1929. He went on to attend Harvard Law School, receiving his law degree in 1932. Blackmun returned to Minnesota upon graduation and set up a law practice that ran from 1933 to 1959. He left his private practice to accept an appointment from President Dwight Eisenhower to the U.S. Eighth Circuit Court of Appeals. Blackmun served in that capacity until President Richard Nixon appointed him to the U.S. Supreme Court in 1970, where he served for twenty-four years. He retired in 1994. Blackmun is most noted for his controversial authorship of the Court's opinion in *Roe v. Wade* in 1973. That decision took the privacy rights established in the case of *Griswold v. Connecticut* and extended them to establish a constitutional right to an abortion. In Blackmun's final year on the Court, he authored the majority opinion in *J.E.B. v. Alabama.* In that case, the Court ruled that gender, just as race, cannot be the basis for a prosecutor's decision to strike a potential juror through peremptory challenges.

Julian Bond (1940–)

Julian Bond was born in Nashville, Tennessee, in 1940. He has lived a life dedicated toward advancing the cause of civil rights for oppressed and depressed economic and racial classes of people. As a college student at Morehouse College in Atlanta, Georgia, in the late 1950s, Bond worked as a student activist in the effort to bring about integration in Atlanta's cinemas, restaurants, and other public places. In 1965, Bond was elected to the Georgia House of Representatives. The Georgia House refused to seat him, however, because of his opposition to the Vietnam War. He was elected two more times before he finally was permitted to serve after the legislature was ordered by the Supreme Court to seat him. Bond served in the Georgia House, and then Senate, from 1965 until 1987. He sponsored dozens of bills relating to civil rights that eventually were passed into law in Georgia. While serving in the state legislature of Georgia, Bond also served the cause of civil rights as an official of the Southern Poverty Law Center. In fact, he was appointed the center's first president upon its founding in 1971. For several years, Bond also served on the National Board of the National Association for the Advancement of Colored People (NAACP), which is the oldest and largest civil rights organization in the United States. In 1998, Bond became the NAACP National Board chairman.

Henry Brown (1836–1913)

Henry Brown was born in Massachusetts in 1836. He attended Yale University, graduating in 1856. Brown then pursued a legal education at Harvard and Yale law schools. He received his law degree in 1859. After law school, Brown moved to Michigan and served as a deputy U.S. marshal and as an assistant U.S. attorney in the Eastern District of Michigan. In 1868, Brown began his judicial career as a local judge in Detroit. In 1875, Brown was appointed as a federal district judge in the Eastern District of Michigan. He had served as a district judge for fourteen years when President Benjamin Harrison nominated him to the Supreme Court in 1890. Brown served as a Supreme Court justice for sixteen years and then retired. During those sixteen years, Brown authored more than 450 majority opinions for the Court. One of those, however, stands out more than the others: *Plessy v.*

Ferguson (1896), in which the Supreme Court upheld state-sanctioned race consciousness. In particular, the concept of "separate but equal" was found to be constitutional. This enabled southern and some northern states to lawfully continue the practice of segregation for decades until the landmark decision in *Brown v. Board of Education* in 1956.

Warren E. Burger (1907–1995)

Warren Burger was born in 1907 in St. Paul, Minnesota. He grew up in Minnesota and attended the University of Minnesota as an undergraduate student from 1925 to 1927. Burger went on to attend the St. Paul College of Law (now known as the William Mitchell College of Law) in St. Paul. Upon being admitted to the Minnesota bar, Burger engaged in private practice for over twenty years. He also taught law on the side. In 1953, the Eisenhower administration hired Burger to serve as the assistant attorney general for the Civil Division in the U.S. Department of Justice. In 1956, Burger was nominated and appointed to the U.S. Court of Appeals for the District of Columbia. In 1969, Burger was appointed by President Richard Nixon to the U.S. Supreme Court to replace outgoing Chief Justice Earl Warren. Burger was a strict constructionist in his judicial philosophy, and many conservatives had hopes that he would roll back some the judicial activism seen in the previous decade. Although Burger was generally considered a conservative on the Court, he did not live up to the expectations of countering the more liberal tide on the bench. Many significant civil rights cases were heard during the Burger Court, which spanned the period from 1969 to 1986. During his tenure, Burger authored an opinion upholding the practice of forced busing as a part of desegregation. He also authored the opinion holding valid the subpoena that required Richard Nixon to give up his private tapes concerning Watergate. This led to Nixon's resignation in 1974.

William J. Clinton (1946–)

William (Bill) Clinton was born William Jefferson Blythe III in Hope, Arkansas. His father died in a car accident three months before he was born. His mother married Roger Clinton when Bill was four years old, and Bill took his stepfather's last name. Clinton earned a bachelor's degree from Georgetown University with a major in international relations in 1968. He also attended Oxford University in England as a Rhodes Scholar and received a law degree from Yale University in 1973. Clinton served as governor of Arkansas from 1978 to 1980 and from 1982 to 1988. In 1992, Clinton was elected president of the United States and was reelected in 1996.

The Clinton presidency, which ran from January 1993 until January 2001, is known for many things. One of the legacies of the Clinton years in the White House is the advancement of community policing in the United States. President Clinton established the Community Oriented Policing Service (COPS) office in the U.S. Department of Justice. Through this office, the federal government subsidized the hiring of tens of thousands of police officers around the country. To qualify for the subsidy, local departments would have to commit officers to community policing efforts. Additionally, the Clinton administration began the funding of dozens of regional community policing institutes around the country, the purpose of which was to support community policing efforts through training and technical advising. Still another legacy is the Clinton administration's stepped-up effort to confront illegal police actions through Department of Justice investigation and intervention.

President Clinton set out to end the practice of racial profiling. He directed the Departments of Justice, Treasury, and Agriculture to collect data on race, ethnicity, and gender of individuals subject to stops by federal law enforcement. He also supported legislation encouraging states to collect the same data. During the Clinton years, several consent decrees were entered into between the U.S. Department of Justice and local police departments accused of racial profiling and other biased policing actions. President Clinton's positive relations with African Americans in the area of law enforcement and other areas caused many to dub him America's first black president. President Clinton also developed positive relations with the gay and lesbian community. He instituted a "don't ask, don't tell" policy in the military that resulted in the cessation of screening gays from military service. He also made dozens of appointments in his administration of openly gay or lesbian public officials. Finally, President Clinton sought to include sexual orientation among the categories covered by hate crime and employment discrimination legislation.

John Douglas (1947–)

John Douglas is a name that has long been associated with criminal profiling—particularly behaviorally rooted profiling. As an FBI special agent and head of the FBI's Investigative Support Unit (also known as the Behavioral Science Unit), he pioneered the development of behavioral profiles as investigative tools and has used such profiles in investigating infamous crimes such as the Tylenol poisonings in Chicago, the Green River Killer in Washington State, a serial killer of children in Atlanta, and a serial killer of prostitutes in Alaska. He has also studied and profiled famous criminals such as Charles Manson, Richard Speck, John Wayne Gacy, David Berkowitz, and others. Although many outside of criminal justice circles have never heard of Douglas, most have heard of fictional characters for whom he or his criminal subjects have served as inspiration. Of particular fame are Thomas Harris's books and subsequent movies (including *Red Dragon* and *Silence of the Lambs*) featuring the character Scott Glenn, who was a nemesis of Hannibal Lecter.

W. E. B. DuBois (1868–1963)

William Edward Burghardt DuBois was an African American who defied all stereotypes for the role of blacks in the late nineteenth and early-middle twentieth centuries. He received a bachelor's degree from Fisk University and a Ph.D. from Harvard. He served as a professor of classical languages at the University of Pennsylvania and as a professor of economics and history at Atlanta University. He was a founding member of the National Association for the Advancement of Colored People (NAACP). He wrote several books concerning the struggle of African Americans for equality both before and after slavery. DuBois was also among the first civil rights leaders to address the issue of gender discrimination—particularly as applied against black women. The reputation of DuBois is that he genuinely desired equality for all people, regardless of race, religion, or gender.

Franz Gall (1758–1828)

Franz Joseph Gall was born in Baden, Germany, in 1758. He studied medicine in Austria and became a well-known medical scientist. He is most remembered for his development of "phrenology," the attempted method of determining personality types and traits in individuals by examining the shape and size of their skulls. He believed that personality traits were localized in different modules of the brain and therefore more pronounced areas of one's brain would predict the talents one likely possessed. Likewise, skull depressions would reveal a person's negative behavioral tendencies, including potential criminality. Many ruling-class people in England during the nineteenth century embraced Gall's theories because they could be used to support the notion that colonial subjects and others in lower social classes were biologically inferior. His theories significantly influenced the early "science" of predicting criminality.

Ruth Bader Ginsburg (1933–)

Ruth Bader Ginsburg was born in New York in 1933. She received her bachelor's degree from Harvard University and her law degree from Columbia University School of Law. She attended law school in the 1950s when women were not particularly welcome in the profession and a great deal of hostility toward female law students could be felt. In 1963, Ginsburg joined the faculty of Rutgers University School of Law. She eventually returned to Columbia University to join the law faculty there. As a law professor, Ginsburg became very active in feminist issues and used her standing in the legal profession to advance feminist causes. In 1971, she shepherded the Women's Rights Project of the American Civil Liberties Union (ACLU) and served as the general counsel for the ACLU from 1973 to 1980, all while serving as a tenured professor of law at Columbia. In that capacity, she had the opportunity to argue cases on behalf of women seeking the same suspect class/strict scrutiny that racial minorities had won in the courts. In 1980, Ginsburg was appointed as a federal appellate judge for the District of Columbia federal circuit. In 1993, President Clinton nominated her to the U.S. Supreme Court. She was confirmed and took her seat that year. She was President Clinton's first Supreme Court nominee.

Herman Goldstein (1931–)

Herman Goldstein is the pioneer of the community policing movement. As far back as the 1970s, this University of Wisconsin professor began focusing his writing and research efforts toward developing a model of policing that emphasizes partnership between the police and the community and incorporates principles of empowerment and democracy within the policing structure. His model of police work permits officers to actually solve problems rather than simply react to them. Community policing has become a popular model for law enforcement in urban centers, especially where there exist high concentrations of ethnic or racial minorities. In many urban areas, police have historically been dimly viewed by the public for their heavy-handedness and perceived racism. Community policing seeks to change that perception by involving the community in the law enforcement and crime control process through partnership with the police. Although not perfect, the model has gone a long way to bridging the gulf between minority groups and the law enforcers serving them.

John M. Harlan (1833–1911)

John Harlan was born the son of a lawyer in Boyle County, Kentucky. He graduated from Centre College in 1850 and studied law at Transylvania University. In 1853, Harlan was admitted to the bar in Kentucky and began practicing law. Although a southerner and a slaveholder, Harlan remained loyal to the Union during the Civil War. In fact, Harlan joined the Union army and served as an officer. In 1863, he resigned his army commission to serve as the attorney general for Kentucky. In 1877, President Rutherford B. Hayes nominated Harlan to the U.S. Supreme Court, where he served for thirty-three years. He was known as the "Great Dissenter" for his many often solitary dissents against the majority on the Court. One of his most worthy dissents was in the case of *Plessy v. Ferguson,* where Harlan demonstrated he was ahead of his time. In that case, Harlan wrote that it was not proper under the Constitution for a government organization to know the race of people under its charge. In other words, Harlan believed government should not be race-neutral, but race-blind.

Thomas Hobbes (1588–1679)

Thomas Hobbes was born in Wiltshire, England, in 1588. He lived a long and productive life, dying in 1679. Over his ninety years on earth, he developed into one of the most influential political philosophers of all time. Hobbes believed and wrote that mankind, if left to its own devices in a state of nature, would exist in a very brutal, violent, and selfish way. Hobbes wrote that government is very important in that without it, social order would erode into savagery. He said that there exists a social contract in which individuals subordinate to the government a limited amount of their inherent freedom in exchange for government's protection and maintenance of order. Given that the natural state of mankind, according to Hobbes, was extremely brutal, his vision of government was fairly authoritative. Government was not to be given unlimited and everlasting authority, however. Should government fail in its obligation of protecting the people under its charge or in securing their individual liberties, then the contract would be broken and a different government could appropriately and morally be crafted to replace the old one. Hobbes's works were very influential upon colonists during the run-up to the American Revolution. Although Hobbes was certainly for individual freedom, he was also for a strong enough and effective enough government to overcome humankind's natural tendencies toward violence and mayhem. Therefore, with regard to criminal justice and profiling, one might conclude that Hobbes would encourage government to use whatever tools are reasonably necessary to ensure the public's safety from crime.

J. Edgar Hoover (1895–1972)

John Edgar Hoover was born in Washington, D.C., in 1895. In 1917, he graduated with a law degree from George Washington University. Soon after, Hoover joined the U.S. Justice Department as a special agent. In 1917, the United States entered World War I. Concern over espionage was very high. Hoover quickly became recognized as an accomplished and skilled federal agent and was promoted to head the Enemy Aliens Registration Section. In 1919, he was promoted to the head of the General Intelligence Division within the Department of Justice. In 1921, Hoover joined the Bureau of Investigation as the deputy director. In 1924, at the age of twenty-nine, he became director of the bureau, which had over 400 special agents. In 1935, the Bureau of Investigation was renamed the Federal Bureau of Investigation (FBI) and was given expanded powers as the federal government's premiere law enforcement and domestic intelligence agency.

By all accounts, Hoover ran a "tight ship" at the FBI. It was *his* FBI. He made great strides to professionalize the bureau. He instituted background checks for all special agents, implemented rigorous training and physical fitness requirements, and created a national laboratory for the analysis of forensic evidence. Under Hoover, the FBI became a part of American popular culture in its fight with gangsters of the 1930s. The Bureau's most famous foe was John Dillinger, who was killed in a gun battle with FBI agents in Chicago. Hoover's FBI emerged as the lead agency to enforce civil rights laws in the 1960s and 1970s and had some success in prosecuting violent segregationists in the South when state and local law enforcement were unwilling to take action. Hoover was shrouded in controversy during his forty-eight-year career with the Bureau. Many have speculated that Hoover kept secret files on potential political opponents. Those files presumably contained information that could be used to blackmail opponents into compliance with Hoover's wishes. In some cases, Hoover is alleged to have leveraged the sexual orientation and sexual practices of some opponents. Hoover remained the director of the FBI until his death in 1972.

Jesse Jackson (1941–)

Jesse Louis Jackson Sr. was born in Greenville, South Carolina, in 1941. He grew up in South Carolina and earned a bachelor's degree from North Carolina A & T University in 1964. Jackson began studies at the Chicago Theological Seminary in Illinois, but dropped out owing to his heavy involvement in the civil rights movement. He eventually returned to seminary to receive his Master of Divinity degree in 2000. Jackson became a civil rights activist in 1960 when he led sit-ins to desegregate local public facilities in South Carolina and elsewhere. In 1965, he began working full-time for the Southern Christian Leadership Conference and for Martin Luther King Jr. In 1971, Jackson founded Operation PUSH (which stands for "People United to Serve Humanity") in Chicago. The goal of PUSH was to empower people of color to overcome economic disadvantage. In 1984, Jackson founded the National Rainbow Coalition in Washington, D.C. The Rainbow Coalition was created to advocate social justice and change public policy to that end. In 1996, Jackson's two organizations merged into the Rainbow/PUSH Coalition. Jackson is one of the more controversial figures in the civil rights movement. He has been an outspoken critic of law enforcement and the criminal justice system, conservative politicians, conservative religious groups and denominations, and others. He ran for president of the United States in 1984 and 1988 as an unabashed liberal. He has also inserted himself many times into international crises; in doing so, he has negotiated the release of hostages and prisoners of war from hostile foreign countries. He has also been an ardent supporter of labor unions worldwide. His political activities have won him support from some and criticism from others.

Martin Luther King, Jr. (1929–1968)

Perhaps the most famous and well-regarded American civil rights leader in the nation's history is Martin Luther King, Jr., who was born in 1929 in Atlanta, Georgia. King grew up in Atlanta and eventually attended and graduated from Morehouse College with a bachelor's degree in sociology. He went on to earn a divinity degree from Crozer Theological Seminary in Pennsylvania in 1951 and a Ph.D. in theology from Boston University in 1955. King, like so many African American civil rights champions of his day, began his adult life in the ministry. He was ordained as a Baptist minister and served as a pastor in Alabama before returning to Georgia as the director of the Southern Christian Leadership Conference in 1959. King was very passionate for the cause of civil rights. He was responsible for organizing the Montgomery bus boycott in 1955 and 1956 to protest segregation on the bus. He was jailed dozens of times for his involvement in nonviolent civil disobedience. He was greatly influenced by Gandhi's own example of nonviolence to influence change.

King aggressively sought the help of the federal government in enforcing the right of blacks to register and vote. His efforts, and others, created the impetus for a variety of sweeping civil rights laws. In 1963, King organized and led the March on Washington, where he gave his famous "I have a dream" speech. That speech remains an anthem of the ideal for race relations in the United States. In 1964, King was awarded the Nobel Peace Prize for his efforts to bring justice and equality to the American South and urban North. In 1968, Martin Luther King Jr. visited the city of Memphis for the purpose of leading a protest march in support of striking garbage workers. While standing on the balcony of his hotel room on April 4, 1968, King was shot dead by James Earl Ray. Ray pleaded guilty to the assassination and was sentenced to ninety-nine years in prison, where he died. Since 1994, the third Monday in January each year is a national holiday dedicated in King's honor.

Rodney King (1965–)

Rodney King was born in Sacramento, California, in 1965. He has become one the most visible symbols of police violence against African Americans in today's society. On March 3, 1991, Rodney King was involved in a high-speed pursuit. King had a significant criminal history. He had been convicted of beating his wife. He was on parole for robbery of a convenience store and assault, and he was intoxicated. Consequently, he fled in his vehicle when a California Highway Patrol officer attempted to stop him on a Los Angeles freeway. During the pursuit, the Los Angeles Police Department became involved to assist the highway patrol. When King finally pulled over and exited his vehicle, four Los Angeles police officers used their batons to subdue him. The baton blows were caught on tape by a bystander and made it to the television news. The officers involved in the beating were eventually charged by the Los Angeles district attorney for assault and police misconduct. On April 29, 1992, a jury found the officers not guilty of criminal wrongdoing. The black and Hispanic communities in Los Angeles were outraged at the verdict, and a riot broke out in the south central part of the city. Many storefronts and homes were set on fire and burned to the ground. Damage totaled $16 billion. More important, fifty-two people were killed in the riots by rioters and 3,000 people were injured. Rodney King, already famous from the videotaped beating, solidified his status as an icon when he asked on national television his famous question "Can't we all just get along?" The same four police officers were re-tried for civil rights violations in federal court. Two of the four were found not guilty; the remaining two—Lawrence Powell and Stacey Koon—were found guilty and sentenced to federal prison. In 1994, the city of Los Angeles agreed to pay King $3.8 million in damages. King has continued to have run-ins with the law. Just since 1999, he has been arrested for domestic assault, drug use, and driving while under the influence of drugs.

John Lewis (1940–)

John Lewis was born in rural Alabama in 1940. He attended segregated schools during his elementary and secondary education. He went on to earn a bachelor's degree in religion from Fisk University and a divinity degree from the American Baptist Theological Seminary in Nashville. John Lewis began his long civil rights advocacy career as a freedom rider in the South in the early 1960s. He frequently participated in civil disobedience in order to protest the segregation policies throughout the South. He was recognized at an early age as a leader in the civil rights movement. In fact, at age twenty-three, he helped organize and spoke at the March on Washington in 1963. Lewis was intimately involved in the "Freedom Summer" of 1964 in Mississippi. He led hundreds of marchers across the Edmund Pettus Bridge in Selma, Alabama. That particular march was notoriously confronted by state troopers—an event that came to be known as "Bloody Sunday." Lewis was no stranger to police contacts. He was arrested over forty times for his acts of nonviolent civil disobedience. Lewis served as an activist for twenty more years until he was elected to the U.S. Congress in 1986 by the citizens of Atlanta, Georgia. He has been a leader among the congressional Democrats and has worked very hard to achieve fairness and equity for minorities in the United States, especially within the context of the criminal justice system.

Cesare Lombroso (1835–1909)

Cesare Lombroso was a nineteenth-century Italian criminologist who believed that there existed a relationship between the physical characteristics and features of people and criminal behavior. It is from Lombroso that we have taken the stereotypical notions of "beady eyes" or a "slack jaw" serving as an indicator of criminality. Lombroso was influenced in the development of his theories by Charles Darwin's theory of evolution and Franz Gall's theories of phrenology. Lombroso's theories were popular in Europe and parts of South America into the twentieth century. Criminological theories that focused on social and environmental causes of crime eventually replaced biological and genetic determinants, however, as the mainstream hypotheses concerning crime's origins.

Thurgood Marshall (1908–1993)

Thurgood Marshall was born in Baltimore, Maryland, in 1908. He attended Lincoln University as an undergraduate, receiving a B.A. in 1930. He then studied law at Howard University, a predominantly black university in Washington, D.C. He received a law degree in 1933. After practicing law in Maryland for a couple of years, Marshall became the legal director for the National Association for the Advancement of Colored People (NAACP). He served in that capacity from 1940 to 1961. During that time, Marshall litigated many significant civil rights cases. The most famous civil rights case he successfully litigated was *Brown v. Board of Education* in 1954. In that case, Marshall argued persuasively before the U.S. Supreme Court that racial segregation in public schools was unconstitutional. The Supreme Court agreed and ended the idea of "separate but equal" previously established in the case of *Plessy v. Ferguson.* In 1961, Marshall was appointed by President John F. Kennedy to serve as a judge on the U.S. Court of Appeals for the Second Circuit. In 1965, Marshall became the solicitor general of the United States under President Johnson. The solicitor general is the chief trial lawyer for the U.S. government and has the responsibility of representing the United States before the Supreme Court. In 1967, Johnson nominated Marshall to become the first black justice of the Supreme Court. By the time he took office, he had successfully argued nearly thirty cases before the court on which he now sat. As a Supreme Court justice, Marshall was considered a staunch liberal. He opposed the death penalty because he believed it to be inherently "cruel and unusual" and applied in a discriminatory fashion, both of which would be violations of the Constitution.

Kweisi Mfume (1948–)

Kweisi Mfume was born Frizzell Gray in 1948 in Baltimore, Maryland. He grew up in that city and became active in politics and the civil rights movement. He attended and graduated from Morgan State University, serving as the editor of the college paper and as the president of the Black Student Union on campus. He eventually earned a master's degree in international studies at Johns Hopkins University. In 1979, Mfume was elected to the Baltimore City Council. He served as a council member until 1986, when he was elected to the U.S. House of Representatives. As a congressman, he worked very hard on civil rights legislation. This included legislation relating to affirmative action, protection of Americans with disabilities, reforming financial institutions, reforming the equal employment opportunity laws, and tightening up gun control. Mfume served as chair of the Congressional Black Caucus and as such gained national attention as a spokesperson for issues affecting African Americans. In 1996, Mfume left the Congress to become president of the National Association for the Advancement of Colored People (NAACP). In that capacity, he has continued to champion affirmative action and other civil rights issues, including the elimination of brutality and discrimination inflicted by the criminal justice system on minorities.

Rosa Parks (1913–)

Rosa Parks is an icon in the American civil rights movement. An African American woman born and raised in Alabama, she dared as a forty-two-year-old adult to challenge the absurdity that was segregation in her home state. On December 1, 1955, while riding home from work on a city bus in Montgomery, Alabama, she was ordered by the driver to give up her seat to a white man. She was further told to move from the front of the bus to the back of the bus, where blacks were permitted to sit. She refused to comply, which resulted in her arrest. This high-profile incident resulted in a boycott of the Montgomery city buses. Blacks all across town, led by Martin Luther King Jr., simply refused to give patronage to a transportation system that treated them as second-class citizens. Instead, they walked or helped each other with rides. The boycott lasted over a year. Eventually, the U.S. Supreme Court ruled that segregation in public transportation was unconstitutional. The civil rights activism that started with her refusal to move to the back of the bus gave rise to the Civil Rights Act of 1964 and the Voting Rights Act of 1965. After this incident, Parks began to work full-time on the cause of civil rights. Eventually, due to threats and harassment, Parks and her family left Alabama and moved to Detroit, Michigan, where she has remained.

Lewis Powell (1907–1998)

Lewis Powell was born in Virginia in 1907. He also grew up there. In 1929, Powell graduated with a bachelor's degree from Washington and Lee. He remained there to study law, receiving his degree in 1931. Powell went on to receive a master's degree in law from Harvard University in 1932. Powell practiced law in Virginia from 1933 to 1971, with the exception of four years service as an officer with the U.S. Army Air Corps from 1942 to 1946. In 1972, Powell was appointed from private practice to the U.S. Supreme Court by President Richard Nixon. During his fifteen years on the Court, Powell was considered a moderate and frequently served as a swing vote. Notably, Powell authored the Court's opinion in the case of *Batson v. Kentucky*. This 1986 case resulted in the prohibition of prosecutors' use of the peremptory challenge to eliminate potential jurors from sitting on a case because of their race. Powell retired in 1987.

William H. Rehnquist (1924–)

William H. Rehnquist was born in Milwaukee, Wisconsin, in 1924. Before he could enter college, World War II broke out. Rehnquist enlisted in the U.S. Army Air Corps and served in North Africa. After the war, Rehnquist attended Stanford University, using funds from the GI Bill. He received a bachelor's and a master's degree in political science. He then went to obtain a second master's degree, this time in government, from Harvard University. In 1950, he returned to Stanford University to attend law school and graduated number one in his class. After law school, Rehnquist practiced law in Arizona and became active in the Republican Party. In 1971, President Richard Nixon appointed him to the U.S. Supreme Court. Rehnquist served on the Court as an outspoken, if often solitary, conservative. His dissenting opinions on several cases demonstrated a restrictive view concerning the breadth of the Fourteenth Amendment vis-à-vis nonracial matters. In 1986, President Reagan nominated him to replace the retiring Warren Burger as the chief justice of the U.S. Supreme Court. The Senate confirmed the nomination, and Rehnquist has served as chief justice ever since. Rehnquist has authored or contributed to many significant court opinions. Notably, Rehnquist authored the Court's opinion in *Sokolow*, which upheld the use of objectively constructed profiles to identify possible drug couriers at airports.

Janet Reno (1938–)

Janet Reno became America's first female U. S. attorney general when she was appointed to that post by President Clinton in 1993. She served in that capacity until 2000. Reno was born in Miami in 1938. She grew up in the Miami area and graduated from high school there. In 1956, she enrolled at Cornell University in New York State. In 1960, she was accepted into Harvard Law School. She was one of sixteen women in a class of 500 students. In 1963, she received her law degree and returned to Florida. Prior to becoming the U.S. attorney general, Reno served as a Dade County assistant state's attorney, as a staff member for the Florida legislature, and as the Dade County state's attorney. She helped establish the Miami Drug Court, which served as an alternative to the traditional criminal justice adjudication and punishment process for nonviolent drug offenders. As the U.S. attorney general, Janet Reno set a course for the Justice Department to aggressively enforce civil rights laws, thereby ensuring equal opportunity for all. In particular, her Justice Department entered into several consent decrees with local police agencies, which required those agencies to adhere to predetermined practices and policies in order to avoid federal litigation.

Jean-Jacques Rousseau (1712–1778)

Jean-Jacques Rousseau was born in Geneva, Switzerland, in 1712. He lived there until the age of sixteen, when he moved to Paris. He remained in France until his death in 1778. Rousseau is considered perhaps the most influential philosopher to emerge from the Enlightenment. In Rousseau's earlier works, he wrote that people were basically good and noble but became corrupted and were made unhappy by the influence of a corrupt society upon them. He believed that the social customs of his time, particularly among the aristocracy, were artificial and should be rejected. Rousseau emphasized the notion that people are born free and should be afforded equality within society. Among his later works was his most important publication: *The Social Contract*. In this work, Rousseau reiterated much of what Thomas Hobbes said about the need for government—namely, that it exists to secure personal freedom and keep what would otherwise be a violent, disorderly society in check. Rousseau, however, emphasized the notions of equality, at the expense of majority will, and challenged the right to hold private property. Rousseau's work is considered to have laid the groundwork for the emergence of socialism and communism—particularly given his defense of "Everyman" against society elites who own all the property and hold all the power. Although one cannot be certain, his writings suggest that he would hold disdain for the practice of profiling when done so on the basis of race, religion, or other classifications. Rousseau would likely find profiling to be a tool of the ruling class for keeping elitist social order in place.

Margaret Sanger (1879–1966)

Margaret Sanger is considered a chief pioneer of feminism in the United States. She was born as Margaret Higgins in 1879 to an Irish American, devoutly Catholic family in Coming, New York. Her mother died at the age of fifty after bearing eleven children. Higgins believed that her mother's chronic condition of pregnancy contributed to her relatively early death. This belief helped shape Higgins's views of the pitfalls of "traditional" living for women and contributed to the development of her feminist philosophy. Margaret Higgins attended Claverack College in 1896 and then entered a nursing training program at White Plains Hospital in 1900. In 1902, she married William Sanger, with whom she had three children. Margaret Sanger became an early advocate for women's health issues and the use of birth control. In 1912, she began to publish newspaper columns related to sex education. She actively promoted the ideas of anarchist Emma Goldman and saw birth control as a way to secure freedom from the economic shackles that a family creates. In 1914, Sanger divorced her husband and carried on a sexually liberated life consisting of several affairs. Sanger's driving issue throughout her adult life centered on the right of women to use birth control. In fact, Sanger was the founder of the Planned Parenthood Federation of America. In 1966, her lifelong battle culminated in the U.S. Supreme Court's decision of *Griswold v. Connecticut*, in which a right to privacy and the use of birth control was deemed to be contained in the Constitution. This court decision decriminalized laws in several states that had restricted the use of birth control methods. Sanger was not an uncontroversial figure even by modern standards. She was directly allied with anarchists and socialists of her day. She was a believer in eugenics, which involves the attempt to produce biologically superior humans by socially controlling reproduction—an idea also popularized in Nazi Germany. Even so, Sanger was undeniably a stalwart of early efforts at women's liberation and decriminalization of matters pertaining to women's health.

Antonin Scalia (1936–)

Antonin Scalia was born in Trenton, New Jersey, in 1936. Scalia is considered, even by his critics, to be one of the sharpest justices academically in Supreme Court history. His father was a college professor, and the love for all things intellectual was passed on to him. Scalia received his bachelor's degree in history from Georgetown University. After graduating from Georgetown summa cum laude as valedictorian, he went on to Harvard Law School. There, he served as the *Law Review* editor and graduated magna cum laude in 1960. After practicing law from 1961 to 1967, Scalia joined the faculty of the University of Virginia's Law School. He served there until 1974 and then again as a law professor at the University of Chicago from 1977 to 1982. He served as assistant attorney general during the Ford administration from 1974 to 1977. In 1982, he was appointed by President Reagan to the Federal Court of Appeals for Washington, D.C. There, Scalia established a record of judicial restraint and strict constructionism (that is, belief that government's authorities are only those expressly granted to it in the U.S. Constitution). In 1986, Reagan nominated Scalia to the Supreme Court at the same time William Rehnquist was nominated to become chief justice. Scalia was confirmed unanimously. Scalia is widely known by admirers and critics as the Supreme Court's most conservative justice. His written opinions have demonstrated a belief in states' rights to regulate things such as abortion or consensual sexual relations. He has also challenged the permissibility of programs such as affirmative action that are race conscious. Scalia wrote the opinion of the court in *Whren v. U.S.*

Al Sharpton (1954–)

Alfred Sharpton was born in Brooklyn, New York, in 1954. Sharpton is widely known as a minister, civil rights activist, and presidential candidate. His career has centered around civil rights issues and has included regular confrontations with the criminal justice system when he has perceived abuses or injustices against minorities to have occurred. Sharpton entered politics in 1978 when he ran for a New York state senate seat. He was not elected and so continued his political activism. In 1986, Sharpton gained prominence nationally by organizing demonstrations after an African American man was killed by several whites in the Howard Beach neighborhood of New York City. A couple of years later, Sharpton became an adviser for Tawana Brawley, who claimed to have been sexually assaulted by a group of white people. Sharpton lost considerable credibility in the public eye by defending Brawley, as her claims later turned out to be a hoax.

Sharpton also gained national attention when he led protests in 1989 following the shooting death of a black youth named Yosuf Hawkins by whites in Bensonhurst, another New York City neighborhood. More recently, Sharpton has organized demonstrations after the sexual assault of Haitian immigrant Abner Louima by police officers in 1997 and the police shooting of Amadou Diallo, an unarmed Ghanaian immigrant in 1999. In addition to Sharpton's failed campaign in 1978, he unsuccessfully ran for New York City mayor in 1997 and for the U.S. Senate in 1992 and 1994. Sharpton also ran as a candidate for president of the United States in 2003–2004.

Roger Taney (1777–1864)

Roger Taney was born in Calvert County, Maryland, in 1777. He graduated from Dickinson College in 1795. After studying law on his own, he was admitted to the Maryland bar in 1799. That year, he was also elected to the Maryland House of Delegates, where he served one term. In 1821, he entered into private practice but remained active in politics and political campaigns. In 1831, Taney was appointed as U.S. attorney general by President Andrew Jackson. Five years later, Taney was nominated to be chief justice of the Supreme Court to replace John Marshall. Taney significantly contributed to the Court's early development. He has primarily come to be known, however, for the notorious decision of *Dred Scott v. Sandford* (1856). The Court's opinion in that case, which Taney delivered, officially declared that blacks were not "people" for the purposes of the Constitution and were indeed inferior beings. That decision damaged the credibility of the Court in the minds of many people at that time. Taney served on the Supreme Court until his death in 1864.

August Vollmer (1876–1955)

August Vollmer is often referred to as the father of modern policing. By all accounts, Vollmer was in many ways ahead of his time. He served as the town marshal, and then police chief, for Berkeley, California, from 1905 to 1932. During his tenure there, he instituted many innovations. He collaborated with the University of California at Berkeley to develop a police training program for his officers. He required all of his officers to be formally trained in criminology and the social and physical sciences. He also developed a code of ethics for his department, which, among other things, eliminated the acceptance of gratuities or favors. Other innovations of his and his department included being first to hire a female police officer; first to use automobiles and motorcycles for patrol; first to use crystal radios for dispatched communications; first to rely on scientific investigative techniques (for example, analysis of blood, fibers, and soil); and among the first to require new recruits to pass psychological screenings and intelligence tests. In 1936, Vollmer published a book entitled *The Police and Modern Society* in which he explained his vision for the emerging profession of law enforcement. Vollmer was an advocate for advancing the goal of impartial police work. Many departments today that still have difficulties navigating through issues of community relations and relations with minority groups would still find Vollmer to be innovative.

Earl Warren (1891–1974)

Earl Warren was born in Los Angeles in 1891. He grew up in Bakersfield, California, and attended the University of California at Berkeley. He received his bachelor's degree from that institution in 1912 and his Juris Doctor degree from there in 1914. He worked in private practice in the San Francisco Bay area for three years before entering the U.S. Army as a lieutenant in 1917. His early career in civilian government included several terms as Alameda County's (Oakland, California) district attorney. Serving as a prosecutor proved to be a good career to come from when entering politics. Warren, a moderate to liberal Republican, was elected governor of California three successive times: . . .in 1942, 1946, and 1950. In 1948, Warren ran unsuccessfully as the vice presidential candidate for Thomas Dewey, who narrowly lost to Harry Truman. In 1953, President Dwight Eisenhower appointed Warren as the chief justice for the U.S. Supreme Court. President Eisenhower would later call the appointment of Warren, as well as his appointment of William Brennan, among the biggest mistakes he ever made. Warren proved to be very liberal and judicially activist on the Supreme Court. It was during his tenure as chief justice that the Bill of Rights was incorporated into the Fourteenth Amendment through one case after another, thereby requiring state and local authorities to abide by the provisions of the Fourth, Fifth, Sixth, and Eighth Amendments in particular. The Warren Court also oversaw the end of legal segregation and a host of other civil rights advances. Despite being a liberal, Warren wrote the opinion of the Court in *Terry v. Ohio*, in which the conviction of armed, would-be robbers was upheld after a police officer patted them down for weapons without a warrant.

Ida B. Wells (1862–1931)

Ida B. Wells is also known as Ida B. Wells-Barnett and was born into a Mississippi slave family in 1862. Wells learned to read as a child owing to the emphasis her parents placed on hard work and education. She went on to receive her college training at Fisk University. In 1884, Wells was traveling on a train and was forcibly removed from first class and placed into the "Jim Crow" car (a blacks-only car), despite having paid for a first class ticket. Wells sued the railroad company over this incident and won the case. The Tennessee Supreme Court reversed, however, in favor of the railroad. She then dedicated her life to confronting racial injustice and bigotry. She did this primarily through writing and giving speeches. One injustice Wells frequently decried was the substandard facilities and supplies for black school children as compared to white children in the same school districts. Wells was also touched by violence against blacks. Three of her friends in Memphis, Tennessee, were killed by whites, and she herself was threatened with death for continuing to write about segregation. She eventually moved to Chicago and wrote several pieces on lynchings and mob rule in the South. In Chicago, Wells worked aggressively for equality for blacks and equality for women. Wells became a very influential civil rights leader in Chicago and wielded that influence until her death in 1931.

Byron White (1917–2002)

Byron White was born in Colorado in 1917. He grew up there and attended the University of Colorado. He played football, basketball and baseball for the university, earning ten varsity letters. He was also an outstanding student and won the Rhodes Scholarship to Oxford University in England in 1939. From 1942 to 1946, White served as a naval intelligence officer. Once World War II ended and he was released from active duty, he attended Yale Law School. Amazingly, while at Yale, he played professional football for the Detroit Lions on the weekends. After graduating from law school, White clerked for U.S. Supreme Court justice Fred Vinson and then returned to Colorado to practice law. He was in private practice in Colorado for fourteen years before being selected to serve as deputy attorney general in Robert Kennedy's Justice Department. Less than a year later, in 1962, White was selected by President John F. Kennedy to take a seat on the U.S. Supreme Court. White developed a reputation on the court as a moderate. His views may have been more liberal than moderate, but compared to the overall tenor of the truly liberal Warren Court, it didn't take much judicial restraint to be considered a moderate. White authored a couple of court opinions directly impacting the issue of profiling. In 1975 he authored the Court's opinion in *Taylor v. Louisiana,* in which the systematic exclusion of women from potential jury duty was ruled unconstitutional. He also authored the opinion of the Court in *Delaware v. Prouse,* in which a police officer's stop of a motorist without an objective basis for the stop was ruled unconstitutional.

Christine Todd Whitman (1947–)

Christine Todd Whitman is well known in political circles for a variety of accomplishments. Most recently, she served as the head of the U.S. Environmental Protection Agency under President George W. Bush. She first gained wide, national notoriety, however, when she was elected governor of New Jersey in 1993, defeating incumbent Jim Florio. Whitman was considered a moderate to liberal Republican by national party standards. She was not as conservative as the national Republican Party on many social issues such as abortion. She believed sincerely in the need to cut taxes, however, as the number-one priority in putting an overall budget together. Whitman cut state income taxes by 30 percent in just two years, something for which she remains well known in New Jersey to this day. Whitman did not shy away from controversy in the criminal justice arena either. As governor, Whitman aggressively sought to end racial profiling in her state—particularly as practiced by the state police. The New Jersey State Police had been regularly accused by civil rights groups of targeting blacks for traffic stops. In 1999, that accusation gained some footing when the New Jersey attorney general concluded the same thing. Whitman, who had been a long-time supporter of law enforcement, then became very loud and visible in her opposition to racial profiling—even to the point of angering many police officers and troopers. Her crusade against profiling hit a bump in the road in 2000 when a 1996 photo of Whitman surfaced, showing her frisking a black male, spread-eagled against the wall, with a state trooper by her side. She was smiling in the picture, seemingly enjoying the encounter. Whitman was in the situation in the first place because she was engaged in a ride-along with that particular trooper. It turned out the subject, who had been stopped for acting "suspiciously," had no weapons or contraband in his possession and was not eventually arrested. Whitman received considerable criticism for her participation in this apparent act of racial profiling. Despite this public relations setback, Whitman's reforms that she forced upon the state police and the antiprofiling legislation she pushed through the legislature have remained.

James Q. Wilson (1931–)

James Q. Wilson is one of the premier criminal justice and public policy scholars of modern times. He attended the University of Redlands in southern California, graduating with a bachelor's degree in 1952. He then went on to earn a master's degree and Ph.D. at the University of Chicago in 1957 and 1959, respectively. Wilson has served on numerous commissions concerning crime and criminal justice. He has also published several books on crime, law enforcement, and other social issues. He is best known for his "broken windows" theory of crime. That theory hypothesizes that ignoring public and social order matters, such as prostitution, abandoned buildings, and small-time drug dealers, sends the message that "crime and the criminal element are welcome here." Instead, police should address those quality-of-life and social order issues. In doing so, more serious crime will be rooted out or will not emerge in those areas to begin with. The application of the broken windows theory has been varied over the years. Some departments have embraced the theory as a reason for community policing, which is a model of law enforcement geared toward solving problems—including social order problems. Others have embraced broken windows as a justification for aggressive policing strategies—that is, aggressively arresting minor offenders in hopes of uncovering or preventing more serious criminal conduct. The latter response has typically been received poorly by communities of color in urban areas.

O. W. Wilson (1900–1972)

O. W. Wilson was one of the most significant police reformers of the twentieth century. A protégé of August Vollmer in Berkeley, California (see Vollmer entry), Wilson went on to influence police professionalism greatly in his own right. Wilson served as a scholar of police studies and as a police administrator over his long career. He served as the police chief for Fullerton, California; Wichita, Kansas; and Chicago. He also served as the first dean of the School of Criminology at the University of California, Berkeley. Wilson is well known for having implemented a professional style of policing everywhere he served as chief. His leadership style is reflected in the well-known text he published in 1950 entitled *Police Administration.* In that book, Wilson argued for the true bureaucratic model of organization for police departments, including strict adherence to rules and regulations, a clear and hierarchical chain of command, division of responsibilities, and impartiality in providing service. His book also outlined principles for building relations with the public. Wilson also is noted for having refined the practice of preventative patrol, that is, fielding roving police officers in squad cars in an effort to deter crime through presence or to intercept crime in the act. He believed that aggressively policing a neighborhood or city could in fact reduce crime. This model of policing continues to be common today but is generally considered to be at odds with community policing.

6

Selected Cases and State Statutes

In this chapter, readers have an opportunity to examine a sampling of proclamations from two distinct governmental venues that have weighed in on the issue of profiling and other discriminating behaviors—legitimate and otherwise—by the criminal justice system in the United States. These two venues are the courts and state legislatures.

These two venues are included together in this chapter because when proclamations emerge from either one, considerable influence is exerted in shaping criminal justice practices and procedures. Furthermore, court rulings and state statutes often and openly draw from each other in reaching conclusions (which is kind of amazing since many think judges and politicians are too arrogant to look beyond their own incumbent wisdom).

What follows are excerpts from some of the most significant U.S. Supreme Court cases and reprints of existing state laws relating to criminal justice profiling and ancillary practices and issues.

Cases

In this section, seven selected U.S. Supreme Court cases related in some way to the issue of profiling have been highlighted. Four of the cases relate to profiling by race, one case relates to gender, one case relates to sexual orientation, and finally one case relates to the permissibility of criminal profiling generally.

Excerpts of the important and historic opinions for each case are reprinted in the pages that follow. Despite the wealth of information and the gist of the court's logic in each excerpted opinion, readers are encouraged to obtain and read these opinions in their entirety. Supreme Court decisions represent mines full of information. In its opinions, the Supreme Court explains its logic for its decisions in light of judicial history. Prior cases that relate to each decision are cited. The reliance on precedence, that is, previously decided cases, is known as stare decisis. In reading the excerpts that follow, you will see that the Supreme Court, in overturning or upholding a particular law or practice, heavily relies on what it has said in the past.

Each case below is preceded by a brief summary of the issues in the case and the Court's opinion. The opinions reprinted below represent the majority opinion of the Court in each case. Not included are the concurring or dissenting opinions. With the name of any party contained in the case heading, or with the case number, one may download majority and dissenting opinions of the U.S. Supreme Court by accessing its website at http://www.supremecourtus.gov or by going to http://www.findlaw.com.

Korematsu v. United States, 323 U.S. 214 (1944)

Korematsu was a U.S. citizen of Japanese descent during World War II. On December 8, 1941, the United States declared war on Japan, Germany, and Italy. In February 1942, President Franklin Roosevelt issued an executive order authorizing the creation of military zones that persons of Japanese descent could not enter. The motive behind the order was to prevent sabotage by people loyal to the Empire of Japan. By March, the entire West Coast of the United States to a depth of about forty miles inland was designated as such a military zone. Eventually, about 112,000 persons of Japanese descent were involuntarily relocated from the West Coast to war relocation camps run by the military. Korematsu was prosecuted for remaining in a prohibited area when relocation was ordered.

This case is significant for profiling in that it involves the single most egregious and massive act of racial profiling that ever occurred in this country—the mass internment of Japanese Americans solely on the basis of their race. In this case, the Supreme Court upheld the conviction of Korematsu for remaining in a prohibited area—namely, his home. Indeed, the mass evacuation of all Japanese Americans from the West Coast was deemed constitutional. The Court did, however, declare that the involuntary internment of Japanese Americans whose loyalty to the United States was established was unconstitutional. It ordered that such people be immediately and unconditionally released, as they posed no threat of sabotage.

JUSTICE BLACK delivered the opinion of the Court.

The petitioner, an American citizen of Japanese descent, was convicted in a federal district court for remaining in San Leandro, California, a "Military Area", contrary to Civilian Exclusion Order No. 34 of the Commanding General of the Western Command, U.S. Army, which directed that after May 9, 1942, all persons of Japanese ancestry should be excluded from that area. No question was raised as to petitioner's loyalty to the United States. The Circuit Court of Appeals affirmed, [1] and the importance of the constitutional question involved caused us to grant certiorari.

It should be noted, to begin with, that all legal restrictions which curtail the civil rights of a single racial group are immediately suspect. That is not to say that all such restrictions are unconstitutional. It is to say that courts must subject them to the most rigid scrutiny. Pressing public necessity may sometimes justify the existence of such restrictions; racial antagonism never can.

In the instant case prosecution of the petitioner was begun by information charging violation of an Act of Congress, of March 21, 1942, 56 Stat. 173, 18 U.S.C.A. 97a, which provides that

> . . . whoever shall enter, remain in, leave, or commit any act in any military area or military zone prescribed, under the authority of an Executive order of the President, by the Secretary of War, or by any military commander designated by the Secretary of War, contrary to the restrictions applicable to any such area or zone or contrary to the order of the Secretary of War or any such military commander, shall, if it appears that he knew or should have known of the existence and extent of the restrictions or order and that his act was in violation thereof, be guilty of a misdemeanor and upon conviction shall be liable to a fine of not to exceed $5,000 or to imprisonment for not more than one year, or both, for each offense. . . .

One of the series of orders and proclamations, a curfew order, which like the exclusion order here was promulgated pursuant to Executive Order 9066, subjected all persons of Japanese ancestry in prescribed West Coast military areas to remain in their residences from 8 P.M. to 6 A.M. As is the case with the exclusion order here, that prior curfew order was designed as a "protection against espionage and against sabotage." In Kiyoshi Hirabayashi v. United States, 320 U.S. 81, 63 S.Ct. 1375, we sustained a conviction obtained for violation of the curfew order. The Hirabayashi conviction and this one thus rest on the same 1942 Congressional Act and the same basic executive and military orders, all of which orders were aimed at the twin dangers of espionage and sabotage.

The 1942 Act was attacked in the Hirabayashi case as an unconstitutional delegation of power; it was contended that the curfew order and other orders on which it rested were beyond the war powers of the Congress, the military authorities and of the President, as Commander in Chief of the Army; and finally that to apply the curfew order against none but citizens of Japanese ancestry amounted to a constitutionally prohibited discrimination solely on account of race. To these questions, we gave the serious consideration which their importance justified. We upheld the curfew order as an exercise of the power of the government to take steps necessary to prevent espionage and sabotage in an area threatened by Japanese attack.

In the light of the principles we announced in the Hirabayashi case, we are unable to conclude that it was beyond the war power of Congress and the Executive to exclude those of Japanese ancestry from the West Coast war area at the time they did. True, exclusion from the area in which one's home is located is a far greater deprivation than constant confinement to the home from 8 P.M. to 6 A.M. Nothing short of apprehension by the proper military authorities of the gravest imminent danger to the public safety can constitutionally justify either. But exclusion from a threatened area, no less than curfew, has a definite and close relationship to the prevention of espionage and sabotage. The military authorities, charged with the primary responsibility of defending our shores, concluded that curfew provided inadequate protection and ordered exclusion. They did so, as pointed out in our Hirabayashi opinion, in accordance with Congressional authority to the military to say who should, and who should not, remain in the threatened areas. . . .

[In this case as with] curfew, exclusion of those of Japanese origin was deemed necessary because of the presence of an unascertained number of disloyal members of the group, most of whom we have no doubt were loyal to this country. It was because we could not reject the finding of the military authorities that it was impossible to bring about an immediate segregation of the disloyal from the loyal that we sustained the validity of the curfew order as applying to the whole group. In the instant case, temporary exclusion of the entire group was rested by the military on the same ground. The judgment that exclusion of the whole group was for the same reason a military imperative answers the contention that the exclusion was in the nature of group punishment based on antagonism to those of Japanese origin. That there were members of the group who retained loyalties to Japan has been confirmed by investigations made subsequent to the exclusion. Approximately five thousand American citizens of Japanese ancestry refused to swear unqualified allegiance to the United States and to renounce allegiance to the Japanese Emperor, and several thousand evacuees requested repatriation to Japan.

We uphold the exclusion order as of the time it was made and when the petitioner violated it. . . . In doing so, we are not unmindful of the hardships imposed by it upon a large group of American citizens. . . . But hardships are part of war, and war is an aggregation of hardships. All citizens alike, both in and out of uniform, feel the impact of war in greater or lesser measure. Citizenship has its responsibilities as well as its privileges, and in time of war the burden is always heavier. Compulsory exclusion of large groups of citizens from their homes, except under circumstances of direst emergency and peril, is inconsistent with our basic governmental institutions. But when under conditions of modern warfare our shores are threatened by hostile forces, the power to protect must be commensurate with the threatened danger. . . .

It is said that we are dealing here with the case of imprisonment of a citizen in a concentration camp solely because of his ancestry, without evidence or inquiry concerning his loyalty and good disposition towards the United States. Our task would be simple, our duty clear, were this a case involving the imprisonment of a loyal citizen in a concentration camp because of racial prejudice. Regardless of the true nature of the assembly and relocation centers—and we deem it unjustifiable to call them concentration camps with all the ugly connotations that term implies—we are dealing specifically with nothing but an exclusion order. To cast this case into outlines of racial prejudice, without reference to the real military dangers which were presented, merely confuses the issue. Korematsu was not excluded from the Military Area because of hostility to him or his race. He was excluded because we are at war with the Japanese Empire, because the properly constituted military authorities feared an invasion of our West Coast and felt constrained to take proper security measures, because they decided that the military urgency of the situation demanded that all citizens of Japanese ancestry be segregated from the West Coast temporarily, and finally, because Congress, reposing its confidence in this time of war in our military leaders—as inevitably it must—determined that they should have the power to do just this. There was evidence of disloyalty on the part of some, the military authorities considered that the need for action was great, and time was short. We cannot—by availing ourselves of the calm perspective of hindsight—now say that at that time these actions were unjustified.

Affirmed.

Hoyt v. Florida, 368 U.S. 57 (1961)

Much of the profiling debate relates to race and ethnicity. In this case, however, the debate revolves around gender. Although for over 100 years the Supreme Court had held that the systematic exclusion of a particular race from a jury was unconstitutional, there had never been the same logic extended to gender. In the present case, Gwendolyn Hoyt was convicted by an all-male jury of killing her husband. Under Florida law at the time, male citizens were automatically subject to jury duty, whereas females had to register an interest in serving on juries. In other words, women had to actively seek eligibility for jury duty. This resulted in very few women actually being listed among eligible jurors. In Hoyt's view, this amounted to the systematic exclusion of women from jury duty based on their gender.

This case was one of several in the 1950s and 1960s that sought to overturn so-called "Jane Crow" laws, that is, laws that made women essentially second-class citizens. In this case and others, the Supreme Court refused to adopt the idea that gender was a suspect class similar to race and therefore required a strict scrutiny test for any laws implicating gender. Eventually, federal and state equal rights legislation would accomplish what the Supreme Court would not do in this and other cases.

MR. JUSTICE HARLAN delivered the opinion of the Court.

Appellant, a woman, has been convicted in Hillsborough County, Florida, of second degree murder of her husband. On this appeal under 28 U.S.C. 1257 (2) from the Florida Supreme

Court's affirmance of the judgment of conviction, 119 So.2d 691, we noted probable jurisdiction, 364 U.S. 930, to consider appellant's claim that her trial before an all-male jury violated rights assured by the Fourteenth Amendment. The claim is that such jury was the product of a state jury statute which works an unconstitutional exclusion of women from jury service.

The jury law primarily in question is Fla. Stat., 1959, 40.01 (1). This Act, which requires that grand and petit jurors be taken from "male and female" citizens of the State possessed of certain qualifications, contains the following proviso:

> provided, however, that the name of no female person shall be taken for jury service unless said person has registered with the clerk of the circuit court her desire to be placed on the jury list.

Showing that since the enactment of the statute only a minimal number of women have so registered, appellant challenges the constitutionality of the statute both on its face and as applied in this case. For reasons now to follow we decide that both contentions must be rejected.

At the core of appellant's argument is the claim that the nature of the crime of which she was convicted peculiarly demanded the inclusion of persons of her own sex on the jury. She was charged with killing her husband by assaulting him with a baseball bat. An information was filed against her under Fla. Stat., 1959, 782.04, which punishes as murder in the second degree "any act imminently dangerous to another, and evincing a depraved mind regardless of human life, although without any premeditated design to effect the death of any particular individual. . . ." As described by the Florida Supreme Court, the affair occurred in the context of a marital upheaval involving, among other things, the suspected infidelity of appellant's husband, and culminating in the husband's final rejection of his wife's efforts at reconciliation. It is claimed, in substance, that women jurors would have been more understanding or compassionate than men in assessing the quality of appellant's act. . . .

Of course, these premises misconceive the scope of the right to an impartially selected jury assured by the Fourteenth Amendment. That right does not entitle one accused of crime to a jury tailored to the circumstances of the particular case, whether relating to the sex or other condition of the defendant, or to the nature of the charges to be tried. It requires only that the jury be indiscriminately drawn from among those eligible in the community for jury service, untrammelled by any arbitrary and systematic exclusions. . . .

Several observations should initially be made. We of course recognize that the Fourteenth Amendment reaches not only arbitrary class exclusions from jury service based on race or color, but also all other exclusions which "single out" any class of persons "for different treatment not based on some reasonable classification." . . .

Manifestly, Florida's 40.01 (1) does not purport to exclude women from state jury service. Rather, the statute "gives to women the privilege to serve but does not impose service as a duty." Fay v. New York, supra, at 277. It accords women an absolute exemption from jury service unless they expressly waive that privilege. This is not to say, however, that what in form may be only an exemption of a particular class of persons can in no circumstances be regarded as an exclusion of that class. Where, as here, an exemption of a class in the community is asserted to be in substance an exclusionary device, the relevant inquiry is whether the exemption itself is based on some reasonable classification and whether the manner in which it is exercisable rests on some rational foundation.

In the selection of jurors Florida has differentiated between men and women in two respects. It has given women an absolute exemption from jury duty based solely on their sex, no similar exemption obtaining as to men. And it has provided for its effectuation in a manner less onerous than that governing exemptions exercisable by men: women are not to be put on the jury list unless they have voluntarily registered for such service; men, on the other hand, even if entitled to an exemption, are to be included on the list unless they have filed a written claim of exemption as provided by law.

In neither respect can we conclude that Florida's statute is not "based on some reasonable classification," and that it is thus infected with unconstitutionality. Despite the enlightened emancipation of women from the restrictions and protections of bygone years, and their entry into many parts of community life formerly considered to be reserved to men, woman is still regarded as the center of home and family life. We cannot say that it is constitutionally impermissible for a State, acting in pursuit of the general welfare, to conclude that a woman should be relieved from the civic duty of jury service unless she herself determines that such service is consistent with her own special responsibilities. . . .

Appellant argues that whatever may have been the design of this Florida enactment, the statute in practical operation results in an exclusion of women from jury service, because women, like men, can be expected to be available for jury service only under compulsion. In this connection she points out that by 1957, when this trial took place, only some 220 women out of approximately 46,000 registered female voters in Hillsborough County—constituting about 40 per cent of the total voting population of that county [10]—had volunteered for jury duty since the limitation of jury service to males, see Hall v. Florida, 136 Fla. 644. 662–665, 187 So. 392, 400–401, was removed by 40.01 (1) in 1949. Fla. Laws 1949. c. 25,126.

This argument, however, is surely beside the point. Given the reasonableness of the classification involved in 40.01 (1), the relative paucity of women jurors does not carry the constitutional consequence appellant would have it bear. "Circumstances or chance may well dictate that no persons in a certain class will serve on a particular jury or during some particular period." Hernandez v. Texas, supra, at 482.

We cannot hold this statute as written offensive to the Fourteenth Amendment.

Appellant's attack on the statute as applied in this case fares no better.

In the year here relevant Fla. Stat., 1955, 40.10 in conjunction with 40.02 required the jury commissioners, with the aid of the local circuit court judges and clerk, to compile annually a jury list of 10,000 inhabitants qualified to be jurors. In 1957 the existing Hillsborough County list had become exhausted to the extent of some 3,000 jurors. The new list was constructed by taking over from the old list the remaining some 7,000 jurors, including 10 women, and adding some 3,000 new male jurors to build up the list to the requisite 10,000. At the time some 220 women had registered for jury duty in this county, including those taken over from the earlier list . . . .

This case in no way resembles those involving race or color in which the circumstances shown were found by this Court to compel a conclusion of purposeful discriminatory exclusions from jury service . . . There is present here neither the unfortunate atmosphere of ethnic or racial prejudices which underlay the situations depicted in those cases, nor the long course of discriminatory administrative practice which the statistical showing in each of them evinced.

In the circumstances here depicted, it indeed "taxes our credulity," Hernandez v. Texas, supra, at 482, to attribute to these administrative officials a deliberate design to exclude the very class whose eligibility for jury service the state legislature, after many years of contrary policy, had declared only a few years before. It is sufficiently evident from the record that the presence on the jury list of no more than ten or twelve women in the earlier years, and the failure to add in 1957 more women to those already on the list, are attributable not to any discriminatory motive, but to a purpose to put on the list only those women who might be expected to be qualified for service if actually called. Nor is there the slightest suggestion that the list was the product of any plan to place on it only women of a particular economic or other community or organizational group.

Finally, the disproportion of women to men on the list independently carries no constitutional significance. In the administration of the jury laws proportional class representation is not a constitutionally required factor. . . .

Finding no substantial evidence whatever in this record that Florida has arbitrarily undertaken to exclude women from jury service, a showing which it was incumbent on appellant to make, we must sustain the judgment of the Supreme Court of Florida.

Affirmed.

Delaware v. Prouse, 440 U.S. 648 (1979)

Leading up to this case in 1979, it had been a common practice in police work to conduct motor vehicle stops without any specific violation. In such cases, the stop would still have to be brief absent the emergence of evidence of a crime. But the stop itself was considered within the purview of legitimate proactive police work. If an officer thought something looked funny with a particular vehicle or occupant, then on the officer's hunch, he or she could stop the vehicle and investigate. In the present case, a police officer pulled over a vehicle because, in the officer's words, the officer wasn't doing anything else, had no calls waiting, and thought he would check the identification and registration.

This practice of pulling over vehicles solely at the discretion of the officer, even when no observed violation existed, certainly had its critics. However noble it was for police officers to be proactive in their fight against crime, the practice litigated in Delaware v. Prouse *certainly lent itself to abuse—particularly against individuals who matched whatever personal profiles officers held regarding likely offenders. For many officers, such profiles included young adult males of color. Hence, this case was particularly important for criminal profiling in that the Supreme Court here first noted that random stops of vehicles simply to "check things out" without articulable suspicion of criminal activity are unconstitutional. Neither the whim of the officer, nor the mere status of driving one's vehicle on a public road, would qualify as a legitimate basis for pulling a vehicle over.*

The logic the Supreme Court followed in this case sets up the Whren *decision nearly two decades later, in which the Court emphasized the fact that an officer must have reasonable suspicion of a violation to pull over a vehicle and that reasonable suspicion is the only element that matters with regard to the legality of a stop.*

MR. JUSTICE WHITE delivered the opinion of the Court.

The question is whether it is an unreasonable seizure under the Fourth and Fourteenth Amendments to stop an automobile, being driven on a public highway, for the purpose of checking the driving license of the operator and the registration of the car, where there is neither probable cause to believe nor reasonable suspicion that the car is being driven contrary to the laws governing the operation of motor vehicles or that either the car or any of its occupants is subject to seizure or detention in connection with the violation of any other applicable law.

At 7:20 P.M. on November 30, 1976, a New Castle County, Del., patrolman in a police cruiser stopped the automobile occupied by respondent. [1] The patrolman smelled marihuana smoke as he was walking toward the stopped vehicle, and he seized marihuana in plain view on the car floor. Respondent was subsequently indicted for illegal possession of a controlled substance. At a hearing on respondent's motion to suppress the marihuana seized as a result of the stop, the patrolman testified that prior to stopping the vehicle he had observed neither traffic or equipment violations nor any suspicious activity, and that he made the stop only in order to check the driver's license and registration. The patrolman was not acting pursuant to any standards, guidelines, or procedures pertaining to document spot checks, promulgated by either his department or the State Attorney General. Characterizing the stop as "routine," the patrolman explained, "I saw the car in the area and wasn't answering any complaints, so I decided to pull them off." The trial court granted the motion to suppress, finding the stop and detention to have been wholly capricious and therefore violative of the Fourth Amendment.

The Delaware Supreme Court affirmed, noting first that "[t]he issue of the legal validity of systematic, roadblock-type stops of a number of vehicles for license and vehicle registration check is not now before the Court." . . . The court held that "a random stop of a motorist in the absence of specific articulable facts which justify the stop by indicating a reasonable suspicion that a violation of the law has occurred is constitutionally impermissible and violative of the Fourth and Fourteenth Amendments to the United States Constitution." . . .

The Fourth and Fourteenth Amendments are implicated in this case because stopping an automobile and detaining its occupants constitute a "seizure" within the meaning of those Amendments, even though the purpose of the stop is limited and the resulting detention quite brief. . . . The essential purpose of the proscriptions in the Fourth Amendment is to impose a standard of "reasonableness" upon the exercise of discretion by government officials, including law enforcement agents, in order "'to safeguard the privacy and security of individuals against arbitrary invasions. . . .'" Thus, the permissibility of a particular law enforcement practice is judged by balancing its intrusion on the individual's Fourth Amendment interests against its promotion of legitimate governmental interests. Implemented in this manner, the reasonableness standard usually requires, at a minimum, that the facts upon which an intrusion is based be capable of measurement against "an objective standard," whether this be probable cause or a less stringent test. In those situations in which the balance of interests precludes insistence upon "some quantum of individualized suspicion," other safeguards are generally relied upon to assure that the individual's reasonable expectation of privacy is not "subject to the discretion of the official in the field." . . .

In this case, however, the State of Delaware urges that patrol officers be subject to no constraints in deciding which automobiles shall be stopped for a license and registration check because the State's interest in discretionary spot checks as a means of ensuring the safety of its roadways outweighs the resulting intrusion on the privacy and security of the persons detained. . . .

The question remains, however, whether in the service of these important ends [particularly, safety on the state roadways]

the discretionary spot check is a sufficiently productive mechanism to justify the intrusion upon Fourth Amendment interests
which such stops entail. On the record before us, that question
must be answered in the negative. Given the alternative mechanisms available, both those in use and those that might be
adopted, we are unconvinced that the incremental contribution
to highway safety of the random spot check justifies the practice
under the Fourth Amendment.

The marginal contribution to roadway safety possibly resulting from a system of spot checks cannot justify subjecting every
occupant of every vehicle on the roads to a seizure—limited in
magnitude compared to other intrusions but nonetheless constitutionally cognizable—at the unbridled discretion of law
enforcement officials. To insist neither upon an appropriate factual basis for suspicion directed at a particular automobile nor
upon some other substantial and objective standard or rule to
govern the exercise of discretion "would invite intrusions upon
constitutionally guaranteed rights based on nothing more substantial than inarticulate hunches. . . ."

An individual operating or traveling in an automobile does
not lose all reasonable expectation of privacy simply because the
automobile and its use are subject to government regulation.
Automobile travel is a basic, pervasive, and often necessary
mode of transportation to and from one's home, workplace, and
leisure activities. Many people spend more hours each day traveling in cars than walking on the streets. Undoubtedly, many find
a greater sense of security and privacy in traveling in an automobile than they do in exposing themselves by pedestrian or
other modes of travel. Were the individual subject to unfettered
governmental intrusion every time he entered an automobile, the
security guaranteed by the Fourth Amendment would be seriously circumscribed. As Terry v. Ohio, supra, recognized, people
are not shorn of all Fourth Amendment protection when they
step from their homes onto the public sidewalks. Nor are they
shorn of those interests when they step from the sidewalks into
their automobiles. . . .

Accordingly, we hold that except in those situations in which
there is at least articulable and reasonable suspicion that a
motorist is unlicensed or that an automobile is not registered, or
that either the vehicle or an occupant is otherwise subject to
seizure for violation of law, stopping an automobile and detaining the driver in order to check his driver's license and the regis-

tration of the automobile are unreasonable under the Fourth Amendment. This holding does not preclude the State of Delaware or other States from developing methods for spot checks that involve less intrusion or that do not involve the unconstrained exercise of discretion. [26] Questioning of all oncoming traffic at roadblock-type stops is one possible alternative. We hold only that persons in automobiles on public roadways may not for that reason alone have their travel and privacy interfered with at the unbridled discretion of police officers. The judgment below is affirmed.

So ordered.

Bowers v. Hardwick, 478 U.S. 186 (1986)

In this case, Hardwick, a male, was charged under the criminal code of the State of Georgia for committing sodomy with another adult male. The act was consensual and took place in Hardwick's bedroom at his home. Hardwick believed that the Georgia statute barring homosexual conduct was unconstitutional and filed suit in federal court. The Federal District Court hearing the case upheld the constitutionality of the statute. Hardwick appealed that decision and won a victory with the Eleventh Circuit Court of Appeals. The Appellate Court ruled that the Georgia statute against sodomy was indeed unconstitutional as it violated the right of privacy developed and affirmed by the U.S. Supreme Court in several previous cases ... most notably Griswold v. Connecticut *(1965). The Supreme Court, however, ruled with a five-to-four margin that the U.S. Constitution does not grant a fundamental right upon homosexuals to engage in homosexual acts. In short, the Court affirmed a state's right to criminalize homosexual conduct. This obviously posed some serious problems for those concerned about discrimination against gays by the criminal justice system. It is difficult for advocates against profiling on the basis of sexual orientation to get a foothold when the very acts associated with gay living remain criminalized with the Supreme Court's blessing.*

This case represented settled law for seventeen years until the Supreme Court found in Lawrence v. Texas *(2003) that a constitutional right to sexual privacy exists for all consenting adults of any sex and of any sexual orientation.*

JUSTICE WHITE delivered the opinion of the Court.

In August 1982, respondent Hardwick (hereafter respondent) was charged with violating the Georgia statute criminalizing sodomy by committing that act with another adult male in the bedroom of respondent's home. After a preliminary hearing, the District Attorney decided not to present the matter to the grand jury unless further evidence developed.

Respondent then brought suit in the Federal District Court, challenging the constitutionality of the statute insofar as it criminalized consensual sodomy. He asserted that he was a practicing homosexual, that the Georgia sodomy statute, as administered by the defendants, placed him in imminent danger of arrest, and that the statute for several reasons violates the Federal Constitution. The District Court granted the defendants' motion to dismiss for failure to state a claim, relying on Doe v. Commonwealth's Attorney for the City of Richmond. . . .

This case does not require a judgment on whether laws against sodomy between consenting adults in general, or between homosexuals in particular, are wise or desirable. It raises no question about the right or propriety of state legislative decisions to repeal their laws that criminalize homosexual sodomy, or of state-court decisions invalidating those laws on state constitutional grounds. The issue presented is whether the Federal Constitution confers a fundamental right upon homosexuals to engage in sodomy and hence invalidates the laws of the many States that still make such conduct illegal and have done so for a very long time. The case also calls for some judgment about the limits of the Court's role in carrying out its constitutional mandate.

We first register our disagreement with the Court of Appeals and with respondent that the Court's prior cases have construed the Constitution to confer a right of privacy that extends to homosexual sodomy and for all intents and purposes have decided this case. The reach of this line of cases was sketched in Carey v. Population Services International, 431 U.S. 678, 685 (1977). Pierce v. Society of Sisters, 268 U.S. 510 (1925), and Meyer v. Nebraska, 262 U.S. 390 (1923), were described as dealing with child rearing and education; Prince v. Massachusetts, 321 U.S. 158 (1944), with family relationships; Skinner v. Oklahoma ex rel. Williamson, 316 U.S. 535 (1942), with procreation; Loving v. Virginia, 388 U.S. 1 (1967), with marriage; Griswold v. Connecticut, supra, and Eisenstadt v. Baird, supra, with contraception; and Roe v. Wade, 410 U.S. 113 (1973), with abortion. The latter three cases were interpreted as construing the Due Process Clause of the Fourteenth Amendment to confer a fundamental individual right to decide whether or not to beget or bear a child. Carey v. Population Services International. . . .

Accepting the decisions in these cases and the above description of them, we think it evident that none of the rights announced in those cases bears any resemblance to the claimed constitutional right of homosexuals to engage in acts of sodomy that is asserted in this case. No connection between family, marriage, or procreation on the one hand and homosexual activity on the other has been demonstrated, either by the Court of Appeals or by respondent. Moreover, any claim that these cases nevertheless stand for the proposition that any kind of private sexual conduct between consenting adults is constitutionally insulated from state proscription is unsupportable. Indeed, the Court's opinion in Carey twice asserted that the privacy right, which the Griswold line of cases found to be one of the protections provided by the Due Process Clause, did not reach so far.

Precedent aside, however, respondent would have us announce, as the Court of Appeals did, a fundamental right to engage in homosexual sodomy. This we are quite unwilling to do. It is true that despite the language of the Due Process Clauses of the Fifth and Fourteenth Amendments, which appears to focus only on the processes by which life, liberty, or property is taken, the cases are legion in which those Clauses have been interpreted to have substantive content, subsuming rights that to a great extent are immune from federal or state regulation or proscription. Among such cases are those recognizing rights that have little or no textual support in the constitutional language. Meyer, Prince, and Pierce fall in this category, as do the privacy cases from Griswold to Carey.

Striving to assure itself and the public that announcing rights not readily identifiable in the Constitution's text involves much more than the imposition of the Justices' own choice of values on the States and the Federal Government, the Court has sought to identify the nature of the rights qualifying for heightened·judicial protection. In Palko v. Connecticut (1937), it was said that this category includes those fundamental liberties that are "implicit in the concept of ordered liberty," such that "neither liberty nor justice would exist if [they] were sacrificed."

It is obvious to us that neither of these formulations would extend a fundamental right to homosexuals to engage in acts of consensual sodomy. Proscriptions against that conduct have ancient roots. Sodomy was a criminal offense at common law and was forbidden by the laws of the original 13 States when they ratified the Bill of Rights. In 1868, when the Fourteenth Amendment was ratified, all but 5 of the 37 States in the Union had criminal sodomy laws. In fact, until 1961, all 50 States outlawed sodomy, and today, 24 States and the District of Columbia continue to provide criminal penalties for sodomy performed in private and between consenting adults. Against this background, to claim that a right to engage in such conduct is "deeply rooted in this Nation's history and tradition" or "implicit in the concept of ordered liberty" is, at best, facetious.

Nor are we inclined to take a more expansive view of our authority to discover new fundamental rights imbedded in the Due Process Clause. The Court is most vulnerable and comes nearest to illegitimacy when it deals with judge-made constitutional law having little or no cognizable roots in the language or design of the Constitution.

Respondent, however, asserts that the result should be different where the homosexual conduct occurs in the privacy of the home. He relies on Stanley v. Georgia, 394 U.S. 557 (1969), where the Court held that the First Amendment prevents conviction for possessing and reading obscene material in the privacy of one's home: "If the First Amendment means anything, it means that a State has no business telling a man, sitting alone in his house, what books he may read or what films he may watch."

Stanley did protect conduct that would not have been protected outside the home, and it partially prevented the enforcement of state obscenity laws; but the decision was firmly grounded in the First Amendment. The right pressed upon us here has no similar support in the text of the Constitution, and it does not qualify for recognition under the prevailing principles for construing the Fourteenth Amendment. Its limits are also difficult to discern. Plainly enough, otherwise illegal conduct is not always immunized whenever it occurs in the home. Victimless crimes, such as the possession and use of illegal drugs, do not escape the law where they are committed at home.

Even if the conduct at issue here is not a fundamental right, respondent asserts that there must be a rational basis for the law and that there is none in this case other than the presumed belief of a majority of the electorate in Georgia that homosexual sodomy is immoral and unacceptable. This is said to be an inadequate rationale to support the law. The law, however, is constantly based on notions of morality, and if all laws representing essentially moral choices are to be invalidated under the Due Process Clause, the courts will be very busy indeed. Even respondent makes no such claim, but insists that majority sentiments about the morality of homosexuality should be declared inadequate. We do not agree, and are unpersuaded that the sodomy laws of some 25 States should be invalidated on this basis. [8]

Accordingly, the judgment of the Court of Appeals is Reversed.

Batson v. Kentucky, 476 U.S. 79 (1986)

The Supreme Court's decision in this case represents an extension of the long-established position of the Court that systematic exclusion of people of a particular race from jury duty is a violation of the Constitution. Here, the Court applied this principle to peremptory challenges. Prosecutors and defense attorneys are both granted a limited number of peremptory challenges (that is, the opportunity to strike a potential juror from the jury pool for no particular reason whatsoever) for any given trial. Traditionally, the right of criminal lawyers on both sides of the case to exercise their peremptory challenges without any oversight has always been upheld.

In Batson, *however, the Supreme Court said that exclusion of people from the jury, even through a peremptory challenge, was not constitutional if the exclusion was because of race. The Supreme Court did not require that attorneys have a good reason for excluding people. Indeed, the reasons could be quite silly—as always—except that the reason had to be race neutral. This opinion represents one of the Court's more contemporary statements outlawing racial profiling during the trial process.*

JUSTICE POWELL delivered the opinion of the Court.

This case requires us to reexamine that portion of Swain v. Alabama, 380 U.S. 202 (1965), concerning the evidentiary burden placed on a criminal defendant who claims that he has been denied equal protection through the State's use of peremptory challenges to exclude members of his race from the petit jury.

Petitioner, a black man, was indicted in Kentucky on charges of second-degree burglary and receipt of stolen goods. On the first day of trial in Jefferson Circuit Court, the judge conducted voir dire examination of the venire, excused certain jurors for cause, and permitted the parties to exercise peremptory challenges. The prosecutor used his peremptory challenges to strike all four black persons on the venire, and a jury composed only of white persons was selected. Defense counsel moved to discharge the jury before it was sworn on the ground that the prosecutor's removal of the black veniremen violated petitioner's rights under the Sixth and Fourteenth Amendments to a jury drawn from a cross section of the community, and under the Fourteenth Amendment to equal protection of the laws. Counsel requested a hearing on his motion. Without expressly ruling on the request for a hearing, the trial judge observed that the parties were entitled to use their peremptory challenges to "strike anybody they want to." The judge then denied petitioner's motion, reasoning that the cross-section requirement applies only to selection of the venire and not to selection of the petit jury itself.

The jury convicted petitioner on both counts.

In Swain v. Alabama, this Court recognized that a "State's purposeful or deliberate denial to Negroes on account of race of participation as jurors in the administration of justice violates the Equal Protection Clause." This principle has been "consistently and repeatedly" reaffirmed in numerous decisions of this Court both preceding and following Swain. We reaffirm the principle today.

More than a century ago, the Court decided that the State denies a black defendant equal protection of the laws when it puts him on trial before a jury from which members of his race have been purposefully excluded. Strauder v. West Virginia. That decision laid the foundation for the Court's unceasing efforts to eradicate racial discrimination in the procedures used to select the venire from which individual jurors are drawn. In Strauder, the Court explained that the central concern of the recently ratified Fourteenth Amendment was to put an end to governmental discrimination on account of race. Exclusion of black citizens from service as jurors constitutes a primary example of the evil the Fourteenth Amendment was designed to cure. . . .

Purposeful racial discrimination in selection of the venire violates a defendant's right to equal protection because it denies him the protection that a trial by jury is intended to secure. "The very idea of a jury is a body . . . composed of the peers or equals of the person whose rights it is selected or summoned to determine; that is, of his neighbors, fellows, associates, persons having the same legal status in society as that which he holds." The petit jury has occupied a central position in our system of justice by safeguarding a person accused of crime against the arbitrary exercise of power by prosecutor or judge. Those on the venire must be "indifferently chosen" to secure the defendant's right under the Fourteenth Amendment to "protection of life and liberty against race or color prejudice."

Racial discrimination in selection of jurors harms not only the accused whose life or liberty they are summoned to try. Competence to serve as a juror ultimately depends on an assessment of individual qualifications and ability impartially to consider evidence presented at a trial. A person's race simply "is unrelated to his fitness as a juror." (Frankfurter, J., dissenting). As long ago as Strauder, therefore, the Court recognized that by denying a person participation in jury service on account of his race, the State unconstitutionally discriminated against the excluded juror.

The harm from discriminatory jury selection extends beyond that inflicted on the defendant and the excluded juror to touch the entire community. Selection procedures that purposefully exclude black persons from juries undermine public confidence in the fairness of our system of justice. Discrimination within the judicial system is most pernicious because it is "a stimulant to that race prejudice which is an impediment to securing to [black citizens] that equal justice which the law aims to secure to all others." . . .

In Strauder, the Court invalidated a state statute that provided that only white men could serve as jurors. We can be confident that no State now has such a law. The Constitution requires, however, that we look beyond the face of the statute defining juror qualifications and also consider challenged selection practices to afford "protection against action of the State through its administrative officers in effecting the prohibited discrimination." Thus, the Court has found a denial of equal protection where the procedures implementing a neutral statute operated to exclude persons from the venire on racial grounds, and has made clear that the Constitution prohibits all forms of purposeful racial discrimination in selection of jurors. While decisions of this Court have been concerned largely with discrimination during selection of the venire, the principles announced there also forbid discrimination on account of race in selection of the petit jury. Since the Fourteenth Amendment protects an accused throughout the proceedings bringing him to justice, the State may not draw up its jury lists pursuant to neutral procedures but then resort to discrimination at "other stages in the selection process."

Accordingly, the component of the jury selection process at issue here, the State's privilege to strike individual jurors through peremptory challenges, is subject to the commands of the Equal Protection Clause. Although a prosecutor ordinarily is entitled to exercise permitted peremptory challenges "for any reason at all, as long as that reason is related to his view concerning the outcome" of the case to be tried . . . the Equal Protection Clause forbids the prosecutor to challenge potential jurors solely on account of their race or on the assumption that black jurors as a group will be unable impartially to consider the State's case against a black defendant. . . .

Since the ultimate issue is whether the State has discriminated in selecting the defendant's venire, however, the defendant may establish a prima facie case "in other ways than by evidence of long-continued unexplained absence" of members of his race "from many panels." Cassell v. Texas, 339 U.S. 282, 290 (1950) (plurality opinion). In cases involving the venire, this Court has found a prima facie case on proof that members of the defendant's race were substantially underrepresented on the venire from which his jury was drawn, and that the venire was selected under a practice providing "the opportunity for discrimination." Whitus v. Georgia, supra, at 552; see Castaneda v. Partida, supra, at 494; Washington v. Davis, supra, at 241; Alexander v. Louisiana, supra, at 629–631. This combination of factors raises the necessary inference of purposeful discrimination because the Court has declined to attribute to chance the absence of black citizens on a particular jury array where the selection mechanism is subject to abuse. When circumstances suggest the need, the trial court must undertake a "factual inquiry" that "takes into account all possible explanatory factors" in the particular case. Alexander v. Louisiana, supra, at 630.

Thus, since the decision in Swain, this Court has recognized that a defendant may make a prima facie showing of purposeful racial discrimination in selection of the venire by relying solely on the facts concerning its selection in his case. These decisions are in accordance with the proposition, articulated in Arlington Heights v. Metropolitan Housing Development Corp., that "a consistent pattern of official racial discrimination" is not "a necessary predicate to a violation of the Equal Protection Clause. A single invidiously discriminatory governmental act" is not "immunized by the absence of such discrimination in the making of other comparable decisions." 429 U.S., at 266, n. 14. For evidentiary requirements to dictate that "several must suffer discrimination" before one could object, McCray v. New York, 461 U.S., at 965 (MARSHALL, J., dissenting from denial of certiorari), would be inconsistent with the promise of equal protection to all. [19]

In deciding whether [purposeful discrimination in jury selection has taken place], the trial court should consider all relevant circumstances. For example, a "pattern" of strikes against black jurors included in the particular venire might give rise to an inference of discrimination. Similarly, the prosecutor's questions and statements during voir dire examination and in exercising his challenges may support or refute an inference of discriminatory purpose. These examples are merely illustrative. We have confidence that trial judges, experienced in supervising voir dire, will be able to decide if the circumstances concerning the prosecutor's use of peremptory challenges creates a prima facie case of discrimination against black jurors.

Once the defendant makes a prima facie showing [of discrimination], the burden shifts to the State to come forward with a neutral explanation for challenging black jurors. Though this requirement imposes a limitation in some cases on the full peremptory character of the historic challenge, we emphasize that the prosecutor's explanation need not rise to the level justifying exercise of a challenge for cause. But the prosecutor may not rebut the defendant's prima facie case of discrimination by stating merely that he challenged jurors of the defendant's race on the assumption—or his intuitive judgment—that they would be partial to the defendant because of their shared race.

The State contends that our holding will eviscerate the fair trial values served by the peremptory challenge. Conceding that the Constitution does not guarantee a right to peremptory challenges and that Swain did state that their use ultimately is subject to the strictures of equal protection, the State argues that the privilege of unfettered exercise of the challenge is of vital importance to the criminal justice system.

While we recognize, of course, that the peremptory challenge occupies an important position in our trial procedures, we do not agree that our decision today will undermine the contribution the challenge generally makes to the administration of justice. The reality of practice, amply reflected in many state- and federal-court opinions, shows that the challenge may be, and unfortunately at times has been, used to discriminate against black jurors. By requiring trial courts to be sensitive to the racially discriminatory use of peremptory challenges, our decision enforces the mandate of equal protection and furthers the ends of justice. In view of the heterogeneous population of our Nation, public respect for our criminal justice system and the rule of law will be strengthened if we ensure that no citizen is disqualified from jury service because of his race. . . .

In this case, petitioner made a timely objection to the prosecutor's removal of all black persons on the venire. Because the trial court flatly rejected the objection without requiring the prosecutor to give an explanation for his action, we remand this case for further proceedings. If the trial court decides that the facts establish, prima facie, purposeful discrimination and the prosecutor does not come forward with a neutral explanation for his action, our precedents require that petitioner's conviction be reversed.

It is so ordered.

United States v. Sokolow, 490 U.S. 1 (1989)

The case of Sokolow was heard by the Supreme Court during the height of the drug war in the United States. Indeed, as discussed earlier in the book, the use of profiles to identify potential criminals was expanded and popularized by the successful use of drug courier profiles. Such a profile was used in this case.

Here, the Supreme Court made it clear that profiling is a permissible police tactic for generating the reasonable suspicion required for an investigatory stop and detention. It reaffirmed its position in Prouse *that the discretionary reliance on hunches is not enough for the officer to detain. Profiles that are built upon articulable facts and probabilities and that do not rely primarily on the protected status of a suspect—particularly race or ethnicity—are however acceptable and indeed valuable.*

CHIEF JUSTICE REHNQUIST delivered the opinion of the Court.

Respondent Andrew Sokolow was stopped by Drug Enforcement Administration (DEA) agents upon his arrival at Honolulu International Airport. The agents found 1,063 grams of cocaine in his carry-on luggage. When respondent was stopped, the agents knew, inter alia, that (1) he paid $2,100 for two airplane tickets from a roll of $20 bills; (2) he traveled under a name that did not match the name under which his telephone number was listed; (3) his original destination was Miami, a source city for illicit drugs; (4) he stayed in Miami for only 48 hours, even though a round-trip flight from Honolulu to Miami takes 20 hours; (5) he appeared nervous during his trip; and (6) he checked none of his luggage. A divided panel of the United States Court of Appeals for the Ninth Circuit held that the DEA agents did not have a reasonable suspicion to stop respondent, as required by the Fourth Amendment. We take the contrary view.

This case involves a typical attempt to smuggle drugs through one of the Nation's airports. On a Sunday in July 1984, respondent went to the United Airlines ticket counter at Honolulu Airport, where he purchased two round-trip tickets for a flight to Miami leaving later that day. The tickets were purchased in the names of "Andrew Kray" and "Janet Norian" and had open return dates. Respondent paid $2,100 for the tickets from a large roll of $20 bills, which appeared to contain a total of $4,000. He also gave the ticket agent his home telephone number. The ticket agent noticed that respondent seemed nervous; he was about 25 years old; he was dressed in a black jumpsuit and wore gold jewelry; and he was accompanied by a woman, who turned out to be Janet Norian. Neither respondent nor his companion checked any of their four pieces of luggage.

After the couple left for their flight, the ticket agent informed Officer John McCarthy of the Honolulu Police Department of respondent's cash purchase of tickets to Miami. Officer McCarthy determined that the telephone number respondent gave to the ticket agent was subscribed to a "Karl Herman," who resided at 348-A Royal Hawaiian Avenue in Honolulu. Unbeknownst to McCarthy (and later to the DEA agents), respondent was Herman's roommate. The ticket agent identified respondent's voice on the answering machine at Herman's number. Officer McCarthy was unable to find any listing under the name "Andrew Kray" in Hawaii. McCarthy subsequently learned that return reservations from Miami to Honolulu had been made in the names of Kray and Norian, with their arrival scheduled for July 25, three days after respondent and his companion had left. He also learned that Kray and Norian were scheduled to make stopovers in Denver and Los Angeles.

On July 25, during the stopover in Los Angeles, DEA agents identified respondent. He "appeared to be very nervous and was looking all around the waiting area." App. 43–44. Later that day, at 6:30 P. M., respondent and Norian arrived in Honolulu. As before, they had not checked their luggage. Respondent was still

wearing a black jumpsuit and gold jewelry. The couple pro-
ceeded directly to the street and tried to hail a cab, where Agent
Richard Kempshall and three other DEA agents approached
them. Kempshall displayed his credentials, grabbed respondent
by the arm, and moved him back onto the sidewalk. Kempshall
asked respondent for his airline ticket and identification; respondent said that he had neither. He told the agents that his name
was "Sokolow," but that he was traveling under his mother's
maiden name, "Kray."

Respondent and Norian were escorted to the DEA office at the
airport. There, the couple's luggage was examined by "Donker," a
narcotics detector dog, which alerted on respondent's brown
shoulder bag. The agents arrested respondent. He was advised of
his constitutional rights and declined to make any statements. The
agents obtained a warrant to search the shoulder bag. They found
no illicit drugs, but the bag did contain several suspicious documents indicating respondent's involvement in drug trafficking.
The agents had Donker reexamine the remaining luggage, and this
time the dog alerted on a medium-sized Louis Vuitton bag. By
now, it was 9:30 P.M., too late for the agents to obtain a second warrant. They allowed respondent to leave for the night, but kept his
luggage. The next morning, after a second dog confirmed
Donker's alert, the agents obtained a warrant and found 1,063
grams of cocaine inside the bag.

Respondent was indicted for possession with the intent to
distribute cocaine in violation of 21 U.S.C. 841(a)(1). The United
States District Court for Hawaii denied his motion to suppress
the cocaine and other evidence seized from his luggage, finding
that the DEA agents had a reasonable suspicion that he was
involved in drug trafficking when they stopped him at the airport. Respondent then entered a conditional plea of guilty to the
offense charged.

The United States Court of Appeals for the Ninth Circuit
reversed respondent's conviction by a divided vote, holding that
the DEA agents did not have a reasonable suspicion to justify the
stop. The majority divided the facts bearing on reasonable suspicion into two categories. In the first category, the majority placed
facts describing "ongoing criminal activity," such as the use of an
alias or evasive movement through an airport; the majority
believed that at least one such factor was always needed to support a finding of reasonable suspicion. In the second category, it
placed facts describing "personal characteristics" of drug couriers,

such as the cash payment for tickets, a short trip to a major source city for drugs, nervousness, type of attire, and unchecked luggage. The majority believed that such characteristics, "shared by drug couriers and the public at large," were only relevant if there was evidence of ongoing criminal behavior and the Government offered "[e]mpirical documentation" that the combination of facts at issue did not describe the behavior of "significant numbers of innocent persons." Ibid. Applying this two-part test to the facts of this case, the majority found that there was no evidence of ongoing criminal behavior, and thus that the agents' stop was impermissible. The dissenting judge took the view that the majority's approach was "overly mechanistic" and "contrary to the case-by-case determination of reasonable articulable suspicion based on all the facts." We granted certiorari to review the decision of the Court of Appeals because of its serious implications for the enforcement of the federal narcotics laws. We now reverse.

The Court of Appeals held that the DEA agents seized respondent when they grabbed him by the arm and moved him back onto the sidewalk. The Government does not challenge that conclusion, and we assume—without deciding—that a stop occurred here. Our decision, then, turns on whether the agents had a reasonable suspicion that respondent was engaged in wrongdoing when they encountered him on the sidewalk. In Terry v. Ohio, we held that the police can stop and briefly detain a person for investigative purposes if the officer has a reasonable suspicion supported by articulable facts that criminal activity "may be afoot," even if the officer lacks probable cause.

The officer, of course, must be able to articulate something more than an "inchoate and unparticularized suspicion or 'hunch.'" The Fourth Amendment requires "some minimal level of objective justification" for making the stop. INS v. Delgado (1984). That level of suspicion is considerably less than proof of wrongdoing by a preponderance of the evidence. We have held that probable cause means "a fair probability that contraband or evidence of a crime will be found," and the level of suspicion required for a Terry stop is obviously less demanding than that for probable cause.

The concept of reasonable suspicion, like probable cause, is not "readily, or even usefully, reduced to a neat set of legal rules." We think the Court of Appeals' effort to refine and elaborate the requirements of "reasonable suspicion" in this case creates unnecessary difficulty in dealing with one of the relatively simple concepts embodied in the Fourth Amendment. In evaluating the validity of a stop such as this, we must consider "the totality of the circumstances—the whole picture." As we said in Cortez:

> The process does not deal with hard certainties, but with probabilities. Long before the law of probabilities was articulated as such, practical people formulated certain common-sense conclusions about human behavior; jurors as factfinders are permitted to do the same—and so are law enforcement officers.

The rule enunciated by the Court of Appeals, in which evidence available to an officer is divided into evidence of "ongoing criminal behavior," on the one hand, and "probabilistic" evidence, on the other, is not in keeping with the quoted statements from our decisions. It also seems to us to draw a sharp line between types of evidence, the probative value of which varies only in degree. The Court of Appeals classified evidence of traveling under an alias, or evidence that the suspect took an evasive or erratic path through an airport, as meeting the test for showing "ongoing criminal activity." But certainly instances are conceivable in which traveling under an alias would not reflect ongoing criminal activity: for example, a person who wished to travel to a hospital or clinic for an operation and wished to conceal that fact. One taking an evasive path through an airport might be seeking to avoid a confrontation with an angry acquaintance or with a creditor. This is not to say that each of these types of evidence is not highly probative, but they do not have the sort of ironclad significance attributed to them by the Court of Appeals.

On the other hand, the factors in this case that the Court of Appeals treated as merely "probabilistic" also have probative significance. Paying $2,100 in cash for two airplane tickets is out of the ordinary, and it is even more out of the ordinary to pay that sum from a roll of $20 bills containing nearly twice that amount of cash. Most business travelers, we feel confident, purchase airline tickets by credit card or check so as to have a record for tax or business purposes, and few vacationers carry with them thousands of dollars in $20 bills. We also think the agents had a reasonable ground to believe that respondent was traveling under an alias; the evidence was by no means conclusive, but it was sufficient to warrant consideration. [3] While a trip from Honolulu to Miami, standing alone, is not a cause for any sort of suspicion, here there was more: surely few residents of Honolulu travel from that city for 20 hours to spend 48 hours in Miami during the month of July.

We do not agree with respondent that our analysis is somehow changed by the agents' belief that his behavior was consistent with one of the DEA's "drug courier profiles." [6] Brief for Respondent 14–21. A court sitting to determine the existence of reasonable suspicion must require the agent to articulate the factors leading to that conclusion, but the fact that these factors may be set forth in a "profile" does not somehow detract from their evidentiary significance as seen by a trained agent.

We hold that the agents had a reasonable basis to suspect that respondent was transporting illegal drugs on these facts. The judgment of the Court of Appeals is therefore reversed, and the case is remanded for further proceedings consistent with our decision.

It is so ordered.

Whren et al. v. United States (1996)

No case has received as much attention within the context of discussions about racial profiling, and other unlawful profiling, as has the present case. The facts in Whren *are as follows: Plainclothes police officers were on patrol in a neighborhood considered to be a "high drug area." The officers observed a vehicle in which Whren was a passenger stopped at a stop sign for an unusually long period of time. The vehicle then made the turn without signaling and sped off. The police officers stopped the vehicle, using the unlawful turn as the basis for the stop. Upon approaching the vehicle, officers observed crack cocaine being held by passenger Whren.*

Whren argued that the officers used the minor traffic violation to investigate other crimes for which they had no probable cause. He urged the Supreme Court to require demonstration that a reasonable officer would make a traffic stop for the purpose of enforcing the traffic violation in question in any given traffic stop situation. The Supreme Court ruled unanimously that the traffic stop and subsequent arrest and prosecution of Whren were legal. Where probable cause exists that a traffic violation has occurred, police are not required to demonstrate that they did not have ulterior motives in the stop.

JUSTICE SCALIA delivered the opinion of the Court.

In this case we decide whether the temporary detention of a motorist who the police have probable cause to believe has committed a civil traffic violation is inconsistent with the Fourth Amendment's prohibition against unreasonable seizures unless a reasonable officer would have been motivated to stop the car by a desire to enforce the traffic laws.

On the evening of June 10, 1993, plainclothes vice-squad officers of the District of Columbia Metropolitan Police Department were patrolling a "high drug area" of the city in an unmarked car. Their suspicions were aroused when they passed a dark Pathfinder truck with temporary license plates and youthful occupants waiting at a stop sign, the driver looking down into the lap of the passenger at his right. The truck remained stopped at the intersection for what seemed an unusually long time—more than 20 seconds. When the police car executed a U-turn in order to head back toward the truck, the Pathfinder turned suddenly to its right, without signaling, and sped off at an "unreasonable" speed. The policemen followed, and in a short while overtook the Pathfinder when it stopped behind other traffic at a red light. They pulled up alongside, and Officer Ephraim Soto stepped out and approached the driver's door, identifying himself as a police officer and directing the driver, petitioner Brown, to put the vehicle in park. When Soto drew up to the driver's window, he immediately observed two large plastic bags of what appeared to be crack cocaine in petitioner Whren's hands. Petitioners were arrested, and quantities of several types of illegal drugs were retrieved from the vehicle.

Petitioners were charged in a four-count indictment with violating various federal drug laws, including 21 U. S. C. Section(s) 844(a) and 860(a). At a pretrial suppression hearing, they challenged the legality of the stop and the resulting seizure of the drugs. They argued that the stop had not been justified by probable cause to believe, or even reasonable suspicion, that petitioners were engaged in illegal drug-dealing activity; and that Officer Soto's asserted ground for approaching the vehicle—to give the driver a warning concerning traffic violations—was pretextual. The District Court denied the suppression motion, concluding that "the facts of the stop were not controverted," and "[t]here was nothing to really demonstrate that the actions of the officers were contrary to a normal traffic stop."

Petitioners were convicted of the counts at issue here. The Court of Appeals affirmed the convictions, holding with respect to the suppression issue that, "regardless of whether a police officer subjectively believes that the occupants of an automobile may be engaging in some other illegal behavior, a traffic stop is permissible as long as a reasonable officer in the same circumstances could have stopped the car for the suspected traffic violation."

The Fourth Amendment guarantees "[t]he right of the people to be secure in their persons, houses, papers, and effects, against unreasonable searches and seizures." Temporary detention of individuals during the stop of an automobile by the police, even if only for a brief period and for a limited purpose, constitutes a "seizure" of "persons" within the meaning of this provision. An automobile stop is thus subject to the constitutional imperative that it not be "unreasonable" under the circumstances. As a general matter, the decision to stop an automobile is reasonable where the police have probable cause to believe that a traffic violation has occurred.

Petitioners accept that Officer Soto had probable cause to believe that various provisions of the District of Columbia traffic code had been violated. They argue, however, that "in the unique context of civil traffic regulations" probable cause is not enough. Since, they contend, the use of automobiles is so heavily and minutely regulated that total compliance with traffic and safety rules is nearly impossible, a police officer will almost invariably be able to catch any given motorist in a technical violation. This creates the temptation to use traffic stops as a means of investigating other law violations, as to which no probable cause or even articulable suspicion exists. Petitioners, who are both black, further contend that police officers might decide which motorists to stop based on decidedly impermissible factors, such as the race of the car's occupants. To avoid this danger, they say, the Fourth Amendment test for traffic stops should be, not the normal one (applied by the Court of Appeals) of whether probable cause existed to justify the stop; but rather, whether a police officer, acting reasonably, would have made the stop for the reason given.

Petitioners contend that the standard they propose is consistent with our past cases' disapproval of police attempts to use valid bases of action against citizens as pretexts for pursuing other investigatory agendas. We are reminded that in Florida v. Wells (1990), we stated that "an inventory search must not be used as a ruse for a general rummaging in order to discover incriminating evidence"; that in Colorado v. Bertine (1987), in approving an inventory search, we apparently thought it significant that there had been "no showing that the police, who were following standard procedures, acted in bad faith or for the sole purpose of investigation"; and that in New York v. Burger (1987), we observed, in upholding the constitutionality of a warrantless administrative inspection, that the search did not appear to be "a 'pretext' for obtaining evidence of ... violation of ... penal laws." But only an undiscerning reader would regard these cases as endorsing the principle that ulterior motives can invalidate police conduct that is justifiable on the basis of probable cause to believe that a violation of law has occurred. In each case we were addressing the validity of a search conducted in the absence of probable cause. Our quoted statements simply explain that the exemption from the need for probable cause (and warrant), which is accorded to searches made for the purpose of inventory or administrative regulation, is not accorded to searches that are not made for those purposes.

... Not only have we never held, outside the context of inventory search or administrative inspection (discussed above), that an officer's motive invalidates objectively justifiable behavior under the Fourth Amendment; but we have repeatedly held and asserted the contrary. In United States v. Villamonte-Marquez (1983), we held that an otherwise valid warrantless boarding of a vessel by customs officials was not rendered invalid "because the customs officers were accompanied by a Louisiana state policeman, and were following an informant's tip that a vessel in the ship channel was thought to be carrying marihuana." We flatly dismissed the idea that an ulterior motive might serve to strip the agents of their legal justification. In United States v. Robinson (1973), we held that a traffic-violation arrest (of the sort here) would not be rendered invalid by the fact that it was "a mere pretext" for a narcotics search and that a lawful postarrest search of the person would not be rendered invalid by the fact that it was not motivated by the officer-safety concern that justifies such searches. In rejecting the contention that wiretap evidence was subject to exclusion because the agents conducting the tap had failed to make any effort to comply with the statutory requirement that unauthorized acquisitions be minimized, we said that "[s]ubjective intent alone ... does not make otherwise lawful conduct illegal or unconstitutional." We described Robinson as having established that "the fact that the officer does not have the state of mind which is hypothecated by the reasons which provide the legal justification for the officer's action does not invalidate the action taken as long as the circumstances, viewed objectively, justify that action."

We think these cases foreclose any argument that the constitutional reasonableness of traffic stops depends on the actual motivations of the individual officers involved. We of course agree with petitioners that the Constitution prohibits selective enforcement of the law based on considerations such as race. But the constitutional basis for objecting to intentionally discriminatory application of laws is the Equal Protection Clause, not the Fourth Amendment. Subjective intentions play no role in ordinary, probable-cause Fourth Amendment analysis.

Recognizing that we have been unwilling to entertain Fourth Amendment challenges based on the actual motivations of individual officers, petitioners disavow any intention to make the individual officer's subjective good faith the touchstone of "reasonableness." They insist that the standard they have put forward—whether the officer's conduct deviated materially from usual police practices, so that a reasonable officer in the same circumstances would not have made the stop for the reasons given—is an "objective" one.

But although framed in empirical terms, this approach is plainly and indisputably driven by subjective considerations. Its whole purpose is to prevent the police from doing under the guise of enforcing the traffic code what they would like to do for different reasons. Petitioners' proposed standard may not use the word "pretext," but it is designed to combat nothing other than the perceived "danger" of the pretextual stop, albeit only indirectly and over the run of cases. Instead of asking whether the individual officer had the proper state of mind, the petitioners would have us ask, in effect, whether (based on general police practices) it is plausible to believe that the officer had the proper state of mind.

Why one would frame a test designed to combat pretext in such fashion that the court cannot take into account actual and admitted pretext is a curiosity that can only be explained by the fact that our cases have foreclosed the more sensible option. If those cases were based only upon the evidentiary difficulty of establishing subjective intent, petitioners' attempt to root out subjective vices through objective means might make sense. But they were not based only upon that, or indeed even principally upon that. Their principal basis—which applies equally to attempts to reach subjective intent through ostensibly objective means—is simply that the Fourth Amendment's concern with "reasonableness" allows certain actions to be taken in certain circumstances, whatever the subjective intent. But even if our concern had been only an evidentiary one, petitioners' proposal would by no means assuage it. Indeed, it seems to us somewhat easier to figure out the intent of an individual officer than to plumb the collective consciousness of law enforcement in order to determine whether a "reasonable officer" would have been moved to act upon the traffic violation. While police manuals and standard procedures may sometimes provide objective assistance, ordinarily one would be reduced to speculating about the hypothetical reaction of a hypothetical constable—an exercise that might be called virtual subjectivity.

Moreover, police enforcement practices, even if they could be practicably assessed by a judge, vary from place to place and from time to time. We cannot accept that the search and seizure protections of the Fourth Amendment are so variable and can be made to turn upon such trivialities. The difficulty is illustrated by petitioners' arguments in this case. Their claim that a reasonable officer would not have made this stop is based largely on District of Columbia police regulations which permit plainclothes officers in unmarked vehicles to enforce traffic laws "only in the case of a violation that is so grave as to pose an immediate threat to the safety of others." This basis of invalidation would not apply in jurisdictions that had a different practice. And it would not have applied even in the District of Columbia, if Officer Soto had been wearing a uniform or patrolling in a marked police cruiser. . . .

In what would appear to be an elaboration on the "reasonable officer" test, petitioners argue that the balancing inherent in any Fourth Amendment inquiry requires us to weigh the governmental and individual interests implicated in a traffic stop such as we have here. That balancing, petitioners claim, does not support investigation of minor traffic infractions by plainclothes police in unmarked vehicles; such investigation only minimally advances the government's interest in traffic safety, and may indeed retard it by producing motorist confusion and alarm—a view said to be supported by the Metropolitan Police Department's own regulations generally prohibiting this practice. And as for the Fourth Amendment interests of the individuals concerned, petitioners point out that our cases acknowledge that even ordinary traffic stops entail "a possibly unsettling show of authority"; that they at best "interfere with freedom of movement, are inconvenient, and consume time" and at worst "may create substantial anxiety. . . ." That anxiety is likely to be even more pronounced when the stop is conducted by plainclothes officers in unmarked cars. . . .

Petitioners urge as an extraordinary factor in this case that the "multitude of applicable traffic and equipment regulations" is so large and so difficult to obey perfectly that virtually everyone is guilty of violation, permitting the police to single out almost whomever they wish for a stop. But we are aware of no principle that would allow us to decide at what point a code of law becomes so expansive and so commonly violated that infraction itself can no longer be the ordinary measure of the lawfulness of enforcement. And even if we could identify such exorbitant codes, we do not know by what standard (or what right) we would decide, as petitioners would have us do, which particular provisions are sufficiently important to merit enforcement.

For the run-of-the-mine case, which this surely is, we think there is no realistic alternative to the traditional common-law rule that probable cause justifies a search and seizure.

Here the District Court found that the officers had probable cause to believe that petitioners had violated the traffic code. That rendered the stop reasonable under the Fourth Amendment, the evidence thereby discovered admissible, and the upholding of the convictions by the Court of Appeals for the District of Columbia Circuit correct.

Judgment affirmed.

State Statutes

Although many state executives and legislatures have proposed legislation concerning profiling, fewer than half of them have actually enacted related legislation. At the time of this writing, twenty states had enacted laws directly related to profiling by the criminal justice system—usually with specific attention to law enforcement.

To aid the reader interested in such resources, statutes relating to profiling from these twenty states are reprinted below. As is evident, some states address the issue through prohibition; other states simply have made it a legal obligation for government agencies to collect information concerning profiling so that future legislative decisions can be made. Depending on the intent of legislatures, the laws reprinted below can and do serve as models for future legislation in those remaining states lacking such laws.

California

Section 13519.4 of the Penal Code is amended to read:

13519.4. (a) On or before August 1, 1993, the commission shall develop and disseminate guidelines and training for all law enforcement officers in California as described in subdivision (a) of Section 13510 and who adhere to the standards approved by the commission, on the racial and cultural differences among the residents of this state. The course or courses of instruction and the guidelines shall stress understanding and respect for racial and cultural differences, and development of effective, noncombative methods of carrying out law enforcement duties in a racially and culturally diverse environment.

(b) The course of basic training for law enforcement officers shall, no later than August 1, 1993, include adequate instruction on racial and cultural diversity in order to foster mutual respect and cooperation between law enforcement and members of all racial and cultural groups. In developing the training, the commission shall consult with appropriate groups and individuals having an interest and expertise in the field of cultural awareness and diversity.

(c) For the purposes of this section, "culturally diverse" and "cultural diversity" include, but are not limited to, gender and sexual orientation issues. The Legislature finds and declares as follows:

(1) Racial profiling is a practice that presents a great danger to the fundamental principles of a democratic society. It is abhorrent and cannot be tolerated.

(2) Motorists who have been stopped by the police for no reason other than the color of their skin or their apparent nationality or ethnicity are the victims of discriminatory practices.

(3) It is the intent of the Legislature in enacting the changes to Section 13519.4 of the Penal Code made by the act that added this subdivision that more than additional training is required to address the pernicious practice of racial profiling and that enactment of this bill is in no way dispositive of the issue of how the state should deal with racial profiling.

(4) The working men and women in California law enforcement risk their lives every day. The people of California greatly appreciate the hard work and dedication of law enforcement officers in protecting public safety. The good name of these officers should not be tarnished by the actions of those few who commit discriminatory practices.

(d) "Racial profiling," for purposes of this section, is the practice of detaining a suspect based on a broad set of criteria which casts suspicion on an entire class of people without any individualized suspicion of the particular person being stopped.

(e) A law enforcement officer shall not engage in racial profiling.

(f) Every law enforcement officer in this state shall participate in expanded training as prescribed and certified by the Commission on Peace Officers Standards and Training. Training shall begin being offered no later than January 1, 2002. The curriculum shall be created by the commission in collaboration with a five-person panel, appointed no later than March 1, 2001, as follows: the Governor shall appoint three members and one member each shall be appointed by the Senate Committee on Rules and the Speaker of the Assembly. Each appointee shall be appointed from among prominent members of the following organizations:

(1) State Conference of the NAACP.

(2) Brotherhood Crusade.

(3) Mexican American Legal Defense and Education Fund.

(4) The League of United Latin American Citizens.

(5) American Civil Liberties Union.

(6) Anti-Defamation League.

(7) California NOW.

(8) Asian Pacific Bar of California.

(9) The Urban League.

(g) Members of the panel shall not be compensated, except for reasonable per diem expenses related to their work for panel purposes.

(h) The curriculum shall utilize the Tools for Tolerance for Law Enforcement Professionals framework and shall include and examine the patterns, practices, and protocols that make up racial profiling. This training shall prescribe patterns, practices, and protocols that prevent racial profiling. In developing the training, the commission shall consult with appropriate groups and individuals having an interest and expertise in the field of racial profiling. The course of instruction shall include, but not be limited to, adequate consideration of each of the following subjects:

(1) Identification of key indices and perspectives that make up cultural differences among residents in a local community.

(2) Negative impact of biases, prejudices, and stereotyping on effective law enforcement, including examination of how historical perceptions of discriminatory enforcement practices have harmed police-community relations.

(3) The history and the role of the civil rights movement and struggles and their impact on law enforcement.

(4) Specific obligations of officers in preventing, reporting, and responding to discriminatory or biased practices by fellow officers.

(5) Perspectives of diverse, local constituency groups and experts on particular cultural and police-community relations issues in a local area.

(i) Once the initial basic training is completed, each law enforcement officer in California as described in subdivision (a) of Section 13510 who adheres to the standards approved by the commission shall be required to complete a refresher course every five years thereafter, or on a more frequent basis if deemed necessary, in order to keep current with changing racial and cultural trends.

(j) The Legislative Analyst shall conduct a study of the data being voluntarily collected by those jurisdictions that have instituted a program of data collection with regard to racial profiling, including, but not limited to, the California Highway Patrol, the City of San Jose, and the City of San Diego, both to ascertain the incidence of racial profiling and whether data collection serves to address and prevent such practices, as well as to assess the value and efficacy of the training herein prescribed with respect to preventing local profiling. The Legislative Analyst may prescribe the manner in which the data is to be submitted and may request that police agencies collecting such data submit it in the requested manner. The Legislative Analyst shall provide to the Legislature a report and recommendations with regard to racial profiling by July 1, 2002.

Colorado

24-31-309—Profiling—officer identification—training.

(1) (a) The general assembly finds, determines, and declares that profiling is a practice that presents a great danger to the fundamental principles of our constitutional republic and is abhorrent and cannot be tolerated.

(b) The general assembly further finds and declares that motorists who have been stopped by peace officers for no reason other than the color of their skin or their apparent race, ethnicity, age, or gender are the victims of discriminatory practices.

(c) The general assembly further finds and declares that Colorado peace officers risk their lives every day. The people of Colorado greatly appreciate the hard work and dedication of peace officers in protecting public safety. The good name of these peace officers should not be tarnished by the actions of those who commit discriminatory practices.

(d) It is therefore the intent of the general assembly in adopting this section to provide a means of identification of peace officers who are engaging in profiling, to underscore the accountability of those peace officers for their actions, and to provide training to those peace officers on how to avoid profiling.

(2) For purposes of this section, "profiling" means the practice of detaining a suspect based on race, ethnicity, age, or gender without the existence of any individualized suspicion of the particular person being stopped.

(3) Any peace officer certified pursuant to this part 3 shall not engage in profiling.

(4) (a) A peace officer certified pursuant to this part 3 shall provide, without being asked, his or her business card to any person whom the peace officer has detained in a traffic stop, but has not cited or arrested. The business card shall include identifying information about the peace officer including, but not limited to, the peace officer's name, division, precinct, and badge or other identification number and a telephone number that may be used, if necessary, to report any comments, positive or negative, regarding the traffic stop. The identity of the reporting person and the report of any such comments that constitutes a complaint shall initially be kept confidential by the receiving law enforcement agency, to the extent permitted by law. The receiving law enforcement agency shall be permitted to obtain some identifying information regarding the complaint to allow initial processing of the complaint. If it becomes necessary for the further processing of the complaint for the complainant to disclose his or her identity, the complainant shall do so or, at the option of the receiving law enforcement agency, the complaint may be dismissed.

(b) The provisions of paragraph (a) of this subsection (4) shall not apply to authorized undercover operations conducted by any law enforcement agency.

(c) Each law enforcement agency in the state shall compile on at least an annual basis any information derived from telephone calls received due to the distribution of business cards as described in paragraph (a) of this subsection (4) and that allege profiling. The agency shall make such information available to the public but shall not include the names of peace officers or the names of persons alleging profiling in such information. The agency may also include in such information the costs to the agency of complying with the provisions of this subsection (4).

(5) The training provided for peace officers shall include an examination of the patterns, practices, and protocols that result in profiling and prescribe patterns, practices, and protocols that prevent profiling. On or before August 1, 2001, the P.O.S.T. board shall certify the curriculum for such training.

(6) No later than six months after the effective date of this section, each law enforcement agency in the state shall have written policies, procedures, and training in place that are specifically designed to address profiling. Each peace officer employed by such law enforcement agency shall receive such training. The written policies and procedures shall be made available to the public for inspection during regular business hours.

Source: L. 2001: Entire section added, p. 934, § 2, effective June 5.

42-4-115—Information on traffic law enforcement—collection—profiling—annual report—repeal.

(1) The Colorado state patrol and any law enforcement agency per-

forming traffic stops that serves the city and county of Denver shall collect and maintain the following information regarding each traffic stop:

(a) The number of persons detained for routine traffic infractions and whether a citation or warning was issued as a result of the traffic stop;

(b) Identifying characteristics of the persons detained during the traffic stop, including race or ethnicity, age, and gender;

(c) The approximate date, time, and location of the traffic stop;

(d) The reason for the traffic stop;

(e) Whether a search of the person occurred as a result of the traffic stop;

(f) Whether, as a result of the traffic stop, the person's vehicle or personal effects or the vehicle's driver or passengers were searched and the race or ethnicity, age, and gender of any person searched;

(g) Whether the search was conducted pursuant to consent, probable cause, or reasonable suspicion to suspect a crime;

(h) Whether any contraband was found as a result of the traffic stop;

(i) Whether an arrest was made as a result of the traffic stop; and

(j) Whether any property was seized as a result of the traffic stop.

(2) Nothing in this section shall be construed to require the collection and maintenance of information in connection with roadblocks, vehicle checks, or checkpoints, except when such traffic stops result in a warning, search, seizure, or arrest.

(3) Beginning January 1, 2002, and continuing through January 1, 2004, the Colorado state patrol and any law enforcement agency performing traffic stops that serves the city and county of Denver shall annually compile the information gathered pursuant to subsection (1) of this section and shall make such information available to the public.

(4) This section is repealed, effective January 1, 2004.

Source: L. 2001: Entire section added, p. 933, § 1, effective June 5.

Connecticut

Connecticut Public Act No. 99–198

An Act Concerning Traffic Stops Statistics.

Be it enacted by the Senate and House of Representatives in General Assembly convened:

Section 1. (NEW) (a) For the purposes of this section, "racial profiling" means the detention, interdiction or other disparate treatment of an individual solely on the basis of the racial or ethnic status of such individual.

(b) No member of the Division of State Police within the Department of Public Safety, a municipal police department or any other law enforcement agency shall engage in racial profiling. The detention of an individual based on any noncriminal factor or combination of non-criminal factors is inconsistent with this policy.

(c) The race or ethnicity of an individual shall not be the sole factor in determining the existence of probable cause to place in custody or arrest an individual or in constituting a reasonable and articulable suspicion that an offense has been or is being committed so as to justify the detention of an individual or the investigatory stop of a motor vehicle.

Sec. 2. (NEW) (a) Not later than January 1, 2000, each municipal police department and the Department of Public Safety shall adopt a written policy that prohibits the stopping, detention or search of any person when such action is solely motivated by considerations of race, color, ethnicity, age, gender or sexual orientation, and the action would constitute a violation of the civil rights of the person.

(b) Commencing on January 1, 2000, each municipal police department and the Department of Public Safety shall, using the form developed and promulgated pursuant to section 3 of this act, record and retain the following information: (1) The number of persons stopped for traffic violations; (2) characteristics of race, color, ethnicity, gender and age of such persons, provided the identification of such characteristics shall be based on the observation and perception of the police officer responsible for reporting the stop and the information shall not be required to be provided by the person stopped; (3) the nature of the alleged traffic violation that resulted in the stop; (4) whether a warning or citation was issued, an arrest made or a search conducted as a result of the stop; and (5) any additional information that such municipal police department or the Department of Public Safety, as the case may be, deems appropriate.

(c) Each municipal police department and the Department of Public Safety shall provide to the Chief State's Attorney (1) a copy of each complaint received pursuant to this section, and (2) written notification of the review and disposition of such complaint.

(d) Any police officer who in good faith records traffic stop information pursuant to the requirements of this section shall not be held civilly liable for the act of recording such information unless the officer's conduct was unreasonable or reckless.

(e) If a municipal police department or the Department of Public Safety fails to comply with the provisions of this section, the Chief State's Attorney may recommend and the Secretary of the Office of Policy and Management may order an appropriate penalty in the form of the withholding of state funds from such department or the Department of Public Safety.

(f) On or before October 1, 2000, and annually thereafter, each municipal police department and the Department of Public Safety shall provide to the Chief State's Attorney, in such form as the Chief State's

Attorney shall prescribe, a summary report of the information recorded pursuant to subsection (d) of this section.

(g) The Chief State's Attorney shall, within the limits of existing appropriations, provide for a review of the prevalence and disposition of traffic stops and complaints reported pursuant to this section. Not later than January 1, 2002, the Chief State's Attorney shall report to the Governor and General Assembly the results of such review, including any recommendations.

(h) The provisions of subsections (f) and (g) of this section shall be in effect from the effective date of this act until January 1, 2002.

Sec. 3. Not later than January 1, 2000, the Chief State's Attorney, in conjunction with the Commissioner of Public Safety, the Attorney General, the Chief Court Administrator, the Police Officer Standards and Training Council, the Connecticut Police Chiefs Association and the Connecticut Coalition of Police and Correctional Officers, shall develop and promulgate: (1) A form, in both printed and electronic format, to be used by police officers when making a traffic stop to record personal identifying information about the operator of the motor vehicle that is stopped, the location of the stop, the reason for the stop and other information that is required to be recorded pursuant to subsection (b) of section 2 of this act; and (2) a form, in both printed and electronic format, to be used to report complaints pursuant to section 2 of this act by persons who believe they have been subjected to a motor vehicle stop by a police officer solely on the basis of their race, color, ethnicity, age, gender or sexual orientation.

Approved June 28, 1999

Florida

An act relating to law enforcement; amending s. 943.1758, F.S.; providing that instruction in interpersonal skills relating to diverse populations shall consist of a module developed by the Criminal Justice Standards and Training Commission on the topic of discriminatory profiling; amending ss. 30.15 and 166.0493, F.S.; requiring sheriffs and municipal law enforcement agencies to incorporate antiracial or other antidiscriminatory profiling policies into their policies and practices; providing guidelines and requirements for such policies; providing an effective date.

Be It Enacted by the Legislature of the State of Florida:
Section 1. Section 943.1758, Florida Statutes, is amended to read:
943.1758 Curriculum revision for diverse populations; skills training.—

(1) The Criminal Justice Standards and Training Commission shall revise its standards and training for basic recruits and its requirements

for continued employment by integrating instructions on interpersonal skills relating to diverse populations into the criminal justice standards and training curriculum. The curriculum shall include standardized proficiency instruction relating to high-risk and critical tasks which include, but are not limited to, stops, use of force and domination, and other areas of interaction between officers and members of diverse populations.

(2) The commission shall develop and implement, as part of its instructor training programs, standardized instruction in the subject of interpersonal skills relating to diverse populations.

(3) Culturally sensitive lesson plans, up-to-date videotapes, and other demonstrative aids developed for use in diverse population-related training shall be used as instructional materials.

(4) By October 1, 2001, the instruction in the subject of interpersonal skills relating to diverse populations shall consist of a module developed by the commission on the topic of discriminatory profiling.

Section 2. Subsection (3) is added to section 30.15, Florida Statutes, to read:

30.15 Powers, duties, and obligations.—

On or before January 1, 2002, every sheriff shall incorporate an antiracial or other antidiscriminatory profiling policy into the sheriff's policies and practices, utilizing the Florida Police Chiefs Association Model Policy as a guide. Antiprofiling policies shall include the elements of definitions, traffic stop procedures, community education and awareness efforts, and policies for the handling of complaints from the public.

Section 3. Section 166.0493, Florida Statutes, is created to read:

166.0493 Powers, duties, and obligations of municipal law enforcement agencies.—On or before January 1, 2002, every municipal law enforcement agency shall incorporate an antiracial or other anti-discriminatory profiling policy into the agency's policies and practices, utilizing the Florida Police Chiefs Association Model Policy as a guide.

Antiprofiling policies shall include the elements of definitions, traffic stop procedures, community education and awareness efforts, and policies for the handling of complaints from the public.

Section 4. This act shall take effect upon becoming a law.

06/19/01 Approved by Governor; Chapter No. 2001–264

Illinois

Signed into law on July 17, 2003

Section 5. The Department of State Police Law within the Civil Administrative Code of Illinois is amended by adding Section 2605-85 as follows:

Sec. 2605-85. Training; cultural diversity. The Department shall provide training and continuing education to State Police officers concerning cultural diversity, including sensitivity toward racial and ethnic differences. This training and continuing education shall include, but not be limited to, an emphasis on the fact that the primary purpose of enforcement of the Illinois Vehicle Code is safety and equal and uniform enforcement under the law.

Section 10. The Illinois Police Training Act is amended by changing Section 7 as follows:

Sec. 7. Rules and standards for schools. The Board shall adopt rules and minimum standards for such schools which shall include but not be limited to the following:

a. The curriculum for probationary police officers which shall be offered by all certified schools shall include but not be limited to courses of arrest, search and seizure, civil rights, human relations, cultural diversity, including racial and ethnic sensitivity, criminal law, law of criminal procedure, vehicle and traffic law including uniform and non-discriminatory enforcement of the Illinois Vehicle Code . . .

Section 15. The Illinois Vehicle Code is amended by adding Section 11-212 as follows:

Sec. 11-212. Traffic stop statistical study.

(a) From January 1, 2004 until December 31, 2007, whenever a State or local law enforcement officer issues a uniform traffic citation or warning citation for an alleged violation of the Illinois Vehicle Code, he or she shall record at least the following:

(1) the name, address, gender, and the officer's subjective determination of the race of the person stopped; the person's race shall be selected from the following list: Caucasian, African-American, Hispanic, Native American/Alaska Native, or Asian/Pacific Islander;

(2) the alleged traffic violation that led to the stop of the motorist;

(3) the make and year of the vehicle stopped;

(4) the date and time of the stop;

(5) the location of the traffic stop;

(6) whether or not a search contemporaneous to the stop was conducted of the vehicle, driver, passenger, or passengers; and, if so, whether it was with consent or by other means; and

(7) the name and badge number of the issuing officer.

(b) From January 1, 2004 until December 31, 2007, whenever a State or local law enforcement officer stops a motorist for an alleged violation of the Illinois Vehicle Code and does not issue a uniform traffic citation or warning citation for an alleged violation of the Illinois Vehicle Code, he or she shall complete a uniform stop card, which includes field contact cards, or any other existing form currently used by law enforcement containing information required pursuant to this Act, that records at least the following:

(1) the name, address, gender, and the officer's subjective determination of the race of the person stopped; the person's race shall be selected from the following list: Caucasian, African-American, Hispanic, Native American/Alaska Native, or Asian/Pacific Islander;

(2) the reason that led to the stop of the motorist;

(3) the make and year of the vehicle stopped;

(4) the date and time of the stop;

(5) the location of the traffic stop;

(6) whether or not a search contemporaneous to the stop was conducted of the vehicle, driver, passenger, or passengers; and, if so, whether it was with consent or by other means; and

(7) the name and badge number of the issuing officer.

(c) The Illinois Department of Transportation shall provide a standardized law enforcement data compilation form on its website.

(d) Every law enforcement agency shall, by March 1 in each of the years 2004, 2005, 2006, and 2007, compile the data described in subsections (a) and (b) on the standardized law enforcement data compilation form provided by the Illinois Department of Transportation and transmit the data to the Department.

(e) The Illinois Department of Transportation shall analyze the data provided by law enforcement agencies required by this Section and submit a report of the findings to the Governor, the General Assembly, and each law enforcement agency no later than July 1 in each of the years 2005, 2006, 2007, and 2008. The Illinois Department of Transportation may contract with an outside entity for the analysis of the data provided. In analyzing the data collected under this Section, the analyzing entity shall scrutinize the data for evidence of statistically significant aberrations. The following list, which is illustrative, and not exclusive, contains examples of areas in which statistically significant aberrations may be found:

(1) The percentage of minority drivers or passengers being stopped in a given area is substantially higher than the proportion of the overall population in or traveling through the area that the minority constitutes.

(2) A substantial number of false stops including stops not resulting in the issuance of a traffic ticket or the making of an arrest.

(3) A disparity between the proportion of citations issued to minorities and proportion of minorities in the population.

(4) A disparity among the officers of the same law enforcement agency with regard to the number of minority drivers or passengers being stopped in a given area.

(5) A disparity between the frequency of searches performed on minority drivers and the frequency of searches performed on nonminority drivers.

Signed into law on July 17, 2003

Kansas

Session of 2000 Effective: July 1, 2000

Substitute for HOUSE BILL No. 2683 An Act concerning criminal procedure; relating to the collection and reporting of certain statistics involving law enforcement activities.

Be it enacted by the Legislature of the State of Kansas:

Section 1. (a) The governor, with the assistance of the attorney general and the Kansas law enforcement training commission, shall develop a request for a proposal for a system to collect and report statistics relating to the race, ethnicity, gender, age and residency by county and state of those who come in contact with law enforcement activities.

(b) Proposals submitted pursuant to the request shall contain, at a minimum:

(1) A system to collect data on a statistically significant sample of those persons who:

(A) Are arrested;

(B) while operating a motor vehicle, are stopped by a law enforcement officer; and

(C) while a pedestrian, are stopped by a law enforcement officer;

(2) which contains the race, ethnicity, gender, age and residency by county and state of such persons;

(3) which has a schedule and plan of implementation, including training;

(4) other factors which may be relevant to law enforcement officers in stopping or arresting individuals;

(5) civilian complaints received by law enforcement agencies alleging bias based on race, ethnicity, gender, age or residency by county or state; and

(6) a survey of policies of law enforcement agencies relating to the investigation of complaints based on alleged race, ethnicity, gender, age or residency bias.

(c) Data acquired pursuant to this proposal shall not contain any information that may reveal the identity of any individual.

(d) The governor, with the assistance of the attorney general, shall select the most comprehensive proposal and implement such proposal, subject to the availability of any grant or grants for such purpose from the United States department of justice or any other governmental or private agency.

(e) The results of such study shall be submitted to the governor and attorney general within 90 days after conclusion of such study. The governor shall submit the study to the legislature with one or more of the following:

(1) An evaluation of the study;

(2) an implementation plan to expand the data collection and reporting system to other law enforcement agencies and whether such system should be made permanent; and

(3) recommendations to improve law enforcement training and operations to address racial, ethnic, gender, age or residency bias.

Kentucky

15A.195 Prohibition against racial profiling—Model policy—Local law enforcement agencies' policies.

(1) No state law enforcement agency or official shall stop, detain, or search any person when such action is solely motivated by consideration of race, color, or ethnicity, and the action would constitute a violation of the civil rights of the person.

(2) The secretary of the Justice Cabinet, in consultation with the Kentucky Law Enforcement Council, the Attorney General, the Office of Criminal Justice Training, the secretary of the Transportation Cabinet, the Kentucky State Police, the secretary of the Natural Resources and Environmental Protection Cabinet, and the secretary of the Public Protection and Regulation Cabinet, shall design and implement a model policy to prohibit racial profiling by state law enforcement agencies and officials.

(3) The Kentucky Law Enforcement Council shall disseminate the established model policy against racial profiling to all sheriffs and local law enforcement officials, including local police departments, city councils, and fiscal courts. All local law enforcement agencies and sheriffs' departments are urged to implement a written policy against racial profiling or adopt the model policy against racial profiling as established by the secretary of the Justice Cabinet within one hundred eighty (180) days of dissemination of the model policy. A copy of any implemented or adopted policy against racial profiling shall be filed with the Kentucky Law Enforcement Council and the Kentucky Law Enforcement Foundation Program Fund.

(4) (a) Each local law enforcement agency that participates in the Kentucky Law Enforcement Foundation Program fund under KRS 15.420 in the Commonwealth shall implement a policy, banning the practice of racial profiling, that meets or exceeds the requirements of the model policy disseminated under subsection (3) of this section. The local law enforcement agency's policy shall be submitted by the local law enforcement agency to the secretary of the Justice Cabinet within one hundred eighty (180) days of dissemination of the model policy by the Kentucky Law Enforcement Council under subsection (3) of this section. If the local law enforcement agency fails to submit its policy within one hundred eighty (180) days of dissemination of the model

policy, or the secretary rejects a policy submitted within the one hundred and eighty (180) days, that agency shall not receive Kentucky Law Enforcement Foundation Program funding until the secretary approves a policy submitted by the agency.

(b) If the secretary of the Justice Cabinet approves a local law enforcement agency's policy, the agency shall not change its policy without obtaining approval of the new policy from the secretary of the Justice Cabinet. If the agency changes its policy without obtaining the secretary's approval, the agency shall not receive Kentucky Law Enforcement Foundation Program funding until the secretary approves a policy submitted by the agency.

(5) Each local law enforcement agency shall adopt an administrative action for officers found not in compliance with the agency's policy. The administrative action shall be in accordance with other penalties enforced by the agency's administration for similar officer misconduct. Effective: June 21, 2001 History: Created 2001 Ky. Acts ch. 158, sec. 1, effective June 21, 2001.

Maryland

Law Enforcement Officers—Vehicle Laws—Race-Based Traffic Stops

FOR the purpose of requiring certain law enforcement officers to record certain information pertaining to traffic stops; requiring certain law enforcement agencies to report certain information to the Maryland Justice Analysis Center (MJAC); requiring the Police Training Commission to develop a certain format and guidelines and a standardized format for the reporting of certain data; requiring the Police Training Commission to develop a certain model policy; requiring the MJAC to analyze certain data based on a methodology developed in conjunction with the Police Training Commission; requiring the MJAC to make certain reports to the General Assembly, the Governor, and law enforcement agencies; requiring law enforcement agencies to adopt certain policies regarding race-based traffic stops for certain purposes; providing for the phasing in of certain requirements; requiring the MJAC to report to the Police Training Commission law enforcement agencies that fail to comply with certain reporting requirements; requiring specified actions following a report on the failure of a law enforcement agency to comply; providing certain exceptions applicable to law enforcement agencies that have entered into certain agreements; defining certain terms; requiring the Governor to appropriate certain funding in certain fiscal years to assist local law enforcement agencies to implement certain provisions of this Act; providing for the termination of this Act; and generally relating to law enforcement procedures and traffic stops.

BY adding to

Article—Transportation Section 25-113 Annotated Code of Maryland

SECTION 1. Be it enacted by the General Assembly of Maryland that the Laws of Maryland read as follows:

Article—Transportation 25-113.

(a) (1) In this section the following words have the meanings indicated.

(2) "Law enforcement agency" means an agency that is listed in § 3-101(e) of the Public Safety Article and that, in accordance with subsection (c) of this section, is subject to the provisions of this section.

(3) "Law enforcement officer" means any person who, in an official capacity, is authorized by law to make arrests and who is an employee of a law enforcement agency that is subject to this section.

(4) "Maryland Justice Analysis Center" means the center operated by the Department of Criminology and Criminal Justice at the University of Maryland, College Park.

(5) "Police Training Commission" means the unit within the Department of Public Safety and Correctional Services established under § 3-202 of the Public Safety Article.

(6) (i) Subject to subparagraph (ii) of this paragraph, "traffic stop" means any instance when a law enforcement officer stops the driver of a motor vehicle and detains the driver for any period of time for a violation of the Maryland Vehicle Law.

(ii) "Traffic stop" does not include:

1. A checkpoint or roadblock stop;

2. A stop of multiple vehicles due to a traffic accident or emergency situation requiring the stopping of vehicles for public safety purposes; or

3. A stop based on the use of radar, laser, or vascar technology.

(b) The Police Training Commission, in consultation with the Maryland Justice Analysis Center, shall develop:

(1) A model format for the efficient recording of data required under subsection (d) of this section on an electronic device, or by any other means, for use by a law enforcement agency;

(2) Guidelines that each law enforcement agency may use as a management tool to evaluate data collected by its officers for use in counseling and improved training;

(3) A standardized format that each law enforcement agency shall use in reporting data to the Maryland Justice Analysis Center under subsection (e) of this section; and

(4) On or before July 1, 2002, a model policy against race-based traffic stops that a law enforcement agency covered under subsection (c)(1) of this section can use in developing its policy in accordance with subsection (g) of this section.

(c) (1) Subject to paragraph (2) of this subsection, this section applies to each law enforcement agency that:

(i) On January 1, 2002, has 100 or more law enforcement officers;

(ii) On January 1, 2003, has 50 or more law enforcement officers; and

(iii) On January 1, 2004, has 1 or more law enforcement officers.

(2) Except as provided in subsection (e)(2) of this section, this section does not apply to a law enforcement agency that, on or before July 1, 2001, has entered into an agreement with the United States Department of Justice that requires it to collect data on the race or ethnicity of the drivers of motor vehicles stopped.

(d) Each time a law enforcement officer makes a traffic stop, that officer shall report the following information to the law enforcement agency that employs the officer using the format developed by the law enforcement agency under subsection (b)(1) of this section:

(1) The date, location, and the time of the stop;

(2) The approximate duration of the stop;

(3) The traffic violation or violations alleged to have been committed that led to the stop;

(4) Whether a search was conducted as a result of the stop;

(5) If a search was conducted, the reason for the search, whether the search was consensual or nonconsensual, whether the person was searched, and whether the person's property was searched;

(6) Whether any contraband or other property was seized in the course of the search;

(7) Whether a warning, safety equipment repair order, or citation was issued as a result of the stop;

(8) If a warning, safety equipment repair order, or citation was issued, the basis for issuing the warning, safety equipment repair order, or citation;

(9) Whether an arrest was made as a result of either the stop or the search;

(10) If an arrest was made, the crime charged;

(11) The state in which the stopped vehicle is registered;

(12) The gender of the driver;

(13) The date of birth of the driver;

(14) The state and, if available on the driver's license, the county of residence of the driver; and

(15) The race or ethnicity of the driver as:

(i) Asian;

(ii) Black;

(iii) Hispanic;

(iv) White; or

(v) Other.

(e) (1) A law enforcement agency shall:

(i) Compile the data described in subsection (d) of this section for the calendar year as a report in the format required under subsection (b)(3) of this section; and

(ii) Submit the report to the Maryland Justice Analysis Center no later than March 1 of the following calendar year.

(2) A law enforcement agency that is exempt under subsection (c)(2) of this section shall submit to the Maryland Justice Analysis Center copies of reports it submits to the United States Department of Justice in lieu of the report required under paragraph (1) of this subsection.

(f) (1) The Maryland Justice Analysis Center shall analyze the annual reports of law enforcement agencies submitted under subsection (e) of this section based on a methodology developed in consultation with the Police Training Commission.

(2) The Maryland Justice Analysis Center shall submit a report of the findings to the Governor, the General Assembly as provided in § 2-1246 of the State Government Article, and each law enforcement agency before September 1 of each year.

(g) (1) A law enforcement agency shall adopt a policy against race-based traffic stops that is to be used as a management tool to promote nondiscriminatory law enforcement and in the training and counseling of its officers.

(2) The policy shall prohibit the practice of using an individual's race or ethnicity as the sole justification to initiate a traffic stop. However, the policy shall make clear that it may not be construed to alter the authority of a law enforcement officer to make an arrest, conduct a search or seizure, or otherwise fulfill the officer's law enforcement obligations.

(3) The policy shall provide for the law enforcement agency to periodically review data collected by its officers under subsection (d) of this section and to review the annual report of the Maryland Justice Analysis Center for purposes of paragraph (1) of this subsection.

(h) (1) If a law enforcement agency fails to comply with the reporting provisions of this section, the Maryland Justice Analysis Center shall report the noncompliance to the Police Training Commission.

(2) The Police Training Commission shall contact the law enforcement agency and request that the agency comply with the required reporting provisions.

(3) If the law enforcement agency fails to comply with the required reporting provisions within 30 days after being contacted by the Police Training Commission, the Maryland Justice Analysis Center and the Police Training Commission jointly shall report the noncompliance to the Governor and the Legislative Policy Committee of the General Assembly.

Massachusetts

Commonwealth of Massachusetts Acts of 2000 Chapter 228

AN ACT PROVIDING FOR THE COLLECTION OF DATA RELATIVE TO TRAFFIC STOPS.

Be it enacted by the Senate and House of Representatives in General Court assembled, and by the authority of the same, as follows:

SECTION 1. As used in this act, "racial and gender profiling" means the practice of detaining a suspect based on a broad set of criteria which casts suspicion on an entire class of people without any individualized suspicion of the particular person being stopped.

SECTION 2. The executive office of public safety shall work with the department of state police and municipal police departments to ensure that adequate efforts are being made to identify and eliminate any instances of racial and gender profiling by police officers in the performance of their official duties.

SECTION 3. The department of state police and the Massachusetts Chiefs of Police Association, shall develop policies and procedures on how to identify and prevent racial and gender profiling by police officers, and shall submit them to the secretary of public safety for review not later than December 31, 2000. If the secretary approves such policies and procedures, the secretary shall direct the criminal justice training council to include them in (a) the new recruit basic training curriculum under section 116A of chapter 6 of the General Laws; (b) any in-service training for veteran officers; (c) any supervisory training for all superior officers; and (d) any dispatcher and communication officer training.

SECTION 4. The executive office of public safety shall initiate a public awareness campaign on racial and gender profiling not later than January 1, 2001. The campaign shall emphasize the responsibility of public safety officials and residents of the commonwealth to identify unlawful or potentially unlawful behavior by an individual, as opposed to the individual's race or gender, before taking any action. As a part of this public awareness campaign, the executive office of public safety shall establish a procedure whereby motorists who allege that an incident of racial or gender profiling has occurred may register a complaint by calling a toll-free telephone number. The executive office of public safety shall periodically analyze such complaints, and shall share the data with the appropriate state or local police departments.

SECTION 5. The registry of motor vehicles shall revise the Massachusetts Uniform Citation to include a field that allows officers to note whether a search of a vehicle occurred at the time a citation was issued.

SECTION 6. The executive office of public safety shall develop a uniform protocol for state police and municipal police officers on how to use the Massachusetts Uniform Citation to record the race and sex of each individual cited by an officer for a motor vehicle violation, and whether or not a search occurred. The protocol shall be put into effect not later than January 1, 2001.

SECTION 7. The registry of motor vehicles shall, in consultation with the department of state police, incorporate in any driver education manual prepared by the registry a section on how motorists should respond if they are stopped by police officers, including what they can do if they believe they were stopped as a result of racial or gender profiling.

SECTION 8. The registry of motor vehicles shall collect data from any issued Massachusetts Uniform Citation regarding the following information:

(1) identifying characteristics of the individuals who receive a warning or citation or who are arrested, including the race and gender of the individual;

(2) the traffic infraction;

(3) whether a search was initiated as a result of the stop; and

(4) whether the stop resulted in a warning, citation or arrest.

The registry of motor vehicles shall maintain statistical information on the data required by this section and shall report that information monthly to the secretary of public safety, who shall determine when it is also appropriate to transmit such data to the attorney general. The data collection shall commence not later than January 1, 2001.

SECTION 9. Individual data acquired under this section shall be used only for statistical purposes and may not contain information that may reveal the identity of any individual who is stopped or any law enforcement officer.

SECTION 10. Not later than one year after the effective date of this act, the secretary of public safety shall transmit the necessary data collected by the registry of motor vehicles to a university in the commonwealth with experience in the analysis of such data, for annual preparation of an analysis and report of its findings. The secretary shall forthwith transmit the university's annual report to the department of the attorney general, the department of state police, the Massachusetts Chiefs of Police Association, the executive office of public safety and the clerks of the house of representatives and the senate. The executive office of public safety shall, in consultation with the attorney general, if such data suggest that a state police barracks or municipal police department appears to have engaged in racial or gender profiling, require said state police barracks or municipality for a period of one year to collect information on all traffic stops, including those not resulting in a warning, citation or arrest. This information shall include

the reason for the stop in addition to the other information already required under the Massachusetts Uniform Citation. Upon appeal by the colonel of state police or the municipality, respectively, the attorney general may determine that collecting such information is not required.
Approved August 10, 2000.

Minnesota

626.8471 Avoiding racial profiling; policies and learning objectives required.

Subdivision 1. Purpose.
The legislature finds that the reality or public perception of racial profiling alienates people from police, hinders community policing efforts, and causes law enforcement to lose credibility and trust among the people law enforcement is sworn to protect and serve. No stop initiated by a peace officer should be made without a legitimate reason; race, ethnicity, or national origin alone should never provide a sufficient reason. Law enforcement policies and training programs must emphasize the need to respect the balance between the rights of all persons to be free from unreasonable governmental intrusions and law enforcement's need to enforce the law.
Subd. 2. Definition.
"Racial profiling" means any action initiated by law enforcement that relies upon the race, ethnicity, or national origin of an individual rather than: (1) the behavior of that individual; or (2) information that leads law enforcement to a particular individual who has been identified as being engaged in or having been engaged in criminal activity. Racial profiling includes use of racial or ethnic stereotypes as factors in selecting whom to stop and search. Racial profiling does not include law enforcement's use of race or ethnicity to determine whether a person matches a specific description of a particular subject.
Subd. 3. Statewide model policy.
(a) The board of peace officer standards and training shall consult with the Minnesota chiefs of police association, the Minnesota sheriffs association, the racial profiling advisory committee, and the Minnesota police and peace officers association in developing an antiracial profiling model policy governing the conduct of peace officers engaged in stops of citizens. This policy shall define racial profiling and identify conduct that violates the law. The policy must also include a duty to give the officer's name or badge number and identify the officer's department during routine traffic stops.
(b) The board shall adopt a model policy and distribute the model policy to all chief law enforcement officers by August 1, 2001.
Subd. 4. Agency policies required.

(a) By November 1, 2001, the chief law enforcement officer of every state and local law enforcement agency must establish and enforce a written antiracial profiling policy governing the conduct of peace officers engaged in stops of citizens. The chief law enforcement officer shall ensure that each peace officer receives a copy of the agency's antiracial profiling policy. The chief law enforcement officer also must ensure that each peace officer is aware of the policy's purpose and the conduct prohibited by it.

(b) The policy must, at a minimum, comply with the requirements of the model policy adopted by the board under subdivision 3.

(c) Every state and local law enforcement agency must certify to the board that it has adopted a written policy in compliance with the board's model policy.

(d) The board shall assist the chief law enforcement officer of each state and local law enforcement agency in developing and implementing antiracial profiling policies under this subdivision.

Subd. 5. Preservice training learning objectives; requirements.

(a) By August 1, 2001, the board shall prepare learning objectives for preservice training to instruct peace officers in avoiding racial profiling when making stops of citizens. These learning objectives shall be included in the required curriculum of professional peace officer education programs.

(b) An individual is not eligible to take the peace officer licensing examination or the part-time peace officer licensing examination on or after June 1, 2002, unless:

(1) the individual has received the training described in paragraph (a); and

(2) the individual has completed a psychological evaluation demonstrating that the individual is not likely to engage in racial profiling.

Subd. 6. In-service training learning objectives.

By August 1, 2001, the board shall prepare learning objectives for in-service training to instruct peace officers in avoiding racial profiling when making stops of citizens. The board shall evaluate and monitor in-service training courses to ensure they satisfy the learning objectives.

Subd. 7. Chief law enforcement officers and supervisors; requirements.

The executive director of the board of peace officer standards and training shall prepare training materials to provide chief law enforcement officers and other peace officers with supervisory authority with information on how to detect and respond to racial profiling by peace officers under their command. The training materials must address both the agency's antiracial profiling policy and procedural components aimed at eliminating racial profiling in stops of citizens. The materials must include information on federal and state constitutional and statutory laws prohibiting discrimination by law enforcement. The procedural information must describe conduct that is unlawful or inappropriate and present guidelines for reinforcing techniques that are lawful and appropriate. The procedural information shall discuss appropriate search and seizure and interviewing techniques.

Subd. 8. Post board; compliance reviews authorized.

The board has authority to inspect state and local agency policies to ensure compliance with subdivision 4. The board may conduct this inspection based upon a complaint it receives about a particular agency or through a random selection process.

Missouri

Chapter 304 Traffic Regulations Section 304.670

Eff. August 28, 2000

Collection and maintenance of certain information regarding traffic law enforcement, analyses to be Missouri conducted. 304.670. 1. The highway patrol and any local law enforcement agency may collect, correlate and maintain the following information regarding traffic law enforcement:

(1) The number of drivers stopped for routine traffic enforcement and whether or not a citation or warning was issued;

(2) Identifying characteristics of the drivers stopped, including race, ethnicity, age and gender;

(3) The alleged violation that led to the stop;

(4) Whether a search was instituted as a result of the stop;

(5) Whether the vehicle, personal effects, driver or passengers were searched, and the race, ethnicity, age and gender of any person searched;

(6) Whether the search was conducted pursuant to consent, probable cause or reasonable suspicion to suspect a crime, including the basis for the request for consent, or the circumstances establishing probable cause or reasonable suspicion;

(7) Whether any contraband was found and the type and amount of any contraband;

(8) Whether an arrest was made;

(9) Whether any property was seized and a description of such property;

(10) Whether the officers making the stop encountered any physical resistance from the driver or passengers;

(11) Whether the officers making the stop engaged in the use of force against the driver or any passengers;

(12) Whether the circumstances surrounding the stop were the subject of any investigation, and the results of such investigation.

2. The information to be collected pursuant to subsection 1 of this section need not be collected in connection with roadblocks, vehicle checks or checkpoints, except when such stops result in a warning, search, seizure or arrest.

3. The highway patrol shall conduct analyses of the information collected pursuant to this section to determine whether law enforcement officers are using profiles in law enforcement activities.

Nebraska

20-501 Racial profiling; legislative intent.

Racial profiling is a practice that presents a great danger to the fundamental principles of a democratic society. It is abhorrent and cannot be tolerated. Motorists who have been stopped by the police for no reason other than the color of their skin or their apparent nationality or ethnicity are the victims of discriminatory practices.

20-502 Racial profiling prohibited.

(1) No member of the Nebraska State Patrol or a county sheriff's office, officer of a city or village police department, or member of any other law enforcement agency in this state shall engage in racial profiling. The disparate treatment of an individual whose motor vehicle has been stopped by a law enforcement officer is inconsistent with this policy.

(2) Racial profiling shall not be used to justify the detention of an individual or to conduct a motor vehicle stop.

For purposes of sections 20-501 to 20-505:

(1) Disparate treatment means differential treatment of persons on the basis of race, color, or national origin;

(2) Motor vehicle stop means any stop of a motor vehicle; and

(3) Racial profiling means detaining an individual or conducting a motor vehicle stop based upon disparate treatment of an individual.

(1) On or before January 1, 2002, the Nebraska State Patrol, the county sheriffs, all city and village police departments, and any other law enforcement agency in this state shall adopt a written policy that prohibits the detention of any person or a motor vehicle stop when such action is motivated by racial profiling and the action would constitute a violation of the civil rights of the person.

(2) With respect to a motor vehicle stop, on and after January 1, 2002, the Nebraska State Patrol, the county sheriffs, all city and village police departments, and any other law enforcement agency in this state shall record and retain the following information using the form developed and promulgated pursuant to section 20-505:

(a) The number of motor vehicle stops;

(b) The characteristics of race or ethnicity of the person stopped. The identification of such characteristics shall be based on the observation and perception of the law enforcement officer responsible for reporting the motor vehicle stop and the information shall not be required to be provided by the person stopped;

(c) If the stop is for a law violation, the nature of the alleged law violation that resulted in the motor vehicle stop;

(d) Whether a warning or citation was issued, an arrest made, or a search conducted as a result of the motor vehicle stop. Search does not include a search incident to arrest or an inventory search; and

(e) Any additional information that the Nebraska State Patrol, the county sheriffs, all city and village police departments, or any other law enforcement agency in this state, as the case may be, deems appropriate.

(3) The Nebraska Commission on Law Enforcement and Criminal Justice may develop a uniform system for receiving allegations of racial profiling. The Nebraska State Patrol, the county sheriffs, all city and village police departments, and any other law enforcement agency in this state shall provide to the commission

(a) a copy of each allegation of racial profiling received and

(b) written notification of the review and disposition of such allegation. No information revealing the identity of the law enforcement officer involved in the stop shall be used, transmitted, or disclosed in violation of any collective bargaining agreement provision or personnel rule under which such law enforcement officer is employed. No information revealing the identity of the complainant shall be used, transmitted, or disclosed in the form alleging racial profiling.

(4) Any law enforcement officer who in good faith records information on a motor vehicle stop pursuant to this section shall not be held civilly liable for the act of recording such information unless the law enforcement officer's conduct was unreasonable or reckless or in some way contrary to law.

(5) On or before October 1, 2002, and annually thereafter until January 1, 2004, the Nebraska State Patrol, the county sheriffs, all city and village police departments, and all other law enforcement agencies in this state shall provide to the commission, in such form as the commission prescribes, a summary report of the information recorded pursuant to subsection (2) of this section.

(6) On and after January 1, 2002, and until January 1, 2004, the commission may, within the limits of its existing appropriations, provide for a review of the prevalence and disposition of motor vehicle stops based on racial profiling and allegations reported pursuant to this section. The results of such review shall be reported to the Governor and the Legislature on or before April 1, 2004.

On or before January 1, 2002, the Nebraska Commission on Law Enforcement and Criminal Justice, the Superintendent of Law Enforcement and Public Safety, the Attorney General, and the State Court Administrator may adopt and promulgate:

(1) A form, in printed or electronic format, to be used by a law enforcement officer when making a motor vehicle stop to record personal identifying information about the operator of such motor vehicle, the location of the stop, the reason for the stop, and any other information that is required to be recorded pursuant to subsection (2) of section 20-504 and

(2) a form, in printed or electronic format, to be used to report an allegation of racial profiling by a law enforcement officer.

Nevada

NRS 289.820 Peace officer prohibited from engaging in racial profiling; retaliatory or punitive action prohibited against peace officer for disclosure of information concerning racial profiling.

1. A peace officer shall not engage in racial profiling.

2. No retaliatory or punitive action may be taken against a peace officer who discloses information concerning racial profiling.

3. For purposes of this section, "racial profiling" means reliance by a peace officer upon the race, ethnicity or national origin of a person as a factor in initiating action when the race, ethnicity or national origin of the person is not part of an identifying description of a specific suspect for a specific crime.

North Carolina

AN ACT TO REQUIRE THE DIVISION OF CRIMINAL STATISTICS TO COLLECT AND MAINTAIN STATISTICS ON TRAFFIC LAW ENFORCEMENT.

The General Assembly of North Carolina enacts:
Section 1. G.S. 114-10 reads as rewritten:
§ 114-10. Division of Criminal Statistics.
The Attorney General shall set up in the Department of Justice a division to be designated as the Division of Criminal Statistics. There shall be assigned to this Division by the Attorney General duties as follows:

(1) To collect and correlate information in criminal law administration, including crimes committed, arrests made, dispositions on preliminary hearings, prosecutions, convictions, acquittals, punishment, appeals, together with the age, race, and sex of the offender, and such

other information concerning crime and criminals as may appear significant or helpful. To correlate such information with the operations of agencies and institutions charged with the supervision of offenders on probation, in penal and correctional institutions, on parole and pardon, so as to show the volume, variety and tendencies of crime and criminals and the workings of successive links in the machinery set up for the administration of the criminal law in connection with the arrests, trial, punishment, probation, prison parole and pardon of all criminals in North Carolina.

(2) To collect, correlate, and maintain access to information that will assist in the performance of duties required in the administration of criminal justice throughout the State. This information may include, but is not limited to, motor vehicle registration, drivers' licenses, wanted and missing persons, stolen property, warrants, stolen vehicles, firearms registration, sexual offender registration as provided under Article 27A of Chapter 14 of the General Statutes, drugs, drug users and parole and probation histories. In performing this function, the Division may arrange to use information available in other agencies and units of State, local and federal government, but shall provide security measures to insure that such information shall be made available only to those whose duties, relating to the administration of justice, require such information.

(2a) To collect, correlate, and maintain the following information regarding traffic law enforcement by law enforcement officers:

a. The number of drivers stopped for routine traffic enforcement by law enforcement officers and whether or not a citation or warning was issued;

b. Identifying characteristics of the drivers stopped, including the race or ethnicity, approximate age, and gender;

c. The alleged traffic violation that led to the stop;

d. Whether a search was instituted as a result of the stop;

e. Whether the vehicle, personal effects, driver, or passenger or passengers were searched, and the race or ethnicity, approximate age, and gender of each person searched;

f. Whether the search was conducted pursuant to consent, probable cause, or reasonable suspicion to suspect a crime, including the basis for the request for consent, or the circumstances establishing probable cause or reasonable suspicion;

g. Whether any contraband was found and the type and amount of any such contraband;

h. Whether any written citation or any oral or written warning was issued as a result of the stop;

i. Whether an arrest was made as a result of either the stop or the search;

j. Whether any property was seized, with a description of that property;

k. Whether the officers making the stop encountered any physical resistance from the driver or passenger or passengers;

l. Whether the officers making the stop engaged in the use of force against the driver, passenger, or passengers for any reason;

m. Whether any injuries resulted from the stop; and

n. Whether the circumstances surrounding the stop were the subject of any investigation, and the results of that investigation.

o. The geographic location of the stop; if the officer making the stop is a member of the State Highway Patrol, the location shall be the Highway Patrol District in which the stop was made; for all other law enforcement officers, the location shall be the city or county in which the stop was made.

For purposes of this subdivision, "law enforcement officer" means:

1. All State law enforcement officers;

2. Law enforcement officers employed by county sheriffs or county police departments;

3. Law enforcement officers employed by police departments in municipalities with a population of 10,000 or more persons; and

4. Law enforcement officers employed by police departments in municipalities employing five or more full-time sworn officers for every 1,000 in population, as calculated by the Division for the calendar year in which the stop was made.

The information required by this subdivision need not be collected in connection with impaired driving checks under G.S. 20-16.3A or other types of roadblocks, vehicle checks, or checkpoints that are consistent with the laws of this State and with the State and federal constitutions, except when those stops result in a warning, search, seizure, arrest, or any of the other activity described in sub-subdivisions d. through n. of this subdivision.

The identity of the law enforcement officer making the stop required by sub-subdivision a. of this subdivision may be accomplished by assigning anonymous identification numbers to each officer in an agency. The correlation between the identification numbers and the names of the officers shall not be a public record, and shall not be disclosed by the agency except when required by order of a court of competent jurisdiction to resolve a claim or defense properly before the court.

The Division shall publish and distribute by December 1 of each year a list indicating the law enforcement officers that will be subject to the provisions of this subdivision during the calendar year commencing the following January 1.

(3) To make scientific study, analysis and comparison from the information so collected and correlated with similar information gathered by federal agencies, and to provide the Governor and the General

Assembly with the information so collected biennially, or more often if required by the Governor.

(4) To perform all the duties heretofore imposed by law upon the Attorney General with respect to criminal statistics.

(5) To perform such other duties as may be from time to time prescribed by the Attorney General.

(6) To promulgate rules and regulations for the administration of this Article.

Section 2. This act shall not be construed to obligate the General Assembly to make any appropriation to implement the provisions of this act. Each department and agency to which this act applies shall implement the provisions of this act from funds otherwise appropriated to that department or agency.

Oklahoma

Oklahoma Statutes Title 22. Criminal Procedure Chapter 2 § 34.3. Stop Racial Profiling

A. For the purposes of this section, "racial profiling" means the detention, interdiction or other disparate treatment of an individual solely on the basis of the racial or ethnic status of such individual.

B. No officer of any municipal, county or state law enforcement agency shall engage in racial profiling.

C. The race or ethnicity of an individual shall not be the sole factor in determining the existence of probable cause to take into custody or to arrest an individual or in constituting a reasonable and articulable suspicion that an offense has been or is being committed so as to justify the detention of an individual or the investigatory stop of a motor vehicle.

D. A violation of this section shall be a misdemeanor.

E. Every municipal, county, and state law enforcement agency shall adopt a detailed written policy that clearly defines the elements constituting racial profiling. Each agency's policy shall prohibit racial profiling based solely on an individual's race or ethnicity. The policy shall be available for public inspection during normal business hours.

F. If the investigation of a complaint of racial profiling reveals the officer was in direct violation of the law enforcement agency's written policy regarding racial profiling, the employing law enforcement agency shall take appropriate action consistent with applicable laws, rules, ordinances or policy.

Historical Data

Added by Laws 2000, c. 325, § 1, eff. June 5, 2000. Oklahoma Statutes Citationized Title 22. Criminal Procedure Chapter 2 § 34.4. Filing Racial Profiling Complaint

Whenever a person who is stopped or arrested believes the stop or arrest was in violation of Section 1 of this act, that person may file a complaint with the Oklahoma Human Rights Commission and may also file a complaint with the district attorney for the county in which the stop or arrest occurred. A copy of the complaint shall be forwarded to the arresting officer's employer by the Commission. The employer shall investigate the complaint for purposes of disciplinary action and/or criminal prosecution.

Historical Data

Added by Laws 2000, c. 325, § 2, eff. June 5, 2000.

Oklahoma Statutes Citationized Title 22. Criminal Procedure Chapter 2 § 34.5. Procedures for Filing Racial Profiling Complaint—Annual Report

A. The Oklahoma Human Rights Commission shall promulgate rules establishing procedures for filing a racial profiling complaint with the Oklahoma Human Rights Commission and the district attorney and the process for delivering a copy of the complaint by the Commission to the employing agency. The Commission, in consultation with the Governor's Cabinet Secretary for Safety and Security, shall promulgate forms for complaints of racial profiling.

B. The Commission shall compile an annual report of all complaints received for racial profiling and submit the report on or before January 31 of each year to the Governor, the President Pro Tempore of the Senate, and the Speaker of the House of Representatives.

Rhode Island

Enacted 7/13/2000

SECTION 1. Title 31 of the General Laws entitled "Motor and Other Vehicles" is hereby amended by adding thereto the following chapter:

CHAPTER 21.1 TRAFFIC STOP STATISTICS

31-21.1-1. Title.—This Chapter may be cited as the "Traffic Stops Statistics Act."

31-21.1-2. Declaration and Policy.—The General Assembly hereby declares that racial profiling as the sole reason for stopping or searching motorists on our public highways is against public policy and violates the civil rights of the motorist. For purposes of this chapter, "racial profiling" means the detention, interdiction or other disparate treatment of an individual solely on the basis of the racial or ethnic status of such individual. The purpose of this chapter is to conduct a study of the traffic stops by the police to determine whether such racial profiling is occurring and to require that police prohibit the practice of racial profiling.

31-21.1-3. Advisory Committee Established.—There is hereby established an advisory committee to be called the "Traffic Stop Study Advisory Committee." Said committee shall consist of thirteen (13) members: three (3) of whom shall be from the House of Representatives, not more than two (2) from the same political party, to be appointed by the Speaker; three (3) of whom shall be from the Senate, not more than two (2) from the same political party, to be appointed by the Majority Leader; two (2) of whom shall be appointed by the Governor; one (1) of whom shall be the Attorney General's designee, who shall be the president of the Rhode Island Police Chiefs Association; one (1) of whom shall be the executive director of the Urban League of Rhode Island or his or her designee; (1) of whom shall be the executive director of the National Conference for Community and Justice (NCCJ) or his or her designee; one (1) of whom shall be the executive director of the Rhode Island Commission for Human Rights or his or her designee; and one (1) of whom shall be a representative from a college or university in Rhode Island, who shall be a professor of statistics, to be appointed by the Governor.

Said committee shall advise the Attorney General throughout the course of the traffic stop study authorized by this chapter. The Attorney General shall work in cooperation with the committee and shall keep the committee informed on all matters relating to the implementation and enforcement of this chapter, including but not limited to, information on all data collected and budgetary expenditures. The committee is advisory only with all power under the chapter resting with the Attorney General.

31-21.1-4. Traffic Stop Study.—(a) The Attorney General is hereby authorized to and shall conduct a study of routine traffic stops by the Rhode Island State Police and each municipal police department. The study shall include the collection and analysis of the data received from the police department pursuant to this section, which shall include the following information for each traffic stop conducted by the police;

(1) The date, time and general location of the traffic stop;

(2) The race or ethnicity, gender and approximate age of the driver stopped; provided that the identification of such characteristics shall be based on the observation and perception of the police officer making the stop and the information shall not be requested of the person stopped;

(3) The reason for the stop;

(4) Whether a search was instituted as a result of the stop;

(5) The scope of any search conducted;

(6) Whether the search was conducted pursuant to consent, probable cause, or reasonable suspicion to suspect a crime;

(7) Whether any contraband, including money, was seized in the course of the search, and if so, the nature of the contraband;

(8) Whether any warning or citation was issued as a result of the stop;

(9) Whether an arrest was made as a result of either the stop or the search;

(10) The approximate duration of the stop; and

(11) Whether the vehicle is registered in Rhode Island or out of the state;

(b) Not later than ninety (90) days after the passage of this act, the Attorney General, with the advice of the committee, shall develop a form, in both printed and electronic format, to be used by each police officer when making a traffic stop to record the data required under this chapter.

(c) Beginning January 15, 2001, and monthly thereafter, each municipal police department and the Rhode Island State Police shall transmit to the Attorney General a report containing:

(1) All of the forms collected to date of motorists who were stopped;

(2) Any complaints filed by motorists who believed they were the subject of racial profiling, provided that no information revealing the identity of the complainant, witnesses or the law enforcement officer involved in the traffic stop shall be used, transmitted or disclosed in violation of the provisions of Chapter 28.6 of Title 42, the Law Enforcement Officers' Bill of Rights; and

(3) Any other information the police department or Rhode Island State Police deem appropriate.

(d) The study authorized under this chapter shall include a multivariate analysis of the collected data in accordance with general statistical standards. The Attorney General shall collect data for a period of not less than twenty-four (24) months and report its findings and conclusions to the Governor and the General Assembly not later than twenty-eight (28) months after the commencement of the collection of data under this chapter. The report, findings and conclusions submitted pursuant to this subsection shall be deemed a public record.

(e) In addition, the Attorney General, with the advice of the committee, shall prepare, on a quarterly basis, a summary report of the monthly data provided by each police department and the State Police for that quarterly period. Said report shall be a public record. The summary report shall include a monthly breakdown by race for each police department of the number of traffic stops made and of searches conducted, and any other information deemed appropriate by the Attorney General with the advice of the committee. The report shall be released not more than ninety (90) days after the end of each quarterly period. No information revealing the identity of any individual shall be contained in the report.

(f) Upon passage of this Act, the Attorney General with the advice of the committee shall procure the services of an organization, company, person or other entity with sufficient expertise in the field of statistics to assist with the implementation of this chapter. The organization, company, person or other entity so retained shall assist the Attorney General and the committee with the design of the methodology for gathering statistics pursuant to this chapter, monitor compliance with the act throughout the study, and conduct a statistical analysis at the conclusion of the study to determine the extent to which racial profiling exists within the state.

(g) Appropriate funding shall be made available to implement the provisions of this chapter.

(h) The department of attorney general shall be exempt from the provisions of chapter 37-2 of the general laws in connection with its procurement of equipment and services necessary to the implementation of this act.

31-21.1-5. Adoption of Written Policies.—Not later than ninety (90) days after the passage of this act each police department and the State Police shall adopt written policies which shall;

(a) Provide a system for the collection of the data required under section 31–21.1–3 and the transmission of the data to the Attorney General as required; and

(b) Prohibit the use of racial profiling as the sole reason for stopping or searching motorists for routine traffic stops. Copies of the policies adopted pursuant to this section shall be submitted to the Attorney General and the committee, and shall be public records.

31-21.1-6. Data Collection and Use.—(a) Except as otherwise specified herein, data acquired under this section shall be used only for research or statistical purposes. Data acquired under this section shall not be used in any legal or administrative proceeding to establish an inference of discrimination on the basis of particular identifying characteristics, except by court order. Notwithstanding the foregoing, during the collection of data, the information and forms collected pursuant to this chapter shall be public for those stops where a citation was issued or an arrest was made, and said forms shall include a citation or arrest number for reference. All data collected pursuant to this chapter shall be made public upon the completion of the study and the submission of the report; provided, however, that any complaints filed pursuant to 31-21.1-4(c)(2) shall be subject to the provisions of Chapter 28.6 of Title 42.

(b) Any police officer who in good faith records traffic stop information pursuant to the requirements of this chapter shall not be held civilly liable for the act of recording such information unless the officer's conduct was reckless.

31-21.1-7. Penalties for refusal to act.—An organization chartered for the purpose of combating discrimination, racism, or of safeguarding civil liberties, or of promoting full, free, or equal employment opportunities may seek appropriate relief in a civil action against any police department for failing to collect or transmit the data as required herein, and may be awarded its costs, including attorneys' fees, for bringing such an action. As a condition precedent to the filing of a civil action by an organization under this section, the organization shall send a notice to the Attorney General and the committee identifying the police department which is failing to collect or transmit the data and the organization shall then allow fifteen (15) days to elapse to allow the police department to come into compliance or to allow the Attorney General to commence a civil action to enforce compliance with this chapter.

Tennessee

AN ACT To amend Tennessee Code Annotated, Title 4, Chapter 7, Part 1; Title 6, Chapter 54 and Title 8, Chapter 8, Part 2, relative to law enforcement.

BE IT ENACTED BY THE GENERAL ASSEMBLY OF THE STATE OF TENNESSEE:

SECTION 1. It is the intent of the General Assembly that the provisions of this act shall serve as a permissive pilot project and as such shall apply to the Tennessee Highway Patrol and any municipal police department or sheriff's department whose commissioner, safety director, chief or sheriff notifies the Comptroller of the Treasury by September 1, 2000, of its willingness to participate in such project.

SECTION 2. (a) Commencing on January 1, 2001, and continuing through the calendar year, the highway patrol and each municipal police department and sheriff's office to which this act applies, using the form developed and promulgated pursuant to subsection (d) of this section, shall record and retain the following information:

1) The number of persons stopped for traffic violations;

2) Characteristics of race, color, ethnicity, gender and age of such persons, provided the identification of such characteristics shall be based on the observation and perception of the law enforcement officer responsible for reporting the stop and the information shall not be required to be provided by the person stopped;

3) The nature of the alleged traffic violation that resulted in the stop;

4) Whether a warrant or citation was issued, an arrest made or a search conducted as a result of the stop; and

5) If a search was conducted, the type of search and the legal basis for that search, and whether contraband was discovered and property was seized.

(b) The highway patrol and each municipal police department or sheriff's office to which this act applies shall begin submitting such data and information to the Comptroller of the Treasury on a monthly basis, beginning not later than February 1, 2001, by submitting or electronically transferring a copy of the form prescribed by the Comptroller.

(c) Any law enforcement officer who in good faith records traffic stop information pursuant to the requirements of this section shall not be held civilly liable for the act of recording such information.

(d) The Comptroller shall, within the limits of existing resources, provide for a review of the prevalence and disposition of traffic stops reported pursuant to this section and develop and promulgate a form, in both printed and electronic format, to be used by law enforcement officers to which this act applies when making a traffic stop to record personal identifying information about the operator of the motor vehicle that is stopped, the location of the stop, the reason for the stop and other information that is required to be recorded pursuant to subsection (a) of this section. Not later than April 1, 2002, the Comptroller shall report to the Governor and General Assembly the results of such review, including any recommendations.

(e) The provisions of this act shall be in effect from the effective date of this act until July 1, 2002.

APPROVED this 19th day of June 2000

Texas

SECTION 1. Chapter 2, Code of Criminal Procedure, is amended by adding Articles 2.131 through 2.138 to read as follows:

Art. 2.131. RACIAL PROFILING PROHIBITED. A peace officer may not engage in racial profiling.

Art. 2.132. LAW ENFORCEMENT POLICY ON RACIAL PROFILING.

(a) In this article:

(1) "Law enforcement agency" means an agency of the state, or of a county, municipality, or other political subdivision of the state, that employs peace officers who make traffic stops in the routine performance of the officers' official duties.

(2) "Race or ethnicity" means of a particular descent, including Caucasian, African, Hispanic, Asian, or Native American descent.

(b) Each law enforcement agency in this state shall adopt a detailed written policy on racial profiling. The policy must:

(1) clearly define acts constituting racial profiling;

(2) strictly prohibit peace officers employed by the agency from engaging in racial profiling;

(3) implement a process by which an individual may file a complaint with the agency if the individual believes that a peace officer employed by the agency has engaged in racial profiling with respect to the individual;

(4) provide public education relating to the agency's complaint process;

(5) require appropriate corrective action to be taken against a peace officer employed by the agency who, after an investigation, is shown to have engaged in racial profiling in violation of the agency's policy adopted under this article;

(6) require collection of information relating to traffic stops in which a citation is issued and to arrests resulting from those traffic stops, including information relating to:

(A) the race or ethnicity of the individual detained; and

(B) whether a search was conducted and, if so, whether the person detained consented to the search; and

(7) require the agency to submit to the governing body of each county or municipality served by the agency an annual report of the information collected under Subdivision (6) if the agency is an agency of a county, municipality, or other political subdivision of the state.

(c) The data collected as a result of the reporting requirements of this article shall not constitute prima facie evidence of racial profiling.

(d) On adoption of a policy under Subsection (b), a law enforcement agency shall examine the feasibility of installing video camera and transmitter-activated equipment in each agency law enforcement motor vehicle regularly used to make traffic stops and transmitter-activated equipment in each agency law enforcement motorcycle regularly used to make traffic stops. If a law enforcement agency installs video or audio equipment as provided by this subsection, the policy adopted by the agency under Subsection (b) must include standards for reviewing video and audio documentation.

(e) A report required under Subsection (b)(7) may not include identifying information about a peace officer who makes a traffic stop or about an individual who is stopped or arrested by a peace officer. This subsection does not affect the collection of information as required by a policy under Subsection (b)(6).

(f) On the commencement of an investigation by a law enforcement agency of a complaint described by Subsection (b)(3) in which a video or audio recording of the occurrence on which the complaint is based was made, the agency shall promptly provide a copy of the recording to the peace officer who is the subject of the complaint on written request by the officer.

Art. 2.133. REPORTS REQUIRED FOR TRAFFIC AND PEDES-TRIAN STOPS.

(a) In this article:

(1) "Race or ethnicity" has the meaning assigned by Article 2.132(a).

(2) "Pedestrian stop" means an interaction between a peace officer and an individual who is being detained for the purpose of a criminal investigation in which the individual is not under arrest.

(b) A peace officer who stops a motor vehicle for an alleged violation of a law or ordinance regulating traffic or who stops a pedestrian for any suspected offense shall report to the law enforcement agency that employs the officer information relating to the stop, including:

(1) a physical description of each person detained as a result of the stop, including:

(A) the person's gender; and

(B) the person's race or ethnicity, as stated by the person or, if the person does not state the person's race or ethnicity, as determined by the officer to the best of the officer's ability;

(2) the traffic law or ordinance alleged to have been violated or the suspected offense;

(3) whether the officer conducted a search as a result of the stop and, if so, whether the person detained consented to the search;

(4) whether any contraband was discovered in the course of the search and the type of contraband discovered;

(5) whether probable cause to search existed and the facts supporting the existence of that probable cause;

(6) whether the officer made an arrest as a result of the stop or the search, including a statement of the offense charged;

(7) the street address or approximate location of the stop; and

(8) whether the officer issued a warning or a citation as a result of the stop, including a description of the warning or a statement of the violation charged.

Art. 2.134. COMPILATION AND ANALYSIS OF INFORMATION COLLECTED.

(a) In this article, "pedestrian stop" means an interaction between a peace officer and an individual who is being detained for the purpose of a criminal investigation in which the individual is not under arrest.

(b) A law enforcement agency shall compile and analyze the information contained in each report received by the agency under Article 2.133. Not later than March 1 of each year, each local law enforcement agency shall submit a report containing the information compiled during the previous calendar year to the governing body of each county or municipality served by the agency in a manner approved by the agency.

(c) A report required under Subsection (b) must include:

(1) a comparative analysis of the information compiled under Article 2.133 to:

(A) determine the prevalence of racial profiling by peace officers employed by the agency; and

(B) examine the disposition of traffic and pedestrian stops made by officers employed by the agency, including searches resulting from the stops; and

(2) information relating to each complaint filed with the agency alleging that a peace officer employed by the agency has engaged in racial profiling.

(d) A report required under Subsection (b) may not include identifying information about a peace officer who makes a traffic or pedestrian stop or about an individual who is stopped or arrested by a peace officer. This subsection does not affect the reporting of information required under Article 2.133(b)(1).

SECTION 2. Chapter 3, Code of Criminal Procedure, is amended by adding Article 3.05 to read as follows:

Art. 3.05. RACIAL PROFILING. In this code, "racial profiling" means a law enforcement–initiated action based on an individual's race, ethnicity, or national origin rather than on the individual's behavior or on information identifying the individual as having engaged in criminal activity.

SECTION 3. Section 96.641, Education Code, is amended by adding Subsection (j) to read as follows:

(j) As part of the initial training and continuing education for police chiefs required under this section, the institute shall establish a program on racial profiling. The program must include an examination of the best practices for:

(1) monitoring peace officers' compliance with laws and internal agency policies relating to racial profiling;

(2) implementing laws and internal agency policies relating to preventing racial profiling; and

(3) analyzing and reporting collected information.

SECTION 4. Section 1701.253, Occupations Code, is amended by adding Subsection (e) to read as follows:

(e) As part of the minimum curriculum requirements, the commission shall establish a statewide comprehensive education and training program on racial profiling for officers licensed under this chapter. An officer shall complete a program established under this subsection not later than the second anniversary of the date the officer is licensed under this chapter or the date the officer applies for an intermediate proficiency certificate, whichever date is earlier.

SECTION 5. Section 1701.402, Occupations Code, is amended by adding Subsection (d) to read as follows:

(d) As a requirement for an intermediate proficiency certificate, an officer must complete an education and training program on racial profiling established by the commission under Section 1701.253(e).

Washington

Sec. 1. A new section is added to chapter 43.43 RCW to read as follows:

(1) Beginning May 1, 2000, the Washington state patrol shall collect, and report semiannually to the criminal justice training commission, the following information: (a) The number of individuals stopped for routine traffic enforcement, whether or not a citation or warning was issued; (b) Identifying characteristics of the individual stopped, including the race or ethnicity, approximate age, and gender; (c) The nature of the alleged violation that led to the stop; (d) Whether a search was instituted as a result of the stop; and (e) Whether an arrest was made, or a written citation issued, as a result of either the stop or the search. (2) The criminal justice training commission and the Washington state patrol shall compile the information required under subsection (1) of this section and make a report to the legislature no later than December 1, 2000.

Sec. 2. A new section is added to chapter 43.43 RCW to read as follows: (1) The Washington state patrol shall work with the criminal justice training commission and the Washington association of sheriffs and police chiefs to develop (a) further criteria for collection and evaluation of the data collected under section 1 of this act, and (b) training materials for use by the state patrol and local law enforcement agencies on the issue of racial profiling. (2) The Washington state patrol, criminal justice training commission, and Washington association of sheriffs and police chiefs shall encourage local law enforcement agencies to voluntarily collect the data set forth under section 1(1) of this act.

Sec. 3. The Washington association of sheriffs and police chiefs shall report to the legislature by December 1, 2000, the following information: (1) The names and number of local law enforcement agencies voluntarily collecting data on potential racial profiling; (2) The type of data being collected by each participating agency; and (3) The manner in which the agencies are using the data collected.

Sec. 4. This act is necessary for the immediate preservation of the public peace, health, or safety, or support of the state government and its existing public institutions, and takes effect immediately. Passed the Senate February 15, 2000. Passed the House March 1, 2000. Approved by the Governor March 24, 2000. Filed in Office of Secretary of State March 24, 2000.

West Virginia

[Signed by the Governor, March 7, 2002]

AN ACT to amend article twenty-nine, chapter thirty of the code of West Virginia, one thousand nine hundred thirty-one, as amended, by adding thereto a new section, designated section ten, relating to prohibiting racial profiling by law-enforcement officers and agencies.

Be it enacted by the Legislature of West Virginia:

That article twenty-nine, chapter thirty of the code of West Virginia, one thousand nine hundred thirty-one, as amended, be amended by adding thereto a new section, designated section ten, to read as follows:

ARTICLE 29. LAW ENFORCEMENT TRAINING AND CERTIFICATION.

§30-29-10. Prohibition of racial profiling.

(a) The Legislature finds that the use by a law-enforcement officer of race, ethnicity, or national origin in deciding which persons should be subject to traffic stops, stops and frisks, questioning, searches, and seizures is a problematic law-enforcement tactic. The reality or public perception of racial profiling alienates people from police, hinders community policing efforts, and causes law-enforcement officers and law-enforcement agencies to lose credibility and trust among the people law-enforcement is sworn to protect and serve. Therefore, the West Virginia Legislature declares that racial profiling is contrary to public policy and should not be used as a law-enforcement investigative tactic.

(b) For purposes of this section:

(1) The term "law-enforcement officer" means any duly authorized member of a law-enforcement agency who is authorized to maintain public peace and order, prevent and detect crime, make arrests and enforce the laws of the state or any county or municipality thereof.

(2) The term "municipality" means any incorporated town or city whose boundaries lie within the geographic boundaries of the state.

(3) The term "racial profiling" means the practice of a law-enforcement officer relying, to any degree, on race, ethnicity, or national origin in selecting which individuals to subject to routine investigatory activities, or in deciding upon the scope and substance of law-enforcement activity following the initial routine investigatory activity. Racial profiling does not include reliance on race, ethnicity, or national origin in combination with other identifying factors when the law-enforcement officer is seeking to apprehend a specific suspect whose race, ethnicity, or national origin is part of the description of the suspect.

(4) The term "state and local law-enforcement agencies" means any duly authorized state, county or municipal organization employ-

ing one or more persons whose responsibility is the enforcement of laws of the state or any county or municipality thereof.

(c) No law-enforcement officer shall engage in racial profiling.

(d) All state and local law-enforcement agencies shall establish and maintain policies and procedures designed to prevent racial profiling. Policies and procedures shall include the following:

(1) A prohibition on racial profiling;

(2) Independent procedures for receiving, investigating, and responding to complaints alleging racial profiling by law-enforcement officers;

(3) Procedures to discipline law-enforcement officers who engage in racial profiling; and

(4) Any other policies and procedures deemed necessary by state and local law-enforcement agencies to eliminate racial profiling.

7

Organizations and Agencies

M any people interested in criminal justice profiling find themselves unsure of where to turn to research the issue further. Fortunately, there are many government agencies and organizations that are available to serve as resources. In this chapter, a number of the public and private organizations are presented to the reader. The purposes of these organizations are summarized, as are the types of information one can receive from them. Information concerning how to contact these agencies and organizations is provided as well.

When researching an issue that is potentially controversial, as criminal profiling is, it is important to remember that many relevant organizations exist with a specific agenda in mind. This does not mean the information those organizations provide is invalid; but in some cases, the information may not be complete. As with most issues, people and organizations who advocate a particular position are inclined to emphasize information that supports that position.

So, when conducting research using these organizations, readers must be mindful that not all the information they receive is gospel. This caveat now having been given, the organizations that follow in this chapter can serve as a wealth of information and support for those interested in the issue of profiling. In many cases, the organizations summarized below have a broader purpose than simply addressing or responding to the issue of profiling. Nonetheless, these organizations can serve as an invaluable source for becoming thoroughly familiar with profiling and its ramifications.

Private Organizations

Academy of Behavioral Profiling
336 Lincoln Street, P.O. Box 6406
Sitka, AK 99835
http://www.profiling.org

The Academy of Behavioral Profiling is a professional association whose mission is to advance the application of evidence-based criminal profiling techniques within the criminal justice system. The emphasis with this organization is to improve the science behind using offender behavior to predict and solve crimes. The association recognizes that race, gender, sexual orientation, and other such classifications are not sufficient criteria by themselves to build a profile. The association publishes a journal that is available to members.

American Civil Liberties Union
125 Broad Street, 18th Floor
New York, NY 10004
http://www.aclu.org

The American Civil Liberties Union (ACLU) is a nonprofit organization founded in 1920. The purpose of the ACLU is to defend civil liberties—particularly those granted under the U.S. Constitution's Bill of Rights. It was originally founded in response to the widespread jailing of foreign-born political radicals in the early part of the twentieth century as the United States geared up for and then fought World War I. The ACLU advances its agenda through dissemination of information and through legal action. Common issues of importance to the ACLU include immigrant rights, women in prison, police misconduct, and religious liberties (usually seeking the removal of religion from the public square). Information concerning these issues, and on the ACLU's national "Campaign against Racial Profiling" specifically, can be accessed through the ACLU Web site. The Web site also links to ACLU press releases, legal briefs, and legislation around the United States.

American Civil Rights Institute
P.O. Box 188350
Sacramento, CA 95818
http://www.acri.org

The American Civil Rights Institute exists for the purpose of educating the public about race and gender preferences. The Institute publishes summaries of cases relating to the issue of preferences on its Web site. Further, the Web site contains links to pertinent legislation, legal briefs, speeches, and a full bibliography of suggested reading materials. The institute monitors the implementation of legislation and legal decisions concerning race and gender neutrality and then works to educate public officials and private citizens on the issue.

Americans for Effective Law Enforcement
841 W. Touhy Avenue
Park Ridge, IL 60068
http://www.aele.org

Americans for Effective Law Enforcement (AELE) was formed in 1966. It created a legal research center in 1973. AELE is a research-driven educational organization. Its primary mission is to disseminate legal information through seminars, other training, use of the legal center, and through the Web. AELE maintains information concerning law enforcement practice, including the use of profiling. AELE also maintains information concerning jails and prisoner rights issues.

Amnesty International
322 8th Avenue
New York, NY 10001
http://www.amnesty.org

Amnesty International is the premiere privately funded global organization concerned with human rights issues. Amnesty International conducts investigations of alleged abuses around the world. It has chapters located in dozens of countries around the world. From the Web site, a researcher can access reports relating to abuses in the United States and abroad. Frequently, the abuses tie directly to the military and criminal justice authorities of a given country. Amnesty International is a leading opponent of the death penalty. It also fights inhumane treatment of the incarcerated. Reports and other documents concerning racism, sexism, and homophobia are also available through the Web site.

The Cato Institute
1000 Massachusetts Avenue NW

Washington, DC 20001
http://www.cato.org

The Cato Institute is a think tank whose purpose is to promote public policies consistent with the traditional American principles of limited government, individual liberty, free markets, and peace. The Cato Institute pursues this goal through involvement in public presentations and debates, conducting research, publishing, and through maintaining its Web site. Although often considered a conservative organization, the Cato Institute is actually libertarian and a good resource for information concerning the dangers of excessive police authority and actions. A search of the Web site will link to several documents concerning profiling.

Center for Constitutional Rights
666 Broadway, 7th Floor
New York, NY 10012
http:///www.ccr-ny.org

The Center for Constitutional Rights uses litigation and advocacy to advance the law in a direction it views as positive, to empower poor communities and communities of color, and to guarantee the rights of people with few legal resources. The center also seeks to train constitutional and human rights attorneys and to foster a broad movement for constitutional and human rights. Through the center and through its Web site, much information is available concerning constitutional rights generally and profiling specifically.

Center for Equal Opportunity
14 Pidgeon Hill Drive, Suite 500
Sterling, VA 20165
http://www.ceousa.org

The Center for Equal Opportunity is a nonprofit organization established out of devotion to a truly color-blind society in which equal opportunity and racial harmony can reign. The organization maintains an extensive Web site for the research to peruse. The site offers an "in the news" section with current stories relating to equal opportunity. The organization has a significant section relating to immigration issues as well as issues concerning disparate impact between the races.

Commission on the Accreditation of Law Enforcement Agencies

10302 Eaton Place, Suite 100
Fairfax, VA 22030
http://www.calea.org

The Commission on the Accreditation of Law Enforcement Agencies (CALEA) was founded in 1979. It is an organization dedicated to the standardization of professional police practice. CALEA does this by assessing police agencies seeking accreditation against a list of standards. Many of the standards are measured by whether a police agency has adopted certain policies supported by CALEA. Although CALEA officially finds profiling generally to be a potentially useful tool in law enforcement, it requires of its member organizations strict policies governing the misuse of profiling—particularly making law enforcement decisions based solely on race, ethnicity, religion, gender, and sexual orientation. The CALEA Web site offers its model policy concerning profiling for any viewer who wishes to read it.

Community Policing Consortium

1726 M Street NW, Suite 801
Washington, DC 20036
http://www.communitypolicing.org

The Community Policing Consortium is a partnership of five major police executive organizations: the International Association of Chiefs of Police, the National Sheriffs Association, the National Organization of Black Law Enforcement Executives, the Police Executive Research Forum, and the Police Foundation. The consortium is funded and administered by the U.S. Department of Justice, Community Oriented Policing Services (COPS). The consortium was established in 1993 and works to provide community policing training and support to law enforcement agencies. The Web site provides access to a wealth of resources concerning the relationship between police and the communities being served. Links to sites and documents with specific reference to profiling are available through the consortium site.

Congressional Black Caucus Foundation

1720 Massachusetts Avenue NW
Washington, DC 20036
http://www.cbcfonline.org

The Congressional Black Caucus Foundation was established in 1976. It was set up for the purpose of broadening the influence of African Americans in the public policy and legal arenas. The foundation's Web site is an excellent source of information concerning public policies, research, and education in the many areas of importance to the African American community. Through the foundation Web site, a researcher can access audio/video materials and publications relating to bias and discrimination in the criminal justice system, among other topics.

Drug Policy Alliance
70 W. 36th Street, 16th Floor
New York, NY 10018
http://www.drugpolicy.org

This organization's purpose is to primarily focus on drug laws and policies in the United States. The Drug Policy Alliance seeks to reform the drug laws so as to deemphasize the use of punitive criminal justice measures. Key issues for the alliance include sentencing reform, police conduct, and profiling. The alliance publishes position papers on a variety of topics. Additionally, the Web site serves as a portal to an online library, from which documents can be viewed concerning the effect of drugs and drug laws on different communities, including racial minorities, women, and homosexuals.

Drug Reform Coordination Network
1623 Connecticut Avenue NW, 3rd Floor
Washington, DC 20009
http://www.stopthedrugwar.org

The Drug Reform Coordination Network is an organization that seeks to reform U.S. drug laws through decriminalization. The organization's Web site is very thorough, with links to attorney general opinions, research data, and commercial documents relating to drug use and drug crimes. The site permits users to access a citizen's guide to police encounters and also offers information concerning profiling within the context of drug enforcement.

EthnicMajority.com
655 13th Street, Suite 303
Oakland, CA 95612
http://www.ethnicmajority.com

EthnicMajority.com is a privately funded organization committed to exposing discrimination against minorities in various walks of life. The group is funded by an organization called Diverse Strategies. EthnicMajority.com emphasizes minority issues in the workplace, politics, the criminal justice system, housing, and other areas. The organization Web site, which is the group's primary product, provides several links and publications of relevance to profiling.

Human Rights Watch
350 Fifth Avenue, 34th Floor
New York, NY 10118
http://www. hrw.org

The purpose of Human Rights Watch is to advocate on behalf of victims of human rights abuses. The organization investigates various types of abuses and discrimination. It then presents its findings to governmental bodies to encourage them to respect human rights laws that are implicated in their findings. Human Rights Watch also seeks to increase public support for ending various human rights abuses in the United States and around the world. Key issues of interest for this organization include prisoner rights, the rights of immigrants and refugees, and women's rights.

International Association of Chiefs of Police
515 North Washington Street
Alexandria, VA 22314
http://www.theiacp.org

The International Association of Chiefs of Police (IACP) was founded in 1893 for the purposes of advancing police professionalism through modern (at the time) administrative practices and reform, increased use of technology to fight crime, improving training and education among the police ranks, and fostering high ethical standards in policing. The IACP provides a vast array of resources to those interested in researching police practices. It offers police professionals model policies for their departments, including policies concerning the use of profiling. The IACP publishes one of the leading police trade journals available—*Police Chief*. Archived articles from past issues of *Police Chief* can be accessed through the Web site. Additionally, many links are available to other sites and documents concerning police/community encounters and the issue of profiling as a tool for law enforcement.

International Association of Directors of Law Enforcement Standards and Training
2521 Country Club Way
Albion, MI 49224
http://www.iadlest.org

The International Association of Directors of Law Enforcement Standards and Training (IADLEST) is an organization made up of the various state agencies that guide the standards for police training and practice. These agencies generally are responsible for certifying police officers in a given state and revoking that certification or license when officers engage in serious misconduct. The IADLEST Web site provides users links to relevant law enforcement organizations in every state. The site also provides model policies for standards and training boards to use, as well as police agencies. Among the model policies are ones that relate to profiling and traffic stops.

John M. Ashbrook Center for Public Affairs
401 College Avenue
Ashland, OH 44805
http://www.ashbrook.org

The Ashbrook Center for Public Affairs is housed by Ashland University. The purpose of the center is to conduct research and promote discussion of the principles and practices of U.S. constitutional government and politics. The center emphasizes the scholarly defense of individual liberty, limited government, and civil morality—all of which together make up America's "democratic way of life." The Ashbrook Center Web site offers users a search engine through which one can access well over 100 documents relating to profiling.

Leadership Conference on Civil Rights
1629 K Street NW, 10th Floor
Washington, DC 20006
http://www.civilrights.org

The Leadership Conference on Civil Rights is a socially concerned, issue-oriented organization that attempts to promote a civil rights agenda through education. Resources available through the conference include audio resources, videos, and publications. The Web site is intended to serve as an online "nerve center" for people struggling against discrimination of all types and for the public at large to gain a better understanding of the nation's need for social and economic justice. The Web site offers users links to a variety of other relevant sites and organizations, including sites related to profiling.

National Association for the Advancement of Colored People
4805 Mt. Hope Drive
Baltimore, MD 21215
http://www.naacp.org

The National Association for the Advancement of Colored People (NAACP) is a long-standing civil rights organization specifically founded to promote equality and justice among the races and to advance opportunities to succeed for minorities—particularly African Americans. The organization was founded in 1909 by Ida Wells-Barnett, W. E. B. DuBois, and others. The purpose of the organization then was to fight segregation and violence perpetrated against black Americans. Today, the organization continues to be among the premiere civil rights organizations in the United States, representing itself as standing for civil and political liberty. The NAACP maintains volumes of resources governing a wide variety of topics concerning justice and equality. Although headquartered in Baltimore, the organization has chapters in every major urban center in the country. The Web site presents a wealth of resources concerning civil rights matters, including racial profiling. The site also links to many other sources of information. People interested in calling the NAACP twenty-four-hour hotline can do so at (410) 521–4939.

National Coalition on Police Accountability
59 East Van Buren, 2418
Chicago, IL 60605
http://www.websyr.edu/~nkrhodes/N-COPA.html

The National Coalition on Police Accountability (N-COPA) describes itself as an organization of religious, community, and legal groups and progressive law enforcement representatives working to hold police accountable to their communities through public education, community organizing, legislation, litigation, and promotion of empowered independent oversight. It was founded as a subsidiary of Citizen Alert, which is a nonprofit group primarily concerned about environmental justice. The N-COPA site, although dated, links to several publications concerning the oversight of police.

National Organization of Black Law Enforcement Executives
4609 Pinecrest Office Park Drive, Suite F
Alexandria, VA 22312
http://www.noblenatl.org

The National Organization of Black Law Enforcement Executives (NOBLE) was founded in 1976 for the purpose of confronting the issue of high crime in urban, low-income areas. Today, NOBLE sets out to work closely with urban communities to create greater cooperation with the criminal justice system so as to have a favorable impact on crime and violence. The organization also seeks to create a unified front of African American law enforcement executives in order to affect public policy, further opportunities for minorities in policing, and disseminate information, training, and consultation where needed. NOBLE emphasizes the need for law enforcement officers to be respectful of all citizens they deal with and for police personnel and organizations to be accountable to the public. The NOBLE Web site provides a section on "areas of concern," which then link to several documents and publications on biased policing.

National Sheriffs' Association
1450 Duke Street
Alexandria, VA 22314
http://www.sheriffs.org

The National Sheriffs' Association (NSA) is a nonprofit organization founded to advance professionalism and best practices in criminal justice, including both law enforcement and corrections. The NSA focuses on the unique role that sheriffs' departments have in that they serve law enforcement and correctional (through their jail operations) purposes at the same time. The NSA sponsors training around the country to modernize and improve criminal justice practice. The organization also helps local sheriffs' departments to secure grant funding for hot issues of the day (for example, antiterrorism, dealing with methamphetamine labs, and so on). The NSA Web site, like the IACP site, offers useful information to those researching the relationship between the criminal justice system and minority communities.

October 22 National Day of Protest to Stop Police Brutality, Repression and the Criminalization of a Generation
P.O. Box 2627
New York, NY 10009
http://www.october22.org

The October 22 National Day of Protest to Stop Police Brutality, Repression and the Criminalization of a Generation (NDP) was organized in 1995. Its name refers, in part, to the date on which the organization was formed. As the Web site notes, the NDP was initiated by a diverse coalition of organizations and individuals that came together out of a concern that the resistance against police brutality needed to take place at a national level. Every October 22, the NDP organizes a day of protest in several cities across the nation against police misconduct. These protests sometimes involve civil disobedience. The NDP Web site offers a variety of resources concerning the fight against police brutality. The perspective of the organization is radically left but nevertheless can serve as a useful resource site.

Police Complaint Center
1220 L Street NW, Suite 100–164
Washington, DC 20005
http://www.policeabuse.com

The Police Complaint Center (PCC) serves as a clearinghouse for information concerning police misconduct—especially unlawful profiling. The PCC invites victims of police abuse from around the country to report their experiences to the center, which then publishes the alleged abuses online. The PCC works to document the extent of police misconduct in the United States so that public policy may be affected. The PCC assists citizens in filing formal complaints against law enforcement and ensures that those complaints are given fair hearing without falling through the cracks. The PCC maintains a phone number to receive complaints: (202) 359–6406. The PCC Web site publishes several pieces of information concerning racial profiling and other dubious police activities.

Police Executive Research Forum
1120 Connecticut Avenue NW, Suite 930
Washington, DC 20036
http://www.policeforum.org

The Police Executive Research Forum (PERF) describes itself as an organization made up of progressive police executives around the United States. The mission of PERF is to advance professionalism and best practices in policing and to help foster good public policy relating to law enforcement issues. PERF maintains an excellent Web site with an entire online library available to users. A whole section linked to the Web site deals with the issue of profiling. Most of the information concerns racial and ethnic profiling; however, there are items of information that relate to profiling along other lines, for example, gender, sexual orientation, religion, and so on. PERF sponsors many studies and publications. PERF also partners with the U.S. Department of Justice (DOJ). The PERF Web site links to several DOJ publications.

Police Foundation
1201 Connecticut Avenue NW
Washington, DC 20036
http://www.policefoundation.org

The Police Foundation is a nonprofit organization founded in 1970. The foundation is committed to improving the ability of police officers to perform their duties, which cover a wide variety of police practice. The foundation works closely with police organizations around the country to conduct pragmatic and useful research concerning the best practices in policing. Additionally, the Police Foundation produces several practitioner-oriented publications to improve policing. The Police Foundation Web site maintains a whole section dedicated to community policing. Additionally, the Web site links to current and proposed legislation relating to police practices such as profiling.

Public Agenda
6 East 39th Street
New York, NY 10016
http://www.publicagenda.org

Public Agenda is a nonprofit, nonpartisan organization created to address a wide range of policy issues through its research and citizen education programs. Issues the organization regularly confronts include health care, schools, national security matters, acquired immunodeficiency syndrome (AIDS), crime, the environment, and economics. By accessing its Web site and following the links to sections on crime, several documents concerning profiling can be viewed.

The Racial Fairness Project
1027 Superior Avenue, Room 140
Cleveland, OH 44114
http://www.racialfairness.org

The Racial Fairness Project was formed for the purpose of pursuing racial and ethnic justice through education of the public, advocacy efforts, and empowerment of communities and institutions by providing information and support. The project distributes a newsletter that can be delivered to subscribers via e-mail. The project's Web site links to many articles and research data concerning matters of racial justice. The project tends to emphasize the context of Ohio, although the information at the site also has general appeal as well.

Rainbow/PUSH Coalition
930 E. 50th Street
Chicago, IL 60615
http://www.rainbowpush.org

Rainbow/PUSH is a progressive organization founded by Jesse Jackson. The mission of Rainbow/PUSH is to fight for social change and social justice. The organization fields several speakers to events around the country. Many of the speeches can be read online. Additionally, the organization's Web site offers press releases, commentaries, and a weekly newsletter. A search of the documents online will yield several resources concerning profiling—particularly racial profiling.

Southern Poverty Law Center
400 Washington Avenue
Montgomery, AL 36104
http://www.splcenter.org

The Southern Poverty Law Center was founded in 1971 as a small civil rights law firm in the racially tense South. The organization in recent years has come to be known for its aggressive battles against white supremacist organizations on behalf of victims of hate crimes. Law enforcement agencies frequently utilize the center's thorough tracking of hate groups. The center publishes an e-newsletter that contains articles and commentary on the center's work. The center does engage in advocacy relating to the criminal justice system. The Southern Poverty Law Center is an ardent foe of the death penalty and disparate sentencing of minorities.

Federal Government Agencies

U.S. Department of Justice
http://www.usdoj.gov

Easily, the most useful Internet site for the study of police practices generally and profiling specifically is the Web site maintained by the U.S. Department of Justice (DOJ). There are literally dozens of DOJ agencies with their own Web sites that can be accessed through the main DOJ Web site address. The DOJ is the lead federal entity responsible for setting law enforcement practice standards in the United States, gauging the extent of crime in the United States, researching the merits of particular police practices, and researching the extent of police misconduct. Additionally, the DOJ investigates and adjudicates criminal and civil action against law enforcers and their parent organizations when misconduct is alleged.

Some of the many Web sites of interest to those researching biases in the criminal justice system are listed below. Almost an unlimited number of links and publications relating to profiling and police/community relations are available through these sites. Even so, they represent only a partial list.

Bureau of Justice Statistics: http://www.ojp.usdoj.gov/bjs

Bureau of Justice Assistance: http://www.ojp.usdoj.gov/BJA

Bureau of Prisons: http://www.bop.gov

Civil Rights Division: http://www.usdoj.gov/crt/crt-home.html

Community Oriented Policing Services: http://www.cops. usdoj.gov

Community Relations Service: http://www.usdoj.gov/crs/ index.html

Federal Bureau of Investigation: http://www.fbi.gov

National Criminal Justice Reference Service: http://www. ncjrs.org

National Institute of Justice: http://www.ojp.usdoj.gov/nij

Office of Police Corps and Law Enforcement Education: http://www.ojp.usdoj.gov/opclee

Office of Legislative Affairs: http://www. usdoj.gov/ola

U.S. Department of State: http://www.state.gov

The U.S. Department of State represents the United States to the world. Consequently, the State Department is the chief agency in the federal government to advocate America's values to other countries, including values concerning fair and equitable treatment in the criminal justice system. From the State Department Web site, one can navigate to several documents and other sites concerning prosecution and punishment of criminals and dissidents.

Interestingly, the State Department Web site also maintains a section specifically on profiling. From the section, one can link to a variety of government documents, legislation, and opinion on the matter.

The profiling section of the U.S. Department of State Web site is: http://usinfo.state.gov/usa/race/profile/official.htm.

State Government Agencies

It is safe to say that criminal justice practice is a major public policy issue in every state of the union. Many states are presently confronting the issues of discrimination in policing, prosecution, and punishment. Other states have confronted such issues in the past. Still others are exploring these types of issues tangentially while dealing with other criminal justice matters.

The best way to ascertain what a particular state is doing or saying about the issue of criminal justice profiling is to go directly to a state's Web site and do a search. Commonly, the attorney general's office and the Department of Corrections for any given state are good places to start. When accessing a state Web site, there will always be a link to the various state agencies, to include the attorney general and the Corrections Department. Other potentially useful sites in the state's executive branch of government include the Department of Public Safety (or a state's equivalent), the state police or highway patrol, and the state's Peace Officer Standards and Training Board.

Also accessible from a state's Web site are the legislative and judicial branches.

By accessing the state legislature, a researcher will be able to conduct a search for proposed legislation concerning profiling. One could also search for existing statutes as well as studies and working papers commissioned and drafted at the behest of the legislature as a part of the public policy process.

Likewise, by accessing the judicial branch a researcher would be able to search court cases at the state and local level that relate to or involve the issue of profiling, either directly or indirectly. What's more, the judicial branch Web sites may include studies or policies concerning sentencing practices and guidelines.

As can be seen below, most state Web site addresses follow a simple pattern: http://www.state.??.us, where the "??" is simply the mail code for the state. So for Minnesota, the state Web site is http://www.state.mn.us.

The Web site for each state is provided below.

Alabama: http://www.alabama.gov
Alaska: http://www.state.ak.us
Arkansas: http://www.state.ar.us or http://www.arkansas.gov
California: http://www.state.ca.us
Colorado: http://www.state.co.us or http://www.colorado.gov
Connecticut: http://www.state.ct.us or http://www.ct.gov
Delaware: http://www.state.de.us or http://www.delaware.gov

District of Columbia: http://www.dc.gov

Florida: http://www.state.fl.us or http://www.MyFlorida.com

Georgia: http:// www.state.ga.us or http://www.georgia.gov

Hawaii: http://www.state.hi.us

Idaho: http://www.state.id.us

Illinois: http://www.state.il.us or http://www.illinois.gov

Indiana: http://www.state.in.us or http://www.in.gov

Iowa: http://state.ia.us

Kansas: http://www.state.ks.us

Kentucky: http://www.kentucky.gov

Louisiana: http://www.state.la.us

Maine: http://www.state.me.us or http://www.maine.gov

Maryland: http://www.maryland.gov

Massachusetts: http://www.mass.gov

Michigan: http://www.michigan.gov

Minnesota: http://www.state.mn.us

Mississippi: http://www.state.ms.us or http://www.mississippi.gov

Missouri: http://www.state.mo.us or http://www.missouri.gov

Montana: http://www.state.mt.us

Nebraska: http://www.state.ne.us or http://www.nebraska.gov

Nevada: http://www.nv.gov

New Hampshire: http://www.state.nh.us or http://www.nh.gov

New Jersey: http://www.state.nj.us

New Mexico: http://www.state.nm.us

New York: http://www.state.ny.us

North Carolina: http://www.ncgov.com

North Dakota: http://www.discovernd.com

Ohio: http://www.state.oh.us or http://www.ohio.gov

Oklahoma: http://www.state.ok.us

Oregon: http://www.oregon.gov

Pennsylvania: http://www.state.pa.us

Rhode Island: http://www.state.ri.us

South Carolina: http://www.myscgov.com

South Dakota: http://www.state.sd.us

Tennessee: http://www.state.tn.us or http://www.tennessee.gov

Texas: http://www.TexasOnline.com
Utah: http://www.utah.gov
Vermont: http://www.vermont.gov
Virginia: http://www.virginia.gov
Washington: http://www.access.wa.gov
West Virginia: http://www.wv.gov
Wisconsin: http://www.wisconsin.gov
Wyoming: http://www.state.wy.us

8

Print and Nonprint Resources

In this chapter, summaries of pertinent academic studies along with lists of various other print and nonprint resources are provided to those interested in researching further the issue of criminal justice profiling.

Academic Studies

In this section, we will examine several of the most recent studies that in some way relate to profiling in the criminal justice system. Interestingly, very few studies have actually been conducted on profiling specifically. Instead, many studies have set out to examine inequities that may exist in the criminal justice system. According to most of the contemporary criminal justice and criminological research findings, these inequities typically form along racial and gender lines. Most of the research efforts (but not all) summarized below relate to disparities felt between races and gender at the sentencing phase of the criminal justice system. Most of the research (but not all) indeed found that unequal treatment does exist when race or gender is taken into account. Although most researchers do not suggest a purposeful bias, as profiling would necessarily require, they argue that bias does exist nonetheless and constitutes a serious problem for a system that claims to put everyone on equal footing before the law. Let us now take a look at some select studies relating to these areas.

Benda, Brent, and Nancy Toombs. **"Religiosity and Violence: Are They Related after Considering the Strongest Predictors?"** *Journal of Criminal Justice* 28, pp. 483–496 (2000).

Much attention has been paid in this handbook and in the scholarly literature to the interaction of race and, to a lesser (but still significant) extent, gender. But profiling can, of course, involve a variety of suspect variables beyond race and gender. One such variable is the religious background of people under scrutiny. If you ask the average police officer on the street to describe the role religion plays in the officer's enforcement actions, you would get the answer "none." For one thing, the religious background of suspects is not typically known. For another, the religious background, if known, has typically not yet been associated with frequent and particular violations. There is no sense in the law enforcement community that drug use is a Catholic problem, for example. There is no sense that Lutherans make up an inordinate share of prostitutes. Religious background, except for certain types of offenses and cases commonly associated with domestic and international terrorism, is not seen as relevant.

In this study, the authors set out to examine the relationship, if any, between religion and general crime. In doing so, the authors administered a 150-question survey to approximately 600 men housed at the only adult boot camp correctional facility in Arkansas. The questionnaire, among other things, measured religious background, intensity of faith, church attendance, family background, age, and number and type of past criminal acts.

Through regression analysis, the researchers found that church attendance, which was affirmatively defined as attending church more than once a month, was not significantly related to criminal activity. Attending church predicted neither criminal activity nor a lack of crime. Religiosity, however, was found to be significantly and *inversely* related. That is to say, as the religious convictions and personal commitment to one's faith went up, the number and severity of criminal acts went down. Although the authors made no claim that the lack of religious conviction in people makes them more likely to offend, it does appear from the study that the presence of religious conviction makes one less likely to offend.

This finding is particularly interesting given the belief by some in society that devoutly religious people are problematic in the modern, indeed postmodern, United States. The anecdotal stories of Baptist televangelists involved in sex scandals and fraud, radicalized Catholics bombing abortion clinics, or devout American Muslims engaging in terror are just that—anecdotes. These offenses and events have happened, but the research suggests that they are anomalies. In fact, religious people tend to be law abiding and therefore of little or no concern to the police. Perhaps that's why police officers don't spend too much time running a check on license plates in church parking lots on Sunday looking for people with outstanding warrants. Perhaps police officers have always known what this study purports— religious folks are generally not the problem.

Crawford, Charles. **"Gender, Race, and Habitual Offender Sentencing in Florida."** *Criminology* 38, no. 1, pp.263–280 (2000).

In this study, gender was added to the mix in examining sentencing practices and potential disparities. In particular, 1,103 female offenders who were eligible for enhanced penalties under Florida's habitual offender statute in fiscal year 1992–1993 were analyzed and compared against 9,960 male habitual offenders previously studied by the author in 1998.

Under the habitual offender law in Florida, an offender can receive harsher penalties at sentencing than he or she would otherwise be eligible for if the offender had been convicted of two prior felonies within five years of a current felony conviction. All three felonies must be unrelated to each other, that is, three separate offenses.

Of the 1,103 females eligible for sentencing as habitual offenders, only sixty-six women were so sentenced. This represents only 6 percent of the eligible female offenders, compared to 20 percent of the eligible men who were sentenced as habitual offenders according to the author's 1998 study. This does suggest that women in Florida are not as aggressively sentenced as men are.

About two-thirds of the women and 70 percent of men sentenced as habitual offenders were African American. In fact, the study indicated that after controlling for (that is, taking into account) the prior records of the offenders, the seriousness of the crime, the type of crime, and the Florida county in which the sentencing took place, black women were almost twice as likely to be sentenced as habitual offenders as white women.

In sum, the state of Florida appears to avoid targeting women for habitual offender sentencing compared to eligible male offenders. If either gender has a claim that they are subject to profiling in sentencing, this study would suggest it is men. The study also suggested that when the habitual offender law is used against women, however, it is possibly discriminatorily used against black women as opposed to white women.

DeLisi, Matt, and Bob Regoli. **"Race, Conventional Crime, and Criminal Justice: The Declining Importance of Skin Color."** *Journal of Criminal Justice* 27, no. 6, pp. 549–557 (1999).

The authors in this study wanted to examine the truthfulness of the common claim in criminal justice academic literature that racial discrimination explains why blacks are arrested, prosecuted, convicted, and imprisoned in numbers disproportionate to their percentage of the U.S. population.

Going into the study, the authors noted that there was no doubt that blacks were overrepresented participants in the criminal justice system. According to the U.S. Department of Justice, the incarceration rate per 100,000 adults in 1996 was 289 for whites and 1,860 for blacks. The chance of a black male going to prison in his lifetime was 29 percent, whereas for white males it was only 4 percent. Black women were also more likely than white women to be incarcerated in their lifetimes—seven times more likely, to be exact.

These troubling statistics provided the backdrop for the authors' study in exploring the answers to five research questions. They were:

1. Is police discretion racially biased, resulting in higher black arrests?
2. Is the arrest setting an example of the practice of racial bias?
3. Are incarceration rates indicative of racial bias?
4. What do racial victimization rates say about racial bias?
5. Is the war on drugs biased against blacks?

To answer these questions, the authors conducted a secondary analysis of existing data.

In answering question number 1, the authors examined two studies relating to driving under the influence of alcohol (DUI) arrests. It was thought by the authors that DUI enforcement represents an area of significant police discretion. If there were a general tendency or desire within the law enforcement community to discriminate against blacks, one would expect to see greater proportions of blacks arrested for DUI, where police discretion is greatest. The authors, however, did not see a disproportionate level of black arrests. In fact, whites were nine times more likely than blacks to be arrested for DUI.

Regarding the second question, the authors found that arrest data show most arrests emerging out of police response to calls. Police respond to 911 calls, disturbances, and drug-related calls by witnesses. Further, the handling of these calls is frequently hampered by the intoxicating effects of drugs and alcohol among those they are dealing with. In such chaotic and fluid situations as a domestic disturbance involving a drunk, combative boyfriend, the police have little opportunity to be racially selective in whom they arrest.

Regarding question number 3, the authors again found that claims of racism's being behind the incarceration rates of blacks were spurious. The authors examined several studies, some of which supported the notion of disparate treatment against blacks, whereas others suggested harsher treatment (relatively) against whites. For example, one study showed that blacks were more likely than whites to be released from jail without having to post money for bond. Another study showed the average elapsed time from conviction to execution in death penalty cases between 1977 and 1996 was 110 months for whites and 117 months for blacks. The authors noted, however, there is compelling evidence that blacks are improperly sentenced to death at higher rates than whites.

Question number 4 relates to the race of the victim and suggests that the criminal justice system, if it were racist, would ignore victims of color. But according to the authors, the aggressive drug and street crime campaigns of urban law enforcement agencies benefit minority potential victims or actual victims at far greater rates than white victims or potential victims. The authors demonstrated that blacks were more likely to be victimized than whites and therefore the intensification of police efforts, if absent, would demonstrate a lack of interest in the well-being of minorities.

Finally, in answering question number 5, the authors examined studies relating to the harsher penalties associated with crack cocaine over powder cocaine. Crack tends to be the form of choice for black cocaine users, whereas powder tends to be used more by whites. The authors argued that harsher treatment of crack cocaine by the law is not necessarily rooted in racism. Crack is a more transitory and compulsive drug than powder cocaine, said the authors. Its trafficking is also associated with more violence and tends to involve and affect younger people. Therefore, there are alternative public policy explanations for the harsher treatment of crack cocaine than simply institutional racism.

In discussing the findings, the authors pointed out that the racial gap in state prisons in 1932 was 4 black prisoners to every 1 white prisoner., when accounting for their representation in the total population. In 1979, the gap was 8 to 1. And in 1999, there were more than 500,000 blacks in state prisons and just less than 400,000 whites; blacks comprise only 13 percent of the U.S. population whereas whites comprise 82 percent. The authors asked the rhetorical question: does this mean the United States is more racist as a society today than it was in the 1930s? Clearly, something other than racism alone must explain these incarceration rates. From their evaluation of the research questions posed above, the authors determined that the contemporary criminal justice system is essentially fair to minorities. Further, the unspoken implication is conveyed that some minority communities, and African Americans in particular, have a crime problem that must be addressed from within.

Griffin, Timothy, and John Wooldredge. **"Judges' Reactions to Sentencing Reform in Ohio."** *Crime and Delinquency* 47, no. 4, pp. 491–512 (2001).

As you may have already gathered, a very hot topic in the general realm of criminal justice profiling is the way convicted offenders who are persons of color are treated by the system at the point of sentencing. Although we often debate the predisposition of police officers to discriminate against minorities, we rarely talk about the predisposition of judges to do the same. And yet, if discrimination or bias does exist in sentencing, judges are necessarily implicated.

In this study, the authors sought to gauge the feelings that Ohio judges had concerning recent sentencing reforms. Traditionally and predictably, judges tend to vigorously defend their autonomy and discretion in sentencing offenders. Reforms put in place as a check against potential bias necessarily reduce judicial discretion. The authors wanted to test this assumption.

The reform effort, known as Senate Bill 2 and implemented by the Ohio Criminal Sentencing Commission in 1996, did several things. The key element affecting judicial discretion, however, was the implementation of presumptive sentences (that is, judges would be expected to follow the recommended sentence within the guidelines and would have to justify not doing so). Also, "truth-in-sentencing" was a key provision. Offenders would be required to serve the majority of the sentence they received.

The authors crafted a survey and sent it out to 221 judges who presided over felony cases in Ohio courts. A total of 138 usable surveys were eventually returned. The survey measured the degree to which judges viewed the reforms favorably or unfavorably, along with specific elements of the reforms.

The majority of judges who responded to the survey believed that the guidelines diminished judicial authority (68 percent), did not feel their input was considered in the reform process by the Ohio Criminal Sentencing Commission (66 percent), and did not feel the commission understood the perspective of judges (70 percent). Interestingly, a majority (55 percent) responded, however, that the new sentencing guidelines were good for the sentencing process. The 45 percent who did not believe the guidelines were appropriate tended to be against them because of their perceived undue restriction on judicial discretion. Additional statistical analysis demonstrated a significant correlation between the fear of losing judicial authority and a belief that punishment for offenders was not being achieved. This makes sense given that the reforms proscribed a presumptive sentence of community service for less serious offenders.

It was not surprising to the authors that judges would be somewhat reluctant to give up their absolute autonomy in sentencing, even for the noble cause (in part) of ensuring equal application of the law through standardization. The slight majority that generally believed the reforms to be a good idea suggested, however (optimistically perhaps), that judges can be persuaded to passively if not actively endorse self-limiting reforms. To the extent that bias exists at the sentencing phase of the criminal justice system, reforms such as those in Ohio remain among the best hopes for change.

Hebert, Christopher. **"Sentencing Outcomes of Black, Hispanic, and White Males Convicted under Federal Sentencing Guidelines."** *Criminal Justice Review* 22, no. 2, pp. 133–156 (Autumn 1997).

In this study, the author attempted to fill a void perceived to exist in the literature on sentencing disparities. Although much had been written about black and white offenders, little had been done to consider Hispanic offenders side by side with black and white offenders. Given the growth of the Hispanic population in the United States, the author thought that this was an important gap to fill.

The data set relied upon by the author to study sentencing disparities was rooted in federal drug offenses for the calendar year 1989. By choosing to examine the sentences for federal drug law violations, the author was able to examine a set of crimes that is relatively new in U.S. jurisprudence. Also, drug violations tend to be more regulatory in nature and therefore *mens rea*, that is, a criminal state of mind, was less relevant. Rather, federal sentencing guidelines simply call for a certain sentence for a certain amount of a particular drug. If bias in sentencing existed, it would be easy to identify in this context.

In this study, the author examined 5,557 single-count drug charges (that is, cocaine, marijuana, and opiates) through records maintained by the U.S. Sentencing Commission.

After analysis of the data, the author concluded that blacks and Hispanics were *not* more likely than whites to be imprisoned for drug offenses generally; African Americans convicted of cocaine offenses and Hispanics convicted of marijuana offenses, however, *were* more likely than whites convicted of the same offenses to be sentenced to imprisonment. Additionally, African Americans were more likely to receive longer sentences than white offenders.

Three weaknesses of the study, as acknowledged by its author, center on limitations of the U.S. Sentencing Commission data. First, they did not reflect criminal history scores of the offenders. Federal sentencing guidelines and the guidelines of every state in the union provide for higher penalties for prior offenders, with sentences progressively harsher the more serious the offender's criminal history.

A second shortcoming was that the data did not reflect

downward departures from the guidelines for those who cooperated with authorities. Under federal sentencing guidelines, an offender will likely receive less than the normally prescribed penalty if that offender helps the police and/or prosecution in a significant way. These data take no account of that.

Third, the data sometimes miscoded crack cocaine as "other drug" rather than as cocaine. Given that the penalties for crack cocaine are harsher than for powder cocaine, some opportunity was missed in the study to observe an anticipated disparity between black and white cocaine users given that blacks tended to use crack cocaine whereas whites tended to use powder.

Despite these weaknesses, there was general support from the study for the assertion that persons of color are treated differently than whites at the sentencing phase of federal drug offenses, which by design is supposed to be rather mechanical and uniform in its application.

Henderson, Martha, Francis Cullen, Liqun Cao, Sandra Lee Browning, and Renee Kopache. **"The Impact of Race on Perceptions of Criminal Justice."** *Journal of Criminal Justice* 25, no. 6, pp. 447–462 (1997).

Almost as important as the question of whether the criminal justice system is discriminatory against minorities is the perception by minorities of whether the criminal justice system discriminates against them. Research has shown that perception matters. Perception is reality for those holding to the perceptions. A person's perception that crime is at an all-time high and that it is unsafe to walk to the store dramatically affects the quality of life for that person, whether or not the perception is consistent with the facts.

Consequently, an important question when considering the issue of whether criminal justice profiles and treats people differently according to their group affiliation is the perception that people have regarding the fairness of the system. The present study attempted to gauge just that.

In this study, the authors administered a telephone survey to 240 Cincinnati, Ohio, residents about their perceptions of the criminal justice system. Whites totaled 136 of the respondents; blacks totaled 104. Females slightly outnumbered males: 53 percent to 47 percent. All income and education levels were represented.

A number of interesting findings about perceptions of police practice and the courts emerged from the survey. For example, 95 percent of blacks indicated that police officers on patrol are more likely to stop black motorists in white neighborhoods, as opposed to white motorists in black neighborhoods or treating all motorists the same. Whites were evenly split on this question, with 47 percent believing blacks would more likely be stopped and 47 percent believing that black and white motorists would be treated the same.

When asked whom an officer would more likely give a ticket to after pulling a speeding vehicle over, 46 percent of blacks believed that black motorists would most likely get the ticket, whereas 50 percent of blacks believed that whites and blacks would be treated the same. The vast majority of whites (93 percent) believed that blacks and whites would be ticketed in equal proportions after being pulled over for speeding.

Blacks also perceived inequity from the courts. A full 80 percent of black respondents believed that a black person would likely be sentenced to jail for shoplifting. Only 2 percent believed whites were more likely to receive jail time for the same offense. Seventeen percent believed blacks and whites would be treated the same. On the other hand, 59 percent of whites believed that both races would be treated the same.

Eighty-nine percent of blacks surveyed believed that a black person convicted of murder was more likely to receive the death penalty. Forty-one percent of whites agreed with them; 50 percent of whites thought both races would face the death penalty in equal proportions.

As the authors pointed out, the results of the survey pointed to a "deep and persistent racial cleavage in perceptions of racial injustice in the criminal justice system" (p. 455). This cleavage makes achieving common ground between the races on criminal justice matters truly a daunting task, for the very assumptions about the system are dramatically different. It is hard to meet in the middle with an opposing viewpoint when you are not on the same planet.

The implications of this study certainly include the fact that officials in the criminal justice system have a long way to go in winning the trust and confidence of minorities. Simply sending a police officer to a community meeting, or visiting a black church once a year on Martin Luther King Day, is not going to bridge this gap.

Koons-Witt, Barbara A. **"The Effect of Gender on the Decision to Incarcerate before and after the Introduction of Sentencing Guidelines."** *Criminology* 40, no. 2, pp. 297–328 (2002).

A research article discussed later entitled "Gender Bias and Juvenile Justice Revisited" by John MacDonald and Meda Chesney-Lind cites other studies and their research in Hawaii to suggest that females may be treated unfairly at least during certain phases of the criminal justice process. When bias exists against one group or another at the sentencing phase, then talk of establishing or reforming sentencing guidelines invariably comes up.

In the present study, the author sought to determine if the establishment of sentencing guidelines did anything to make the sentencing process fairer in Minnesota. In particular, the author examined the decision to put female offenders behind bars before and after the introduction of sentencing guidelines in Minnesota.

Unlike some other studies, the author first recognized the existence of prior research indicating that women tend to be treated more leniently than men when judges have maximum discretion in sentencing—particularly in urban felony courts. This is not to say there isn't sexism in the criminal justice system, however. Scholars suggest the leniency is afforded especially to those women who meet the gender role expectations of a paternalistic, chivalrous, patriarchal system. In particular, women who live up to their gender roles by being mothers of children are especially likely to receive leniency at sentencing, whereas fathers of children are not.

In testing whether or not the sentencing guidelines have adequately created an equal application of sentences for equal offenses, the author posed two primary research questions: (1) Were Minnesota's female offenders sentenced more leniently than male offenders prior to the establishment of sentencing guidelines, but not after? (2) Did having dependent children result in more lenient sentences for women than for men, both before and after the creation of the guidelines?

Minnesota's sentencing guidelines were adopted in May 1980. The guidelines were intended to uniformly regulate the decision to impose imprisonment and the duration of such imprisonment. The objective of the guidelines was to maintain equality and proportionality in sentencing while assuring that deserving people were still punished.

In this study, the author compiled data from the Minnesota Sentencing Guidelines Commission and the presentencing investigation reports of Hennepin and Ramsey counties (the counties of Minneapolis and St. Paul, respectively). Data for drug and property offenses during three separate time periods were considered (including before, immediately after, and well after the installation of the guidelines).

Interestingly, several significant findings held true across all three periods of time. For one, women were always more likely to be incarcerated than men. Also, men were more likely to have criminal histories and to have committed more serious offenses. And women were more likely to have dependent children than were men.

The authors also found that women, even with dependent children, were more likely to be sentenced to incarceration in the immediate aftermath of the guidelines as compared to similarly situated women before the guidelines. This suggests that the guidelines initially served to turn a blind eye to circumstances that had previously mattered in determining sentencing. By the third time period, however, that is, after the guidelines had been around a while, women with dependent children were incarcerated at no greater rates than before the guidelines. This suggests that judges grew increasingly comfortable returning to making chivalrous decisions, even if it meant departing from the guidelines.

In sum, the answer to the first research question posed by the author is "no." Women were not treated more leniently than men before but not after the guidelines. Rather, women were treated more leniently before and after the guidelines. The guidelines did not correct the gender inequity of sentencing against men. The second question's answer is "yes": having dependent children helped women to receive more lenient sentences in relation to men, both before and after the guidelines. In relation to themselves, however, women were treated most harshly during the immediate period after the establishment of guidelines. That development, depending on one's perspective, could be viewed as a time that was harmful to women and dependent children or as a time when the gender gap at least closed a bit regarding sentencing disparity.

Lahm, Karen. **"Equal or Equitable: An Exploration of Educational and Vocational Program Availability for Male and Female Offenders."** *Federal Probation* 64, no. 2, pp. 39–46 (2000).

Although considerable scholarly effort has been devoted to the existence of inequalities between male and female offenders within the criminal justice system leading up to and including sentencing, there is another body of literature that has examined the quality of programs available to male and female offenders once imprisoned. Historically, very valid claims have been levied against prison officials for devoting more resources per prisoner to males for their rehabilitation than to females.

Researchers in the 1970s found female prisons to be characterized by inadequate health care, stereotypical job training (for example, programs to learn sewing or secretarial skills instead of how to fix electronic components or manufacturing). In light of the past research, and with the female prison population in the United States growing rapidly, the author sought to examine the current status of educational and training programs for female prisoners.

In this study, the author was able to survey 474 correctional institutions, including 47 female-only institutions, in 30 states. The survey simply assessed the presence or absence of various types of educational and vocational programs that prisoners can take part in. The results of the author's findings suggest that opportunities for female prisoners have dramatically increased over the past 30 years.

Specifically, the results showed that 100 percent of both male and female institutions offered general education/high school equivalency programs. Furthermore, female institutions offered greater opportunities than did the male institutions regarding college education, managerial skill training, technical and sales training, service training, and operator/fabricator training. The two areas of training that favored the male institutions were production and farming/forestry/fishing.

The author found that female institutions are offering equal or even superior training and educational opportunities as compared with male prisons. The author also noted with dismay, however, the lingering presence of stereotypical training programs at the female prisons in addition to the other opportunities. The author may be failing to consider the possibility that some women may *want* to learn how to sew or clean or type. Although the author was correct in noting that many of the jobs women train for in prison result in low-paying positions once released and back in society, the same is clearly true of male prisoners who are released. The matriculation of released prisoners into society at the lower socioeconomic rungs is likely a problem across gender.

Lundman, Richard, and Robert Kaufman. **"Driving while Black: Effects of Race, Ethnicity, and Gender on Citizen Self-Reports of Traffic Stops and Police Actions."** *Criminology* 41, no. 1, pp. 195–220 (2003).

At the time of this writing, this study represented the most current academic findings concerning the perceptions of minorities regarding their risk for being subject to police action because of their race or ethnicity. The researchers in this study posed similar questions to those, in part, of Ronald Weitzer and Steven Tuch, in "Perceptions of Racial Profiling," which is discussed later—that is, what do citizens perceive as the basis for police actions taken against them. Unlike the Weitzer and Tuch project, however, this study did not limit the comparison racially by only considering whites and blacks. Instead, the study assessed the opinions of whites, blacks, and Hispanics.

In the present research, the authors sought to answer three specific questions:

1. Are African American men, compared to white men, more likely to report being stopped by police for traffic violations?
2. Are African American and Hispanic drivers less likely to report that police had a legitimate reason to stop them?
3. Are African American and Hispanic drivers less likely to report that police acted properly during an encounter?

Researchers Lundman and Kaufman set out to answer these questions by consulting and analyzing data from a section of the 1999 National Crime Victimization Survey conducted by the U.S. Department of Justice. This section, titled "Contacts between Police and the Public," hereinafter will be referred to as CBPP.

The data Lundman and Kaufman had to work with were very comprehensive. The survey, conducted nationally, required that participants be at least sixteen years old. The CBPP portion of the survey focused on the participants' contacts with the police in the previous twelve months. Over 80,000 subjects were randomly selected for this study; of those, 7,034 (8.7 percent) reported that they had been pulled over by law enforcement at least once in the past year in which they were the driver.

For these respondents, additional questions were then asked concerning the number of stops they had, the nature of the stops, and their perceptions concerning the legitimacy of the stops and the properness of police actions. The researchers also captured data concerning a variety of possible explanatory factors specific to the driver. These factors, which were controlled for, included

- history of police contact with the driver
- geographic location (large city, small town, and so on)
- social class of the driver
- age of the driver
- gender of the driver
- race/ethnicity of the driver
- race/ethnicity of the driver by gender

Using regression analysis, the researchers in this study made several determinations. These included the following:

- Drivers with previous stops were less likely to report legitimate reasons for the stops.
- Drivers in larger geographic settings were less likely to report legitimate reasons for stops than those in smaller settings.
- African Americans and Hispanics were much less likely than whites to report legitimate reasons for stops and to report that police acted properly during stops and encounters.

From these findings, Lundman and Kaufman concluded that police were indeed more likely to use traffic stops as pretexts for pulling over minorities. They argued that despite the serious threats to validity in self-report surveys, the overwhelming difference in responses between African Americans and Hispanics on the one hand and whites on the other cannot be dismissed; where there is smoke, there's fire.

Although some scholars could argue that the methodology of the study did not permit sweeping conclusions about what the police are doing and why they are doing it, the study demonstrated—once again—the undeniable perception that minorities have concerning the legitimacy of policing services they receive. Law enforcement does not fare well in the eyes of minority communities in the United States, especially in urban areas.

The cliché "perception is reality" may not hold up against rigorous scientific inquiry. After all, for the scientist—even the social scientist—reality is reality. But that fact is of little solace to those who understand that community cooperation with the police hinges on quality of life and service satisfaction—important intangibles that do indeed revolve around perceptions. Perhaps perception is reality after all.

MacDonald, John, and Meda Chesney-Lind. **"Gender Bias and Juvenile Justice Revisited: A Multiyear Analysis."** *Crime and Delinquency* 47, no. 2, pp. 173–195 (2001).

A considerable amount of research exists concerning race and the criminal justice system. Many of the preceding studies are sampled from that body of literature. This study focuses on gender bias in the criminal justice system. Specifically, the authors examined the extent of gender bias existing in the juvenile justice system in Hawaii. Based on prior research, the authors entered this study with the theory that female juveniles, once found to be delinquent by a juvenile court, tend to be punished more severely than male juvenile delinquents.

To test this theory, the authors examined data that had been collected by the Hawaii State Judiciary and provided to the National Juvenile Court Data Archive. The data set covered all delinquency cases in the state of Hawaii from 1980 to 1991. In total, 85,692 cases were included for analysis in the study.

As with some of the previously discussed studies, a regression analysis was used to assess the relationship of several variables, including gender, to the severity of punishment one receives. Other variables considered included race/ethnicity, geographic location within Hawaii, urban versus rural areas, the year of adjudication, and so on. Of the 85,000-plus cases examined, 30 percent (nearly 26,000) involved female offenders. From the raw data, the authors noted that in most cases, boys were more likely than girls to be referred to juvenile court for property and violent offenses. The tendency was to handle female delinquency more informally at the early stages of the process.

The analysis showed that once boys and girls who were in the system were found to be delinquent (the juvenile court term for "guilty"), however, girls were treated more harshly. For the authors, this demonstrated a built-in antifemale bias in Hawaii's juvenile justice system. Efforts were taken to control for all relevant factors. If it is true that females are given a pass at the front end of the system while boys are not, however, then perhaps the females making it all the way through to sentencing for their delinquent acts are there precisely because they are more deserving of harsher punishment (otherwise, informal measures to address their misconduct would have been pursued).

In any case, the study certainly does raise the possibility of institutional bias against female offenders, at least in Hawaii, despite the common perception that females always get off more easily for their offenses by the criminal justice system.

Mosher, Clayton. **"Predicting Drug Arrest Rates: Conflict and Social Disorganization Perspectives."** *Crime and Delinquency* 47, no. 1, pp. 84–104 (2001).

Many studies focus on the discretion that takes place by criminal justice officials—particularly judges—at the time of sentencing. And yet profiling is generally associated with law enforcement actions. The present study examines exactly that: law enforcement actions in the field. The author of this research examined 1989 data on illegal drug possession and trafficking arrests against the backdrop of socioeconomic data from the 1990 census in a sample of U.S. cities.

Drug enforcement reached its zenith in the late 1980s and early to mid-1990s. In light of the heightened intensity of enforcement brought on by the war on drugs, many scholars had been concerned about a disproportionate application of the drug enforcement activities against minorities. In 1996, there were approximately 1,500,000 arrests for drug offenses in the United States. That comes to 1,078 arrests per 100,000—about one and a half times the arrest rate of the second-highest crime category: larceny/theft. Interestingly, in California, more than 80 percent of adults arrested for drug violations in the late 1980s were black or Hispanic. In New York State, more than 90 percent were minorities; and in Baltimore, black juveniles were arrested at nearly 100 times the arrest rate for whites. Do these figures amount to a clear case of police bias?

Within the parameters of this study, the authors were able to examine the arrest rates for drug possession and drug trafficking by race against the community variables of geographic region of the country, police-to-population ratio, gender and age makeup, percentage of high school graduates, percentage of population employed, average income, and others.

Using a statistical process known as regression analysis involving the variables listed above, the author found that racial composition of a particular city, even after controlling for all the other community variables, was the strongest predictor of drug arrest rates for that city. Essentially, the greater the black or Hispanic population, the greater were the drug offense arrest rates. Given that other studies cited by the author demonstrated a greater rate of possession by whites compared to minorities and a basically equal rate of drug dealing between the races, the author suggested that a bias exists in police culture that favors enforcement actions against persons of color. The study reinforced the author's position that U.S. drug laws are being used by authorities to control racial minorities in America.

Pratt, Travis. **"Race and Sentencing: A Meta-Analysis of Conflicting Empirical Research Results."** *Journal of Criminal Justice* 26, no. 6, pp. 513–523 (1998).

This study differs from others in that it amounts to a study of the studies. The researcher here conducted a meta-analysis (that is, a grand analysis) of prior research concerning the impact race has on sentencing. As the author noted, prior research over the years had suggested any one of three possibilities explaining the relationship between race in sentencing.

The first explanation is the differential involvement perspective. This perspective says that African Americans are overrepresented in the prisons and receive harsher sentences because they are involved in more crimes than are whites and their crimes are more serious. Theorists who believe this would not deny the existence of racial bias in sentencing in the past. They would argue that at some point in contemporary history, however, the criminal justice system became sufficiently professional, formal, and bureaucratic to eliminate or severely mitigate against overt racism within the system

The second perspective that emerges from the literature is the direct-impact perspective. This approach says that racial bias does indeed exist and exists on purpose, with the goal of keeping minorities powerless and oppressed. This position amounts to a very cynical view of the U.S. criminal justice system, seeing it really as a tool to maintain the power elite's institutions and values in place.

Finally, the interactionist perspective claims that race does play a role in sentencing, but not in isolation. Rather, race in interaction with other variables and varied contexts has been found to be statistically significant in predicting sentences for offenders.

In the study, the author set out to examine the contradictory research findings that propped up the three different perspectives. In doing so, the author attempted to pool the data from prior research and analyze the overall effect of race on sentencing while considering legally relevant variables (for example, prior criminal history, severity of crime, and so on). The analysis examined the data from race and sentencing studies contained in sociological and criminal justice academic journals from 1974 to 1996. The author noted and accounted for the fact that the earlier studies tended to be less statistically rigorous than the latter studies. In total, 48,251 cases were examined from 47 studies.

The author performed regression analysis to determine the effects of race, prior criminal history, and seriousness of the offense on sentencing outcomes. The results showed that race and prior criminal history had a relatively small effect on the sentencing outcomes. The severity of the offense, however, had a very large effect on the variance in sentencing. Put another way, the variations in sentences the people received most often could be explained primarily by the respective difference in the severity of crimes.

The author noted that his findings do not suggest that there is no racial bias in the criminal justice system or in the sentencing process specifically. The evidence from this study, however, supported the idea that legally relevant factors play the greatest role in sentencing outcomes.

Son, In Soo, Mark Davis, and Dennis Rome. **"Race and Its Effects on Police Officers' Perceptions of Misconduct."** *Journal of Criminal Justice* 26, no. 1, pp. 21–28 (1998).

In contrast to studies that focus on the perceptions of minorities toward the criminal justice system, the present study flipped that around. Here, the authors conducted a survey of 718 Ohio police officers to determine if race played a role in how they perceived the seriousness of another officer's misconduct toward a suspect. It was hypothesized by the authors that if the police were biased against minorities, then they would view misconduct directed against minorities as less serious than misconduct directed against white citizens.

To measure police perceptions about misconduct and the influence race has on those perceptions, the researchers developed a survey that included thirty-five short stories or vignettes. In each vignette, a hypothetical police officer engaged in some form of misconduct. Examples of misconduct included drug use, theft from a crime scene, forcing a confession, and so on. Fewer than one-third of the vignettes made any reference to the race of the suspect or officer in the scenario. This was considered an important design feature in the study because the researchers did not want the officers to know the purpose of the survey.

In contradiction to the anticipated results of the study, the researchers found that the citizen's race in each of the vignettes did not play a significant role when officers characterized the seriousness of the misconduct. Rather, the acts of misconduct of the officers in the vignettes and the consequences of the actions played the greatest role in determining how seriously the survey respondents viewed the misconduct. Another factor was the suspect's behavior toward the officer in each vignette. This is consistent with other research that shows officers are harsher with uncooperative citizens than they are with cooperative ones.

The authors noted the cycle that exists when minorities, who presume the existence of police bias, manifest that bias in the form of uncooperativeness. This, of course, is met with harsher tactics, which then only serve to reinforce the idea that it is all about bias.

Thomson, Ernie. **"Discrimination and the Death Penalty in Arizona."** *Criminal Justice Review* 22, no. 1, pp. 65–76 (Spring, 1997).

The author of this study noted that many other studies had been conducted concerning suspected patterns of racial bias in death sentences. Considerable focus has fallen on southern states where the history of racial tension is obvious. Studies on death penalty bias have also been conducted in nonsouthern states, however, and have found similar bias.

In this study, the author examined whether racial and ethnic discrimination in death sentences occurs in the state of Arizona, which has many ethnic groups represented among its population. In particular, the author sought to find out whether African Americans and Hispanics were more likely to be sentenced to death for capital offenses than were white offenders, particularly if the victims were white.

To answer this research question, the author examined the racial and ethnic characteristics of reported homicides in Arizona from 1982 through 1991 and compared that data against the racial or ethnic characteristics of death row inmates in 1993 who were convicted during the 1982–1991 time frame. As the author acknowledged, he made no attempt to evaluate the role that prosecutorial, judicial, or jury discretion played in the sentence. Instead, he focused on the gross "beginning to end disparities."

The study's findings suggested that in Arizona, white murderers were more likely to receive the death penalty than minority murderers. Further, murderers of all ethnic backgrounds were more likely to receive the death penalty if their victims were white.

When the data are taken in combination, the study found that minorities were three times more likely to receive the death penalty if they murdered white victims as opposed to minority victims. And white murderers were twice as likely to receive the death penalty if their victims were white as opposed to minority victims.

The implication of the study is that an inequitable profiling of sorts takes place at sentencing in homicide cases—the profile relates to the victim rather than the offender. The author admitted the study's limitations with regard to details of those homicides, however. Not all homicides are capital offenses eligible for the death penalty. Aggravating circumstance must accompany the crime to elevate it to a capital offense.

Most murders are intraracial—that is, murderers tend to kill victims of the own race. This makes sense given that most murderers and the victims know each other. Typically, the victim is a family member, domestic partner, friend, coworker, or acquaintance of the murderer. On the other hand, most capital offenses, such as those involving murder combined with rape, or murder during a liquor store robbery, are stranger crimes. Further, white individuals are more likely to be in a position to fall prey to a stranger-committed, capital murder because of their socioeconomic status in relation to minorities. Regardless of whether the offender is white, black, or Hispanic, the store owner who is robbed and shot is quite often white. These unforeseen variables may explain some of the tendency to favor capital sentences when white victims are involved—perhaps the killings tended to be capital offenses when those victims were involved.

In any case, the study reminds us of the need to be vigilant in avoiding unfair discrimination against suspects but also in unfairly elevating the value of some victims over others when otherwise the crimes are equally abhorrent.

Weitzer, Ronald, and Steven Tuch. **"Perceptions of Racial Profiling: Race, Class, and Personal Experience."** *Criminology* 40, no. 2, pp. 435–456 (2002).

This study represents one of the few research efforts directly aimed at broadening our understanding of racial profiling by the police. The authors noted early in the article that very little existed in scholarly literature concerning the experiences people have had with profiling or their perceptions of it. One exception is the police-public contact survey conducted by the U.S. Department of Justice (DOJ) in 1999. That study found that blacks were more likely than whites or Hispanics to report being stopped by the police in 1999. Of those citizens stopped by the police, blacks and Hispanics were more likely than whites to report being ticketed, arrested, or searched during the stop. They were also more likely to indicate that officers had used force or threatened to use force during the stop. That study relied on survey respondents who had reported being stopped by the police. The present study sought to expand the DOJ one by analyzing perceptions of police actions according to the wider population.

The data analyzed by the authors came from a 1999 nationwide Gallup survey of 2,006 U.S. residents. The authors restricted their analysis to the 903 whites and 961 blacks who took part in the survey. The survey questionnaire polled respondents about their attitudes toward racial profiling and the police. Additionally, demographic and background data were obtained (for example, education level, income range, gender, where they lived, and so on).

When asked about the use of racial profiling to stop motorists because the police perceive certain racial groups as more likely to be engaged in criminal activity, 94 percent of blacks and 84 percent of whites disapproved of the practice. Among whites, women tended to be slightly more disapproving then men. When asked if they thought the practice was widespread, 82 percent of blacks and 60 percent of whites believed that it was.

When the survey respondents were asked if they had ever been stopped by the police because of their race or ethnic background, 40 percent of blacks said they had. Only 5 percent of whites reported being stopped by the police because of race or ethnicity. The percentage of blacks reporting being stopped by the police went up when just considering males and in particular, the 18 to 34 age range. Seventy-three percent of black males in that age group reported having been stopped because of their race.

The authors pointed out that this last statistic was consistent with other studies that showed young black males more frequently encountered law enforcement. Lost on the authors, ironically, is the fact that these statistics suggest that racial profiling— taking police action solely because of a suspect's race—is not occurring. Race is not the sole criteria if age and gender are playing a significant role. Profiling may indeed be taking place, but not racial profiling. Otherwise, one would expect to see equal percentages claiming victimization of racial profiling by blacks across variables of age, gender, location, and so on.

In any event, the study highlighted the fact that prior personal experiences with law enforcement significantly help shape people's attitudes toward the police and police practice. Officers need to be reminded that however mundane a traffic stop or other minor offense encounter may be for them, such an encounter is a significant event in the lives of most people. Police officers must do their best to demonstrate fairness, professionalism, and solid, legal tactics to leave a lasting favorable impression on members of the public, regardless of race.

Williams, Marian, and Jefferson Holcomb. **"Racial Disparity and Death Sentences in Ohio."** *Journal of Criminal Justice* 29, pp. 207–218 (2001).

In this study, the authors analyzed data from the Supplemental Homicide Report (SHR) for the state of Ohio from 1981 through 1994. The SHR is a database of information gathered by the FBI from police departments around the country. Although not every police agency submits data, the vast majority of police agencies of any size or consequence submit data to be counted in the SHR.

The SHR reflects the number of homicides that took place in any particular jurisdiction, along with specific information about the homicides. This information includes details about the homicide, the classification of the homicide, information about the offenders, and information about the victims. The data from the SHR were then matched against Ohio death penalty information from the same period of time using data from the Office of the Ohio Public Defender.

In their analysis, the authors found that from 1981 through 1994, only 4 percent of the 6,441 cases in which the death sentence could have been imposed actually saw the death sentence handed down. White killers were more likely than black killers to receive the death penalty (5 percent to 3 percent respectively). Not unlike the results shown in Ernie Thomson's study, "Discrimination and the Death Penalty in Arizona," however, murders involving white victims were twice as likely to result in a death sentence for the offender as were murders with victims of color. Additionally, blacks who killed whites were five times more likely to receive the death penalty than were blacks who killed blacks. Not surprisingly, offenders who killed multiple victims of any race were significantly more likely to receive the death sentence than were those who killed only one victim. Further, male offenders who killed female victims were more likely to receive a death sentence than those who murdered male victims. Also, older offenders were more likely than younger offenders to be sentenced to death.

Once again, a significant profiling question that emerges from this study is whether or not offenders are sentenced according to profiles of the victims. The victim's race and gender in these cases seem to have a relationship to the sentencing outcome. Although a relationship may exist, this falls short of claiming causation. There may be additional intervening variables that affect the sentencing outcome that are also related to the variables of victim race and gender. In other words, when A is seen to be related to B, as in this study, further analysis is needed before we can say if A causes B, or B causes A, or C causes A and B. From this study, by the authors' own admission, we just don't know.

Books, Government Publications, and Videos

In this section of the chapter, lists of various print and nonprint resources are provided. The majority of such resources that one can find on profiling tend to address specifically the issue of racial profiling. Unfortunately, few books or documentaries have been produced that confront the criminal justice system's intentional reliance on suspect gender, sexual orientation, or religion in making decisions or arriving at conclusions. What follows is a selected list of recent books, government publications, and video documentaries that may be of interest to one who desires to research a variety of criminal justice profiling issues.

Books

Bireda, Martha. *Eliminating Racial Profiling in School Discipline.* Lanham, MD: Scarecrow Press, 2002. 128 pp. ISBN: 0-8108-4201-7.

This book examined the question of why suspensions, expulsions, and other sanctions were so high for African American students, particularly males. Although the book focused on the secondary education setting, there are parallels to the perceived problem of profiling by the criminal justice system. The book examined cultural assumptions that contribute to the higher rate of punitive interventions against black males. The reader may find these assumptions to likewise be at work in the decisions made by justice officials.

Douglas, John, Ann Burgess, Alan Burgess, and Robert Ressler. *Crime Classification Manual: Standard System for Investigating and Classifying Violent Crimes,* rev. ed. San Francisco, CA: Jossey-Bass, 1997. 400 pp. ISBN: 0-7879-3885-8.

Although last published in 1997, this book is appropriate to list here because it remains a classic in the field of profiling and offender classification. John Douglas is a founding father of the practice as employed in criminal investigative work. The book focused on the criminal intent of offenders and delivered a mechanism for developing a suspect profile within the context of violent crimes. The authors in particular examined the offender "signatures" commonly left behind at violent crime scenes. The book devoted attention to serial types of violent crime, including homicides, sexual offenses, and arson. The book is intended to be a reference manual for criminal justice and forensic mental health practitioners.

Fredrickson, Darin, and Raymond Siljander. *Racial Profiling: Eliminating the Confusion between Racial and Criminal Profiling and Clarifying What Constitutes Unfair Discrimination and Persecution.* Springfield, IL: Charles C. Thomas Publishing, 2002. 170 pp. ISBN: 0-398-07255-8.

This text attempted to distinguish between legitimate criminal profiling techniques and the controversial practice of racial profiling. The position of the authors in this book was that profiling is a legitimate police technique but that bias and prejudice in police officers can spoil or pollute the process and therefore diminish the practice's legitimacy. Solutions, according to the authors, can be found in understanding the issue thoroughly and through hiring unbiased police officers and enforcing stringent antibias policies. Legal remedies, such as consent decrees between police departments and the federal justice department, were also explored.

Fridell, Lorie, Robert Lunney, Drew Diamond, and Bruce Kubu. *"Racially Biased Policing: A Principled Response."* Police Executive Research Forum. http://www.policeforum.org. 2001.

To download this book, one needs the Adobe Acrobat reader program on one's computer. The book critically examined the issue of racially biased policing, encouraging law enforcement administrators to recognize its existence generally and the potential damage it can cause within a department and community. Chapter 4 is key in that it offered up model policies for governing police conduct in this regard. Police executives were advised to embrace the policies in whole or in part, as the needs of their particular departments dictate.

Harris, David. *Profiles in Injustice: Why Racial Profiling Cannot Work.* New York: New Press, 2002. 320 pp. ISBN: 1-56584-818-7.

This book, written by one of the leading thinkers on the issue of racial profiling, confronted the arguments made by law enforcement that profiling is a useful and effective police tool. Profiling is used by local police officers, state troopers, and federal customs and border officials in their respective law enforcement roles, and many argue for the practice. Harris attempted to refute arguments favoring profiling by calling into question the ethical and legal problems that profiling generates. Harris also produced statistical evidence, however, to demonstrate that profiling, apart from questions of legality or morality, was simply ineffective as a law enforcement tool. The book also included a chapter on profiling in the wake of the September 11 terrorist attacks.

Holmes, Ronald, and Stephen Holmes. *Profiling Violent Crimes: An Investigative Tool.* 3rd ed. Thousand Oaks, CA: Sage, 2002. 299 pp. ISBN: 0-761-92593-7.

This is the third edition of what many call a classic work in criminal profiling. The text focused on behavioral and psychological profiling in solving violent crimes. The authors have included a new chapter since previous editions, which addresses crimes and the occult. The dark role that unconventional religious sects and Satanism can play in certain crimes was explored thoroughly. Sexual crimes, and particularly the psychological profile of pedophiles, were also examined. The book is intended to be a resource for the criminal justice practitioner, as well as for students destined for careers in investigating violent and often bizarre crimes.

Jackson, Janet, and Debra Bekerian, eds. *Offender Profiling: Theory, Research, and Practice.* Indianapolis, IN: Wiley Publishing, 1998. 254pp. ISBN: 0-471-97565-6.

This text is a compilation of works by several authors whose expertise lies in profiling as an investigative tool. Among the chapters contained this book are ones focused on the role of personality theories in developing offender profiles, the use of databases in investigatory profiling, and geographic profiling. Although this type of profiling cannot be equated with racial profiling or gender profiling per se, the criteria of race, gender, culture, geography, and other objective factors are potential component parts in developing an offender profile. This text, through its contributors, helped distinguish unlawful and unethical profiling based on prejudice from profiling based on objective observations and facts.

Marks, Kenneth, *Driving while Black: Highways, Shopping Malls, Taxi Cabs, Sidewalks: How to Fight Back if You Are a Victim of Racial Profiling.* New York: Broadway Publishing, 2000. 272 pp. ISBN: 0-7679-0549-0.

This publication was framed as a handbook for surviving police encounters. Its premise was that class, age, race, and dress (such as baggy pants or baseball caps on sideways) are factors in who has an encounter with the police, whether one's objective behavior warrants such an encounter or not. It also speaks to readers who believe they have been discriminated against in other ways outside of the criminal justice system, such as cab drivers failing to stop for a black man on the corner in favor of a white man farther down the street, or a black person being persistently followed by mall or store security when browsing. The book provided guidance on what actions can be taken when one believes one's civil rights have been violated.

Milovanovic, Dragon, and Katheryn Russell, eds. *Petit Apartheid in the U.S. Criminal Justice System.* Durham, NC: Carolina Academic Press, 2001. 124 pp. ISBN: 0-89089-951-7.

This publication took a theoretical approach to explaining the relationship of African Americans to the criminal justice system. Contributions from different authors form the various chapters of the book. The chapters included discussions of racial profiling in the drug war, the perspective of African American officers in policing other African Americans, the interest in law enforcement held by African Americans, and how "petit apartheid" is manifested at the macro as well as micro levels.

O'Reilly, James. *Police Traffic Stops and Racial Profiling: Resolving Management, Labor, and Civil Rights Conflicts.* Springfield, IL: Charles C. Thomas Publishing, 2002. 304 pp. ISBN: 0-398-07295-7.

The book is broken into four main parts. The first part addressed the issue of racial profiling within the specific context of traffic stops. The legal standards necessary for police encounters and detentions were explained, along with the political ramifications that accompany the practice of racial profiling. The second part of the book looked at the multitude of remedies for the practice of profiling, as advocated by civil rights activists, the courts, and politicians. The third part of the text addressed in detail the role of politics and elected officials in responding to racial profiling. Additionally, the role that the police unions play, as a political constituency, was addressed. Last, the book offered preventative steps that police administrations and communities can take to avoid the controversy that invariably comes with the practice of profiling.

Schultz, David, and Christina DeJong. *Good Cop, Bad Cop: Racial Profiling and Competing Views of Justice.* New York: P. Lang Publishing, 2003. 246 pp. ISBN: 0-8204-5829-5.

This book, part of a larger series related to studies on crime and punishment, examined the history of racial profiling. The practice of profiling as a tool for drug enforcement on the highways and airports was highlighted. The authors attempted to provide a balanced view of profiling, examining what the courts have said with regard to racial profiling and how politicians have responded. The book also attempted to convey the arguments for and against the use of racial profiles, particularly in the wake of the terrorist attacks on September 11, 2001.

Turvey, Brent. *Criminal Profiling: An Introduction to Behavioral Evidence Analysis.* London: Academic Press, 2002. 717 pp. ISBN: 0-12-705041-8.

This book is suitable as a text for working criminal investigators as well as would-be sleuths. This text teaches the deductive reasoning approach to investigative work, covering case types such as homicides, arson, stalking, and sex offenses. Turvey's deductive profiling approach treated criminal profiling as an investigative process that requires the investigator to gain a genuine understanding of behavioral and environmental contributions to criminality. This book did not examine profiling from a racial, gender, religious, or sexual orientation consciousness, except insofar as these characteristics inform the investigator about cultural or environmental issues of relevance in a particular instance of criminality.

Vogel, Robert. *Fighting to Win.* Nashville, TN: Turner Publishing, 2001. 248 pp. ISBN: 1-56311-627-8.

In this book, famed Florida law enforcer Robert Vogel described his career as a Florida state trooper and then as a sheriff. Vogel explained his effort to fight drug trafficking throughout his career and addressed the controversy surrounding the practice of profiling. Vogel defended the practice of profiling drug runners as an effective and ethical law enforcement tool. He attempted to debunk the criticisms that his brand of profiling was racist and unfair. The bulk of his book discussed his ultimately successful legal fight with his critics and with the U.S. Department of Justice over the practice of profiling.

Williams, Mary, ed. *Discrimination.* San Diego, CA: Greenhaven Press, 2002. 200 pp. ISBN: 0-7377-1226-0.

This is a compilation of essays addressing the degree of discrimination in society still being felt by racial minorities, women, and homosexuals. Although the book is not exclusively devoted to discrimination within the context of the U.S. criminal justice system, a number of the essays do touch pervasive discrimination by justice officials. Further, the general discussions and arguments that emerged from the various essays have relevance to the justice system if only because the justice system is made up of people, and it is in the hearts of people, either because of malice or unwitting ignorance, that the roots of discrimination are found.

Government Publications

Characteristics of Drivers Stopped by Police in 1999
http://www.ojp.gov/bjs

This Department of Justice publication offered to the reader data concerning the characteristics of traffic stops. The data were collected through a 1999 Police-Public Contact Survey. Factors such as race, gender, age, and driving record were all sorted in this study. Additionally, the outcomes of the stops and the use of force to effect those outcomes, where applicable, were also examined.

Contacts between Police and Public: Findings from the 1999 National Survey
http://www.ojp.gov/bjs

This report provided data from a 1999 national survey in which contacts between the police and citizens were characterized by reason for the contact, circumstances surrounding the contact, characteristics of the citizens and officers, and a variety of other factors.

Differences in the Background and Criminal Justice
Characteristics of Young Black, White, and Hispanic Male
Federal Prison Inmates
http://www.bop.gov

This study looked at a variety of characteristics that describe the federal male inmate population, broken down along racial lines. The offenses that were committed, demographic factors, criminal history, and so on were all examined to get a snapshot of who is in prison and why. A researcher of bias in sentencing will find the raw data contained in this report very informative.

The End Racial Profiling Act of 2001
http://purl.access.gpo.gov/GPO/LPS22239 or /LPS22240

This document serves as the record for the Senate Judiciary Committee, 107th Congress, concerning the hearing for Senate Bill 989, which would ban racial profiling in the United States. This was the Senate's second hearing on the practice of racial profiling in two years. The bill was not passed into law during the 107th Congress. However, a similar bill—S. 2132—known as the "End Racial Profiling Act of 2004" was introduced in the 108th Congress. To date, it has not become law.

Fact Sheet: Racial Profiling
http://www.usdoj.gov

This six-page-long fact sheet summarized the controversy that is racial profiling in law enforcement and made distinctions of when it is legitimate to use race in identifying criminal suspects.

Guidance regarding the Use of Race by Federal Law
Enforcement Agencies
http://www.usdoj.gov/crt

This document represents the law of the land insofar as federal law enforcement and the use of racial profiling are concerned. The document specified when race is a permitted consideration for federal law officers. It also drew a line between the use of race for routine law enforcement purposes and for national security purposes. The federal government permits greater latitude in using race when national security and border security are implicated.

How to Correctly Collect and Analyze Racial Profiling Data: Your Reputation Depends on It!
http://www.ojp.gov/bja

Demonstrative of the importance the U.S. Department of Justice places on data collection techniques for profiling studies, this document serves as an update from previously published ones and provides additional insights from the benefit of hindsight. As the subtitle suggests, emphasis was placed on proper techniques, as the reputation of police administrators or researchers could certainly suffer given the volatility of this issue and the enormous potential for error in collection of key data.

Minnesota Statewide Racial Profiling Report
http://www.umn.edu/irp

Report of a landmark study involving the analysis of traffic stops conducted by sixty-five Minnesota law enforcement agencies. The agencies that participated in the study included urban, suburban, and rural departments. The study involved the analysis of thousands of traffic stops and vehicle searches where whites, blacks, Hispanics, and Native Americans were the drivers and occupants in the vehicles being pulled over. The results of the study indicated that nonwhite motorists were pulled over at greater rates than were white motorists. The study also showed, however, that white motorists were more likely to have drugs or other contraband in their possession inside the motor vehicle as compared to nonwhite motorists. These results tended to debunk the notion that minorities are pulled over at greater rates owing to a greater likelihood that minorities will have contraband in their possession.

Principles of Good Policing: Avoiding Violence between Police and Citizens
http://www.usdoj.gov/crs

This lengthy publication examined the role of the police in contemporary American society and the values of good policing. A number of contemporary issues were explored in light of effective police leadership and practice. Key elements of the report related to the police-community relationship and the need for police to understand the culture, expectations, and environment of those being policed. Also discussed was how to achieve police departments' employment of culturally sensitive officers.

Racial Profiling Studies in Law Enforcement (by Jim Cleary)
http://www.house.leg.state.mn.us/hrd/pubs/raceprof.pdf

This report serves as a "how to" to conduct valid and reliable studies concerning the practice of racial profiling. The report highlighted the history of profiling by law enforcement and reflected on arguments for and against the practice. It provided detailed information on working with law enforcement agencies to construct a study so that the role race plays in discretionary police action could be gauged.

Racial Profiling within Law Enforcement Agencies
http://purl.access.gpo.gov/GPO/LPS15529 or /LPS15530

This document recounted the testimony and findings of the U.S. Senate Judiciary Committee of the 106th Congress concerning the use of racial profiling by American law enforcement. Testimony came from law enforcement officers, victims of profiling, the attorney general, and others. Arguments for and against the use of profiling were also part of the record.

Resource Guide on Racial Profiling Data Collection Systems: Promising Practices and Lessons Learned
http://www.ojp.gov/bja

This publication provided an overview concerning the issue of racial profiling. It also discussed the nature of profiling data collection. The document highlighted data collection activities in California, New Jersey, North Carolina, and even Great Britain. Recommendations for collection procedures were made.

Traffic Stop Data Collection Policies for State Police
http://www.ojp.gov/bjs

In March 2001, sixteen of forty-nine state police agencies required their officers to record data concerning the traffic stops they made. In some cases, the data collection requirement extended to other types of citizen contacts as well. This report examined the methods of collection that were employed and summarized the findings.

Women and Girls in the Criminal Justice System
http://www.ncjrs.org and http://www.ojp.usdoj.gov/nij

This large publication explored the changing involvement of females with the criminal justice system in the United States. The historical trends of women and criminal conduct were discussed, culminating in the recognition of increased levels of female criminal conduct—particularly violent crimes. This document is a must-see for readers interested in the disparate treatment of women by the criminal justice system—sometimes to the benefit of women, and sometimes not.

Videos

Behind the Blue Wall: Police Brutality

Date: 1999
Type: VHS
Length: 50 min.
Cost: $24.95
Source: Distributed by Arts and Entertainment Networks
            http://www.aetv.com

This Arts and Entertainment production explored the issue of police brutality by focusing on two relatively recent, high-profile events involving the New York City Police Department. In particular, the cases of Abner Louima and Amadou Diallo—both black immigrants—were examined. In the Louima case, white police officers were accused and convicted of sexually assaulting Louima with a toilet plunger while he was in custody in 1997. In the Diallo case, four white police officers were accused but acquitted of unlawfully gunning down Diallo in an alleyway in 1999. It was determined that Diallo was incorrectly thought to be reaching for a gun when confronted by the officers; it turned out he was reaching for his wallet. Former New York Police commissioner Howard Safir was interviewed and attempted to explain the perceived police propensity to use violence against suspects, especially minorities.

Cops under Fire

Date: 1996

Type: VHS
Length: 50 min.
Cost: $24.95
Source: Distributed by Arts and Entertainment Networks
http://www.aetv.com

This Arts and Entertainment program, hosted by Mike Wallace, explored the selective targeting of minorities by law enforcement. The program reviewed high profile cases, such as the Rodney King beating and the Amadou Diallo shooting. Wallace interviewed citizens and law enforcers alike to gain their perspectives on the degree to which the problem of biased policing exists and what must be done to end it.

Cultural Diversity for Law Enforcement
Date: 1995
Type: VHS
Length: 23 min.
Cost: $29.95
Source: Distributed by Performance Dimensions
http://www.lawenforcementvideos.com

This police training video was hosted by noted police training expert Ed Nowicki. The video was designed to equip police officers with an understanding of the cultures and subcultures that are found in the areas they police. Issues such as racial profiling, stereotyping, the CARD system (class, age, race, dress), and hate crimes were all explored as practical matters and from the perspective of professional, legal, and moral police work. The video contained scenarios to help facilitate discussion in a training environment.

Cultural Diversity: Myths and Stereotypes
Date: 1999
Type: VHS
Length: 60 min
Cost: $259.00
Source: Distributed by Insight Media
http://www.insight-media.com

This video serves as a tool for police officers by teaching them how to avoid making judgments about others based upon false assumptions. The natural tendency of police officers to draw conclusions about people upon initial contact is addressed. The use of stereotyping to assess not only suspects, but victims and witnesses as well, is confronted in this production. This video can be used alone or in conjunction with *Cultural Diversity: Professionalism* (described below).

Cultural Diversity: Professionalism
Date: 1999
Type: VHS
Length: 60 min
Cost: $259.00
Source: Distributed by Insight Media
http://www.insight-media.com

This police training video addresses the issue of police professionalism. It reveals how the standards of police professionalism are inconsistent with the nature of prejudice and actions that follow. This video can be used alone or in conjunction *with Cultural Diversity: Myths and Stereotypes* (described above).

Protect and Serve: De-Policing in Urban Neighborhoods
Date: 2001
Type: VHS or DVD
Length: 23 min.
Cost: $69.95 (VHS) or $79.95 (DVD)
Source: Distributed by Films for the Humanities and Sciences
http://www.films.com

This ABC News special hosted by Ted Koppel explored the reaction by law enforcement to the criticism of biased policing and racial profiling. Many large cities have seen police department production drop as measured by contacts with public, arrests, citations, and so on. Koppel interviewed several individuals from law enforcement, community organizations, and politics to gauge the degree to which police officers were pulling back under the premise of "no contact, no complaint."

Racial Profiling and Law Enforcement: America in Black and White
Date: 1998
Type: VHS or DVD
Length: 41 min.

Cost: $129.95 (VHS) or $139.95 (DVD)
Source: Distributed by Films for the Humanities and Sciences
           http://www.films.com

This two-part series hosted by Ted Koppel and Michael McQueen of ABC News examined both sides of the "driving while black" (DWB) debate. What law enforcement personnel consider to be a valuable and proven technique of interdicting crime—profiling—community activists decry as racial profiling, claiming it is unfair, humiliating, and often ineffective. Part One of the series investigated this issue from the victim's point of view, that is, innocent black citizens pulled over or otherwise confronted by police because of their race. Part Two examined the issue from the law enforcement perspective and included commentary by former O. J. Simpson prosecutor Christopher Darden.

The Rodney King Incident: Race and Justice in America
Date: 1998
Type: VHS or DVD
Length: 57 min.
Cost: $89.95 (VHS) or $99.95 (DVD)
Source: Distributed by Films for the Humanities and Sciences
           http://www.films.com

This is a fascinating revisitation of the Rodney King beating by four Los Angeles police officers and the subsequent local and federal trials of the officers. All the key individuals involved in the incident were interviewed for the program, including Rodney King, King's attorney, all four police officers charged in the beating, the local prosecutor in the case, former police chief Darrel Gates, and several others. The unedited version of the Rodney King videotape, which captured the beating, was played in its entirety. All sides of the issue were examined. A discussion of the outrage in the community after the initial verdict of not guilty and the resulting riot in South Central Los Angeles was also included in the program.

Serial Killers: Profiling the Criminal Mind
Date: 1998
Type: DVD
Length: 200 min.

Cost: $14.95
Source: Distributed by Arts and Entertainment Networks
http://www.aetv.com

This four-part program examined why serial killers commit the offenses they do. Interviews with a variety of experts, including former FBI agent John Douglas, were the mainstay of the program. Also included were prison interviews with actual offenders, including Charles Manson and John Wayne Gacy. Other serial killers were also considered in the analysis, including Wayne Williams and Jeffrey Dahmer.

Should We Fear the Police?
Date: 1999
Type: VHS
Length: 30 min.
Cost: $99.00
Source: Distributed by Insight Media
http://www.insight-media.com

This video examined two different contexts thought to be representative of police antagonism toward minorities. The first context was in the city of New York, where Amadou Diallo was mistaken for an armed suspect and shot several times by four police officers. The incident was reviewed and the reasons why so many in the African American community believed the shooting was racially motivated were revealed. The second context the video explored is that of the New Jersey State Police. In that segment of the video, black New Jersey state troopers were featured, along with their claims that their white colleagues systematically engaged in racially biased policing.

To Catch a Killer: Use and Abuse of Criminal Profiling
Date: 2001
Type: VHS or DVD
Length: 46 min.
Cost: $149.95 (VHS) or $159.95 (DVD)
Source: Distributed by Films for the Humanities and Sciences
http://www.films.com

In this video, a retired FBI profiler, a police psychologist, and several British law enforcement officials discussed a couple of highly sensationalized cases in England that involved the use of criminal profiling. In one case, involving a serial rapist, profiling was successfully used to identify and apprehend the offender. In another case, this time involving a murder, the use of profiling nearly scuttled the entire investigation.

20th Century with Mike Wallace: Profiling Killers

Date: 1998
Type: VHS
Length: 50 min.
Cost: $24.95
Source: Distributed by Arts and Entertainment Networks
http://www.aetv.com

This episode of *20th Century with Mike Wallace* examined the history of criminal profiling. Pioneering profilers formerly with the FBI, such as John Douglas and Clint Van Zandt, were interviewed about the struggle to legitimacy for profiling as an investigatory tool. The creation of the FBI's Behavioral Science Unit at Quantico, Virginia, in 1972 was also examined. After viewing this video, there will be little doubt that the FBI as an agency remains the premier holding organization of expertise concerning profiling.

Glossary

atavism The theory that criminality is rooted in primitive and savage biological traits.

beat patrol A policing strategy that concentrates an officer's attention on a particular, relatively small geographic location, thus enabling the officer to become very familiar with the area and people being policed.

behavioral profiling A composite of behavioral patterns observed by law enforcement and used to predict future criminality.

Bill of Rights The first ten amendments of the U.S. Constitution, most of which establish the limitations to which government is subject when infringing upon individual freedom.

blue curtain/wall Terms used to describe the culturally ingrained reluctance of police officers to report on the misconduct of other police officers

broken windows A strategy of policing based on the theory that failure to address the minor offenses and public nuisances in a neighborhood will lead to more serious crime problems.

Carroll search A permissible warrantless bumper-to-bumper search of a motor vehicle by law enforcement without the owner's consent, provided probable cause exists that the vehicle contains evidence of a crime.

Civil Rights Act of 1964 A federal act outlawing discrimination in housing, employment, and other areas on the basis of race, ethnicity, religion, and gender.

civilian review board A panel of citizens who are organized to evaluate the legitimacy of specific police-citizen encounters and to make recommendations or impose sanctions (depending on the degree of power conferred upon a board in a particular jurisdiction).

classical criminology Theories of crime rooted in the notion that people commit crimes after making a rational choice of their own free will.

code of ethics A framework for what is considered appropriate, moral, and professional behavior on the part of criminal justice professionals. Police officers, prosecutors, judges, and correctional officials all have standing codes of ethics.

code of silence Similar to the "blue wall" or "blue curtain"; this is an unofficial code of conduct thought to exist in many police organizations that requires officers not to divulge to the public information about conduct or misconduct on the part of other officers.

community-based policing Any police program in place to foster partnerships between the community and police officers for the purpose of reducing crime and the fear of crime.

community policing A strategy of policing that involves connecting specific officers to specific communities and subcommittees over the long term in order to reduce crime and the fear of crime.

conflict model A political philosophy that argues that criminal laws and enforcement mechanisms have been crafted by society's powerful elite and for their benefit.

consensus model A political philosophy that holds to the notion that criminal laws are an expression of society's widely shared values and beliefs.

consent decree An agreement that allows a police department to avoid being sued by the U.S. Justice Department for civil rights violations provided that the police department in question consents to set conditions and oversight by the U.S. Justice Department.

crime control model A conceptualization of the criminal justice system that emphasizes the need for efficiency and effectiveness in catching, punishing, and incapacitating criminals.

criminal justice profiling The activity of criminal justice officials strategically considering characteristics such as race, gender, religion, or sexual orientation as they make discretionary decisions in the course of their duties.

criminal justice system Generally considered to be the combination of law enforcement, the courts, and the correctional system—all working (sometimes at odds with each other) toward the goal of achieving justice.

criminal profiling The term generally used to describe all types of profiling utilized in the investigation of unsolved crime.

criminogenics The theory that some people are just born criminals.

cultural diversity A topic of periodic training for many criminal justice professionals that emphasizes a recognition that society in the United States is made up of people with many different cultural and social backgrounds that impact their behavior and their relationships with the criminal justice system.

driving while black (DWB) A play on the words "driving while intoxicated"; the phrase used to describe the "crime" being committed by black motorists when they are pulled over for no apparent reason by the police.

drug courier profile A composite of traits identified by law enforcement as consistent with those commonly possessed by those engaged in drug trafficking.

due process model A conceptualization of the criminal justice system that emphasizes the need to protect individual rights and freedoms from a potentially overzealous or mistaken government.

ethnicity Generally, the combination of cultural, religious, national, and racial groupings to which one belongs to or from which one comes.

Federal Bureau of Investigation (FBI) The federal law enforcement agency with the broadest federal enforcement powers; it pioneered the use of criminal profiling to solve crime.

Fourteenth Amendment Ratified in 1868, this amendment to the U.S. Constitution declared that the states were prohibited from depriving any person of life, liberty, or property without due process of law; court cases over time used the Fourteenth Amendment to apply the Bill of Rights to state and local government action.

gender One's status of being male or female.

GLBT An acronym meaning "gay, lesbian, bisexual, transgender."

incident-driven policing A reactive style of policing whereby officers merely respond to one incident after another with little or no effort or opportunity to develop relationships with the community.

institutional discrimination The concept that consistent bias is felt by certain groups in the criminal justice system due to otherwise neutral factors, such as criminal record or family status.

legalistic model A style of policing that emphasizes following the letter of the law.

peremptory challenge The ability of a trial attorney to strike a prospective juror from hearing a case for almost any reason or no reason.

phrenology A theory of crime that proposed that deviant thought and behavior were rooted in localized parts of the brain and that, therefore, an examination of one's skull could help predict future criminality.

police brutality A term used to describe unlawful use of force by police officers.

police-community relations A general term referring to the state of understanding and relationship between a police organization and the community it serves.

police discretion   The ability of police officers to make enforcement decisions in the field without consulting others higher up in the chain of command or elsewhere in the criminal justice process.

police misconduct   Nonprofessional, unethical, and/or unlawful conduct by police officers.

problem-oriented policing   A policing strategy that empowers officers to determine the source of problems within their jurisdiction and take sweeping steps to solve those problems, as opposed to repeatedly reacting to the symptoms of those problems.

prosecutorial discretion   The ability of prosecutors to decide whom to prosecute and whom not to prosecute without consulting others in the criminal justice process.

prosecutorial misconduct   Unprofessional, unethical, or unlawful conduct by a prosecutor either while building a case for prosecution or while in trial.

psychological profiling   Drawing conclusions about unidentified criminal offenders through the analysis of psychological traits and application of psychological theories.

race   Distinguishing biological features among human beings that are genetically passed on from generation to generation.

racial profiling   The exclusive use of race by criminal justice officials in identifying criminals or potential criminal activity.

religion   A belief system concerning that which governs nature and the universe.

selective enforcement   A police and prosecutive strategy that aggressively takes enforcement action against particular offenses deemed to be an acute problem.

serial offender   A criminal offender who repeatedly reoffends in a similar manner, often out of compulsion.

service model   A style of policing that emphasizes aiding the community in nonenforcement ways and building relationships.

sexual orientation   The status of sexual preference one has toward either the same or opposite gender.

slave patrols   A law enforcement operation in the American South during the eighteenth and nineteenth centuries devoted to curbing rebellious slave activities and conducting general patrol duties.

social contract   The concept that the people consent to be policed by the government in exchange for protection of individual rights and liberties.

stereotyping   A shortcut to perceiving a person or persons by relying on assumptions about groups to which they belong, whether true or untrue.

street justice   The term used to describe the extralegal remedies taken against criminal offenders by police officers prior to or in lieu of arrest and formal charges; generally involves unlawful use of force.

systematic discrimination   The concept that bias is built into the very processes and mechanisms of the criminal justice system, thus resulting in consistent discrimination against certain groups of people.

Terry search/frisk   A permissible, brief detention and search for weapons by law enforcement if reasonable suspicion exists that a subject has a weapon and is committing or about to commit a crime.

Title 42 USC 1983   A federal law permitting citizens to sue nonfederal law enforcement officers and agencies for violation of one's civil rights.

voir dire   The process by which prospective jurors are selected for or eliminated from jury service in a trial; the process is generally accomplished through questions asked of would-be jurors by the trial attorneys and the judge in the case.

Index

*Page numbers in **bold type** refer to major discussions of topics covered in the text.*

About the Author

Jeffrey B. Bumgarner, Ph.D., is a faculty member within the Department of Political Science and Law Enforcement at Minnesota State University, Mankato. He earned a B.A. in political science from the University of Illinois (Champaign-Urbana), an M.P.A. in public administration from Northern Illinois University, and a Ph.D. in training and organization development from the University of Minnesota.

Dr. Bumgarner is also a licensed Minnesota peace officer and has several years of experience in local and federal law enforcement as an officer, criminal investigator, and trainer. He has written several articles and reports concerning police training and professionalism.

DATE DUE

DEMCO 38-296